ANATOMY OF AN AFRICAN TRAGEDY

D1560143

ANATOMY
OF AN
AFRICAN TRAGEDY:
Political, Economic and
Foreign Policy Crisis
in
Post-Independence Eritrea

Kidane Mengisteab
&
Okbazghi Yohannes

The Red Sea Press, Inc.
Publishers & Distributors of Third World Books

P.O. Box 1892　　　　　　P.O. Box 48
Trenton, NJ 08607　　　Asmara, ERITREA

The Red Sea Press, Inc.
Publishers & Distributors of Third World Books

P.O. Box 1892      P.O. Box 48
Trenton, NJ 08607   Asmara, ERITREA

Book Design: Damola Ifaturoti
Cover Design: Dapo Ojo-Ade

Library of Congress Cataloging-in-Publication Data

Kidane Mengisteab
  Anatomy of an African tragedy : political, economic, and foreign policy crisis in post-independence Eritrea / Kidane Mengisteab & Okbazghi Yohannes.
    p. cm.
  Includes bibliographical references.
  ISBN 1-56902-247-X (hardcover) -- ISBN 1-56902-248-8 (pbk.)
  1. Eritrea--Politics and government--1993- 2. Eritrea--Economic conditions. 3. Eritrea--Foreign relations. I. Yohannes, Okbazghi. II. Title.

DT397.3K53 2005
963.507'2--dc22

                                    2005015158

TABLE OF CONTENTS

CHAPTER ONE
INTRODUCTION
AN EXCEPTIONALIST PROLOGUE OR AN AFRICAN REQUIEM?

An "economic tragedy" is how some observers have described the economic record of post-independence Africa (Artadi and Sala-i-Martin, 2003; Easterly and Levine, 1997). The World Economic Forum has also used the same characterization of African economies in a report it released at the June 2004 Africa Economic Summit held in Maputo, Mozambique. Per capita income in Sub-Saharan African countries has fallen by 11% since 1974. Both food production and industrial production in the region have stagnated and poverty rates have intensified. Given these conditions, the characterization of Africa's economic record as "tragic" is justified.

Unfortunately, sub-Saharan Africa's tragedy is not confined to its economy. Its conditions in the areas of governance and state building, political security and health are equally tragic, as evident by the chronic conflicts that have besieged the region. Since the early 1970s sub-Saharan African countries have experienced civil conflicts which have produced more than half of all war-related deaths worldwide and about 9.5 million refugees (*UN Secretary-General's Report*, April 16, 1998; *Genocide Watch*, 2003). During the 1989-2003 period 56% of sub-Saharan Africa's 48 countries were involved in interstate, intrastate wars or violent communal conflicts that devoured millions of lives (*Genocide Watch*, 2003; *Uppsala Conflict Data*

Project (UCDP), 2004). These conflicts have also produced genocide in Rwanda and "genocidal massacres" in the Sudan, Ethiopia, Burundi, the Democratic Republic of the Congo and Uganda (*Genocide Watch*, 2003). African conflicts have also precipitated gross violations of human rights, including gruesome mutilations of large members of people in Sierra Leone, Rwanda, the Democratic Republic of the Congo, Angola and Uganda. The economic costs of African conflicts are difficult to determine. A typical conflict is, however, estimated to reduce national income by about 10 to 15% (Collier, et al., 2003).

The unfolding health crisis the region is facing is another tragedy. The Commission on Macroeconomics and Health estimates that malaria costs sub-Saharan Africa between 5.8% and 17.4% of annual gross national product, due to lost years of healthy life. The cost from HIV/AIDS is estimated to be between 11.7% and 35.1% of GNP (*Taylor and DeYoung*, 2003-2004). These estimates create a frightening scenario. Even if we take the lower estimates, a combined loss of 23.2% of GNP, along with the costs of the conflicts and political turmoil, is far beyond the continent's ability to bear.

The principal goal of this book is to examine how Africa's development prospects which seemed to have a promising trajectory at the time of decolonization degenerated into the prevailing tragic predicament. Instead of examining the entire sub-Saharan region, however, we take a case study approach and examine how Africa's newest state, Eritrea, which was widely regarded as Africa's bright spot at the time of its independence reverted to a troubled spot just a decade after its independence. We find the lessons we learn from Eritrea's experience to be informative in understanding many of the factors that led to Africa's prevailing predicament.

After one hundred years of successive colonial occupation by Italy, Great Britain and Ethiopia, Eritrea secured its liberation in 1991 by armed means. Two years later, the

Eritrean people overwhelmingly voted in an internationally-supervised referendum to seal a permanent divorce from Ethiopia. With the installation of a *De Jure* government in 1993, Eritrea turned a new chapter in its history.

Like most African countries at the time of their independence, the new Eritrean state faced many challenges. Its birth was contextualized by the sudden collapse of the bipolar international political structure and the consequent unleashing of the forces of globalization, and by the inheritance of a country shattered by thirty years of war and the politics of famine, which left three quarters of a million Eritreans either internally displaced or as refugees in neighboring countries. The changed international geopolitical context immediately presented Eritrea with both opportunities and challenges. One of the opportunities was that Eritrea did not have to choose between two rival superpowers. The challenges of defining its external relations were, however, still enormous since the young country had to craft its own regional identity and international imagery within the context of a radically transformed global configuration of power.

The internal challenges were equally formidable. The country's 750 kilometers of asphalt roads were torn up from years of heavy military vehicle use, the bridges blown up, the nation's railway network that once ran from the port of Massawa on the Red Sea through Asmara in the highland to the western towns was completely dismantled by Ethiopian troops for scrap metal for bunkers, and two-thirds of Eritreans were subsisting on international food aid. Add to the above the necessary task of repatriating hundreds of thousands of refugees from Sudan and demobilizing tens of thousands of liberation fighters. Given the enormity of the challenges, the prospects of rebuilding the country's infrastructure, resuscitating the national economy, and reintegrating repatriated refugees and demobilized fighters into civil society productively required extraordinary vision on the part of the country's leadership and a high level of mobilization of the country's human and material resources. Indeed, the internal challenges coupled with the external dynamics of politics and diplomacy forwarded themselves in the form of questions: how would Eritrea mobilize the internal and international resources necessary for internal rebuilding in a sustained way; how would it define its external relations in the context of the highly globalized structure; and how would Eritrea build a democratic institutional governance in order to give the rebuilding effort and its external relations coherence and sustainability?

Despite the magnitude of the challenges it faced, at the time of its formal independence, Eritrea's future seemed bright. The country emerged from its thirty-year liberation war with a population that was united, highly motivated and mobilized to rebuild the country. Its leadership was also widely viewed as belonging to a small group of new and enlightened African leaders who appeared to be poised to avoid many of the mistakes of the older generation of African leaders. The Eritrean leadership was, for example, hailed for being relatively free of corruption and for involving the population in the crafting of the country's constitution. The participation of the population in the making of the constitution seemed to signal a good start for establishing a democratic system of governance. The country also made significant strides toward economic recovery. In addition, Eritrea appeared to be a catalyst for regional peace and revitalization of the Inter Governmental Authority on Development (IGAD). Eritrea's good relations and open borders with its neighbors seemed to enable it to be a bridge between the two largest countries in the Horn of Africa, Sudan and Ethiopia. This positive image of the country was mellifluently captured in various titles. Charles Cobb and Robert Caputo, for example, entitled their essay: "Eritrea Wins the Peace" (1996). A cover story in the *New York Times* was entitled: "Eritrea: African Success Story Being Written" (McKinley Jr., April 30, 1996). Writing in the

Christian Science Monitor, Arlo Devlin-Brown highlighted the cross-national significance of the Eritrean experiment in an essay entitled: "Eritrea Offers Key Lessons in Nation-Building" (June 18, 1996). Many other reporters and analysts expressed their optimism in equally glowing terms.

To the surprise of many observers, however, seven years after its ratification in May 1997, the Eritrean constitution remains unimplemented and the country's democratization process has come to a grinding halt. The once respected leadership is now accused of authoritarian rule, violations of human rights and suppression of the press (Amnesty International, 2002; *Human Rights Watch*, 2002). The country's economic recovery has also stalled and a rapid rise in inflation has exacerbated an already precarious standard of living of the population. The country's foreign relations, especially relations with its neighbors, are also in flux. With breathtaking speed, many observers have crafted a negative image of the country. "Eritrea's Non-Democracy: We Fought for This? A Once Admired Leader Turns Tyrant" is the title of a report in the *Economist* (November 23, 2002) that best represents the negative depiction of the country today. "Student Program in Eritrea Turns into Forced-Labor Camp" is the title of Wachira Kigotho's essay in the *Chronicle of Higher Education* (November 23, 2001). "What Happened to Self-Reliance?" asked the *New African* (October, 2001). In its *2003 World Report*, Human Rights Watch also described Eritrea as a country that remained "under siege—from its own government" (*IRIN News*, January 24, 2003).

Most African countries which seemed to have a promising future at the time of their independence found themselves engulfed in chronic crises within a decade or so after independence. Eritrea was expected to avoid this fate since it had the benefit of learning from the experiences of other African countries. Unfortunately, it too has degenerated from a bright star into a troubled spot in less than a decade after its independence. This new reality of failure poses a fundamental question of how to explain the abrupt departure from the exuberant expectation of the country's prospects for a smooth and quick transition to sustainable development and governance. Since the purpose of this work is to draw important theoretical and pedagogical lessons from the apparent successes and failures of the Eritrean experience, the perspective offered here is a critical one. Eritrea in many respects has become a microcosm of the African tragedy. A careful study of the Eritrean experience should be useful in our understanding of the African crisis.

For purposes of preliminary exposition of our analytical study, we begin with clarifying the method involved in this volume. Students of comparative politics often debate over whether the idiographic or the nomothetic approaches to the study of a country's political formation are appropriate. Scholars who subscribe to idiographic approaches maintain that every nation can be viewed as a distinct and unique self-contained political system. Thus a focus on its history, state of its economic development, the particulars of its internal makeup and the extent of its social differentiation should yield a superior corpus of scholarship. In this view, a sharper focus on Eritrea's colonial history, the state of its economic and political development, the experiences of the liberation years and the social morphology of its inhabitants would suffice to generate a sound scholarship in the political study of the country. Seen in this light, the search for historical analogues and/or comparative frameworks would not add much to our understanding of the social matrix and political mapping of the country. Indeed, the idiographic perspective did hold sway over both the seasoned scholar and the casual observer alike in the immediate post-liberation years of the country. There were seemingly propitious signs that led to the internalization of the idiographic orientation.

The downside of this methodological orientation is, of course, that it glosses over the fact that the Eritrean crisis, like the crisis in the rest of Africa, has resulted from a complex set of multiple factors. Many of the factors are internal while some are external. Some are structural while others are agency related. Some are primary factors while others are triggering factors. Taking cognizance of the multiplicity and complexity of the factors involved, both idiographic and nomothetic approaches are thus employed in this work. Among the most important internal factors we explore are: the problem of leadership, the absence of public critics, especially within the intelligentsia, and the weakness of civil society, which has been unable to command a private space from which to challenge the self-serving tendencies of those who control state power and becomes an agent in the building of a democratic system.

Idiographers may approach the Eritrean predicament by looking at the biography, nature and composition of the leadership of the country. A weak civil society and the absence of countervailing civic groups and programmatic parties make the role of political leadership particularly critical in Eritrea. According to the new literature on leadership, the character and composition of a country's leadership is arguably decisive in effectuating the transition to an orderly civic governance and consolidation of a legitimated political democracy. After examining a large sample of case studies in Latin America, John Peeler (1998) highlights elite agency as critical during periods of transition and the early phases of democratization. In his view, although structures impose constraints on actors and limit the menu of choices, human agency, mediated by elite character and intra-elite competition, is arguably decisive in shaping and directing the trajectory of a transition to and consolidation of democracy. Larry Diamond and his associates note as well that the qualitative properties of national leadership, although not determinative in themselves, make a substantial difference in the evolution of any political species.

> This is why we take so seriously the character and quality of political leadership. The choices that key political leaders make in managing crises or constructing the patterns and perimeters of a political system have a powerful influence on whether the legitimacy of democracy will be established, maintained or squandered. We do not think that the choices elites make and the strategies they pursue are merely given by the historical or structural situation (Diamond et al., 1999: 5).

To the extent that civil society is weak and the structural impediments are seemingly insurmountable in such countries as Eritrea, a progressively democratic leadership must have as its core objective the duty to inspire an entire nation toward the attainment of collective freedom, liberty and equal justice under the law, manifested in transparent commitment to institutional governance, the rule of law and impartial administration of justice. A leadership with democratic vision is one that negates its self-serving importance by placing inspired and inspiring men and women in positions of responsibility and whose tenure in office is guaranteed by no less than an effective demonstration of competence and performance.

In his attempt to explain why post-independence African political systems collapsed, Ayittey (1998) forwarded the crisis of leadership as a working hypothesis. The Ghanian scholar argues that the socio-temporal conditions and natural resources of Africa were reasonably propitious and abundant enough in the 1960s and 1970s to initiate and sustain an African renaissance, grounded in solid economic prosperity, political democracy and human rights governance. What was missing from the equation was, however, an incorruptible, farsighted and democratic class of leaders. It did not take much time for Africa's post-colonial leaders to turn into "crackpot" democrats and "gangsters" who created "vampire states" throughout the continent as a monument to their utter degeneracy (Ayittey, 1998). In this view, the interiorization of the causes for the betrayal of African leadership and the consequent rise of the "vampire state" presupposes the tangential quality of exterior forces in explaining the utter dysfunctionality of African political systems.

Undoubtedly, leadership quality is only one among many factors, but having a competent and visionary leadership can make a significant difference in success or failure. Especially in the context of the African condition of grim levels of human development, including lack of access to health and education by the general population, a visionary and competent leadership that is prepared to sacrifice its own interests for social interests or "commits class suicide," as Cabral (1969) notes, is essential for the successful transformation of African societies. In the context of the African reality, successful transformation of African societies is rather unlikely to take place without a leadership that has the necessary qualities of vision, commitment to democracy and competence. The failure of leadership may thus be regarded as a primary factor in the African crisis. If seen in this light, one does not have to theoretically travel far to understand and explain the political crisis that characterizes Eritrea today. Arguably, Eritrea's fatal retreat from a democratic vision is a reflection of the simple fact that the Eritrean leadership appears to have internalized the examples of other African leaders. Wholesale emulation of rule by preemption, containment, co-optation and, when necessary, by political ostracism and elimination seem to become integral to the Eritrean political system.

In studying political leadership, the aspect of the political system which is often overlooked is the public administration side of the democratization process. As Werlin (1988) notes, one crucial yardstick by which to evaluate a political system is by examining the nature of its public administration. In this view, the public administration that is simultaneously effective in performance, efficient in using resources and delivering services, and democratic internally is one where authority is widely dispersed within the organization and where the top leadership displays a remarkable degree of willingness to share responsibility with subordinates. Delegation of operational functions to subordinates, the democratic installation of vertical and horizontal channels of communication and having transparent mechanisms of accountability make a nation's public administration effective, efficient and democratic.

If we use this simple and yet useful criterion, the conclusion we reach is that Eritrea's public administration is not only poorly developed but also inefficient and undemocratic both internally and externally. In view of the excessive centralization of administrative functions in the office of the president, the boundaries of authority whether within or between and among ministries do not seem to exist. Anyone from the office of the president can reverse a decision taken by a juridically or functionally competent ministry. Moreover, rectifying administrative failures and abuses is exceedingly difficult because administrative orders are usually given verbally. One intellectual who worked with the government since independence expressed his exasperation with the administrative practice in the country by confiding that government officials at all levels do their best not to leave a paper trail. In consequence, when things go wrong, public administrators not only blame each other but also shift responsibility to others for failures and rush to take credit for effectiveness or efficiency. Perhaps bureaucratic informalism may be the proper term to characterize the nation's public administration, a subsidiary to populist authoritarianism.

In addition to becoming a source of confusion, chaos and internal squabbles, bureaucratic informalism encourages the deployment of coercive methods of control and breeds corruption. In fact, official corruption became overtly so widespread in the country that the president ordered the creation of a special court in 1996 to exclusively try public officials and bureaucrats charged with crimes of corruption.

The crucial point of departure in studying Eritrean politics is perhaps the political culture of the liberation period as a window to look into the history and nature of the leadership. As we shall see in chapter two, in the name of national unity, organizational cohesiveness and internal harmony, the Eritrean People's Liberation Front (EPLF) crafted an ideology that made absolute the centrality of the leadership to the full realization of the Front's historic mission. In the parlance of the age, the Front's leadership and its mode of operation were dubbed democratic- centralism. Despite the external misrepresentation of the EPLF's mode of operation as one embedded in the notion of collective leadership, the affairs of the Front were run under the tight supervision and personal control of the central figure. The vertical line of authority emanating from the central figure and the channels of communication put in place by the Front's politburo might have preempted the prospect for developing and promoting horizontal relationships, critical to innovative political entrepreneurship and democratic experimentation. In the post-liberation years, things appear to have grown worse as the central figure's grip on the body politic grew even wider and tighter with the methodical concentration of the reins of power in the office of the president. Thus the prologue to the leadership crisis seems to have long been written. The Ethio-Eritrean war of 1998-2000 served to amplify and expose the incompetence as well as the authoritarian character of the Eritrean leadership.

Another salient dimension of the political culture of the liberation years was empiricism. The survival of the Eritrean struggle under extraordinary circumstances coupled with the subsequent realization of victory by armed means against one of Africa's largest and over-equipped army could not have failed to shape the political psychology of both the Eritrean leadership and follower-ship. The air of self-confidence surrounding the leadership, bordering on what appeared to be overt arrogance and hubris, was reflected in the elite's contemptuous treatment of the citizenry as well as in its imprudent diplomatic moves. The danger inherent in empiricism is the tendency among leaders to view their narrow personal experiences as the epicenter of all things. The external universe is understood not only by reference to the Front's experiences but also as the dangerous source of threats in terms of contrarian political and cultural influences that might challenge the ruling ethos and the entire political architecture of the new system. The personal experiences of the leadership are seen as distinctly autonomous and superior; external constraints are assumed away as wholly negative. In consequence, the internal capacity to fashion one's future is exaggerated. The Eritrean leadership, for example, continually harped on the notion of uniquely Eritrean-style "self-reliance" as the immutable grid on which both the survival of the Eritrean struggle and its victory hinged. The dangerous extrapolation the Eritrean leadership made from the empiricist dogma since liberation was that the old methods that helped to secure victory would continue to guide the country's progress now and in the future. Internal admonitions and external exhortations were ignored as having no consequence for regime performance and legitimacy.

Another factor that underpinned the drift toward authoritarianism was the conspicuous absence of independent civil society in general and public intellectuals in particular from the Eritrean political landscape. In our judgment, in circumstances where civil society is weak and/or civic groups are in their infancy, the presence of a robust intellectual leadership is critical in a country in transition. Given the history of the liberation front, punctuated by over-centralization of the decision making process and mediated by a sense of urgency to insure internal cohesion, discipline and order, there appears to be little or no room for internal self-reflection and scrutiny or criticism of the Front's operations and the activities of the leadership. As chapter two shows, those critics who attempted to point out the errors of the Front from within were either effectively ostracized or physically liquidated after they were given multifarious labels. In consequence, the ubiquitous presence of fear of political ostracism or physical elimination appears to have preempted the emergence of critics from within.

In retrospect, the exigencies of fighting a war of liberation coupled with the Front's practice seem to have vitiated the prospect of generating a national class of public intellectuals. The only intellectuals who could have played the role of public critics since the country's independence were those who had stayed behind the enemy line or were the intellectual members of the diaspora community. But these intellectuals largely restrained themselves from serving as public critics both during the liberation and post-liberation wars with Ethiopia out of fear that their criticism of the undemocratic behavior of the Eritrean leadership might be opportunistically used by the Ethiopian regimes, and that these same intellectuals might be viewed by the Eritrean leadership and the mass public as undermining the country's cause. Moreover, the intellectuals outside the armed struggle were treated by the Front as having no equal rights with those in the field; if they had wanted to have equal say on the conduct or operations of the Front, they should have joined the Front. Real struggle was defined in terms of carrying weapons and with it came the honor of equal status. By default, Eritrean intellectuals, including those in the diaspora, accepted the Front's definition of struggle and internalized their secondary or even tertiary status.

Civil society in the country was also largely reorganized by the Liberation Front during the era of liberation struggle. There were thus hardly any civil organizations that were independent of the Front in post-independence Eritrea. Thus it happened that the Eritrean leadership proceeded to construct a political architecture outside the framework of national discourse and public scrutiny. Neither internal policies nor external moves were questioned by anyone. Furthermore, policy-making was not based on methodical study, analysis and evaluation of factors germane to the problem in question or by reference to careful considerations of competing choices and options. The capacity for professional research was limited and even when the capacity was available it was scarcely utilized by the regime. In fact, when the regime indulged in distressing excesses, the nation's intellectuals and leaders of civil society treated the excesses with incredulity or apologia.

One of the regime's troubling actions was the order given to the security forces to use lethal ammunition against disabled veterans. One of the enduring scars of a thirty-year long war of liberation was the fact that 12,000 fighters came home disabled. In reality, though, these disabled veterans are concentrated in camps, far removed from the nation's capital; they have yet to come home. In July 1993, the veterans requested that the president himself visit them so that he could personally bear witness to their unbearable conditions of existence. Their voice unheard, the veterans then took to the road in the hope of dramatizing their case. At this point the security forces opened fire on the disabled veterans, killing five and wounding nearly a dozen. Such humiliation of the disabled veterans and the gross violation of their elementary human rights, dignity and self-worth by the government became telling testimony to a political system that had begun going awry, and yet it produced little or no moral indignation or intellectual outrage internally or externally. This act alone, bordering on barbarity, was sufficient to incite conscious intellectuals to demand accountability from the leadership and to call the new system into serious question; but it never happened. No single intellectual bothered to take time out to systematically examine the precipitants and consequences of the tragic event.

Perhaps it is not useful to speak of intellectuals generically as if they are homogenous. Like all social segments in all societies, Eritrean intellectuals are atomized by contradictory interests, orientations and ideological predispositions. When we speak of public intellectuals, we are speaking of those who consciously see their role in society in terms of serving as watchdogs by continually scrutinizing government policies and actions, exposing the uncomfortable truth at the risk to themselves, articulating alternative visions, inciting formation of countervailing social forces and taking public officials to task when they fail to measure up to their responsibilities as public officials. To fulfill such invaluable services, public intellectuals must not only chasten their lives by ideals and values that transcend their narrow self-interests but also recognize the celebration of dissent and the search for justice as the twin pillars on which democracy hinges. In addition to mitigating the association or complicity of other intellectuals with officialdom, public intellectuals are needed to combat the often sentimental and self-serving version of history and politics orchestrated by public officials. Vigilantly keeping their distance from the perimeters of power, they are the anchor of moral conscience and the proverbial voice of dissent. They have also to accept the incontrovertible fact that there is heroism in public criticism and martyrdom in its cause.

Extremely important to bear in mind is that the search for and the realization of justice, the pursuit of happiness and the defense of civil liberties have historically been carried on the shoulders of public intellectuals. Indeed, we owe to John Locke the modern conception of government and society, embedded in the ideas of individual freedom and rule of law, and yet we forget that Locke spent seventeen years of his life in the Netherlands as a refugee rather than capitulating to the absolutism of the age. Likewise, Thomas Payne, through his fiery speeches and writings, was able to capture the imagination and revolutionary zeal of the American people, and yet we forget that Payne fell out of favor with some of the founders of the American republic for his scathing criticism against the system he helped to create, and he died almost destitute. What Locke, Payne and others like them empirically demonstrated was the fact that democracy could never be built nor sustained without the presence of a class of public critics. Precisely this essential ingredient of politics Eritrea lacked and still lacks.

Even after liberation, Eritrea's intellectuals tended to be homogeneously complicitous with government policies by their actions or silence. The fundamental disposition of the nation's intellectuals toward the guerrilla politicians was not only deferential but also subservient in a manner that turned out to be injurious to the profession and to the formation of democracy in the country. In the absence of public scrutiny and criticism, the assumed wisdom of the guerrilla politicians was taken as superior to the collective insights of the Eritrean people and of the nation's intellectuals. In consequence, the leadership claimed for itself omnicompetence in politics, economics, law and diplomacy. Ultimately, the result was that the corporatist infrastructure of control and repression was locked into place with domestic insularity and external adventurism as its dual manifestations. Seminars, workshops and conference papers organized or produced before the year 2000 almost invariably either extolled the virtues of the liberation period or endorsed the regime's vision and action with moral blindness and intellectual indifference; the nation's intellectuals became unwitting defenders and generators of post-hoc justifications and trepid rationalizations of government policies and actions in the cause of what has ended up being a suffocating autocracy. An illuminating case in point is a compilation of essays that appeared in an edited work on how the government was justified in expelling foreign non-governmental organizations from Eritrea in order to shield the presumed virtue of self-reliance from corrosive external penetration (Doornbos and Tesfai, 1999).

Again, consider the officially orchestrated notion of transition. During the liberation years, the masses were extolled as the driving force of history. Since liberation, however, the guerrilla politicians forwarded the proposition that the Eritrean people were uneducated, unable to tell the difference between friends and enemies, divided by region and religion and incapable of organizing themselves for self-government. Awakening the Eritrean masses, as the tortured logic went, would take a long period of time. The 1994 party manifesto lavishly squandered so many words to drive this point home. No intellectual dared to challenge this orchestration of staged periods of transition or suspect that the country was on the path to tyranny and that the guerrilla politicians were preparing the country for an over-reaching despotism. In the early 1990s, the concomitant circumstances of liberation had offered a paradigm of infinite possibilities for the country; Eritrea was, to use the Maoist aphorism, a blank sheet of paper on which anyone could write virtually anything. This objective reality should have necessitated the vigilant presence of public intellectuals to watch and monitor what the guerrilla politicians were about to write on this blank sheet or how they were going about managing the possibilities offered by the seminal moment. True intellectual patriotism must have as its focus the recognition of the fact that love of country involves the simultaneous celebration of freedom and vigilance against its potential loss. However, betrayed by their romantic hopes and acting in ways the regime attributed to the masses, Eritrea's intellectuals mistook the false horizon offered by the guerrilla politicians for a bright light.

The lamentable truth was that the liberators were trained in the art of warfare and steeped in a culture that was subsidiary to and supportive of war fighting capability. The translation of such training and culture into civic governance was by no means automatic. In fact, the guerrilla politicians' open rejection of civil administration and the exclusion of civilian experts from positions of responsibility should have come to all as an ominous warning of the potential slide toward authoritarianism. We all missed the clues. Following the end of the 1998-2000 war with Ethiopia, the nascent Eritrean private press began to create a platform where national discourse on the state of the country's affairs and public scrutiny of policies could take place. Unfortunately, the platform was nipped in the bud when the government quickly closed all private press and jailed many journalists in September 2001. The journalists remain in prison and the country has no private press at the time of writing.

The ritualization of martyrdom was another sign-post of danger. Upon liberation, the guerrilla politicians recast the military culture into a national culture, an unquestioning one, deeply infused with symbols and myths of heroism, sentimental and martial songs, orienting the whole nation toward the past. In commemoration of the past and its sons and daughters, meetings would be opened or closed with a moment of silence. Because the regime was installed in the name of the martyrs and every government action was defended in the name of the martyrs—even the exclusive monopoly of power by the guerrilla politicians was justified in their name—the climate created by the ritualization of martyrdom ended up producing an unquestioning collective mind.

This new culture oriented toward the past was part of the regime's effort to cope with the dilemma of transition. Upon liberation, the leadership found itself having to make a dual transition simultaneously from a popular liberation-regime type to civic governance and a legitimated political democracy. One needs to bear in mind that, during the liberation era, the fighting forces and the broad masses were told that the present was a moment of necessity: one in which self-sacrifice and discomfort were the defining features in order to give birth to a future of freedom, abundance and happiness. After the dawn of liberation, however, the Eritrean leadership found itself unable to deliver on that promised future in time as the gap between regime performance and the unfulfilled expectations of the liberators and the unmet needs of the masses began to widen. This prompted the regime to make a transition from what Claude Ake (1978) called a period of politicization, when advance mega-promises are given to the masses as a price for their participation in the struggle, to one of de-politicization, when the masses are reprogrammed in such a way as to make them forget about past promises and, instead, focus on the need for more present sacrifices.

Illustrative of this point is the confrontation that took place in April 1993 between the ordinary liberators and the leadership over the definition and duration of transition. That year, the regime communicated to the fighting units in the country that the plan to demobilize the liberators was postponed, which meant that the members of the liberation army would continue serving the nation without pay for two more years. In response, the elite units of the army took control of key installations in the capital to show their displeasure with the decision and confronted the president to change course. The units returned to their barracks after receiving assurances that their concerns would be legitimately addressed. Soon thereafter, however, those considered key leaders in the quasi-coup found themselves under martial proceedings. Over 120 of them were sentenced to jail and hard labor, and the units which conceived and carried out the mutiny were dispersed and kept on a constant move in remote regions of the country. Against this backdrop the political deactivation of the liberators and the depoliticization of the broad masses were developed as a solution to the transition dilemma. The expedient argument now became that the processes of articulation and representation of freedom, abundance and happiness would take even longer; consolidating independence and rehabilitating the nation's infrastructure still required collective sacrifices and enduring hardships, by definition making political democracy an article of luxury given the enormity of the problems shadowing the nation. Mass mobilization of the nation's adult youth under the guise of national service for development was also conceived in the context of the necessity called for by the moment. Both decisions to postpone demobilizing the liberators and to make the youth participate in nation-building were taken without national discourse and public input. Precisely this combination of compulsion from above and the new art of reprogramming the masses invites the typological characterization of the post-liberation Eritrean political order as populist authoritarianism, whose justification and maintenance require constantly reminding the living of the huge sacrifices the martyrs made in blood.

From the standpoint of the new architects, the overarching aim of ritualizing martyrdom was thus to produce a favorable psychological change in mass orientation toward the populist authoritarian state and by extension to provide the necessary psychological context to its new institutions. Frederich Hayek (1944: XIV) is right when he notes:

> that the most important change which extensive government control produces is a psychological change and alteration in the character of the people…. The important point is that the political ideas of a people and its attitude toward authority are as much the effect as the cause of the political institutions under which it lives. This means, among other things, even a strong tradition of political liberty is no safeguard if the danger is precisely that new institutions and policies will gradually undermine and destroy that spirit. The consequences can, of course, be averted if that spirit reasserts itself in time and the people not only throw out the party, which has been leading them further and further in the dangerous direction, but also recognize the nature of the danger and resolutely change their course.

Intellectual leadership prepares a population to recognize the nature of actual or potential danger that might face it and to struggle to change its course before it gives way to hopelessness and powerlessness. Eritrea's intellectuals, their thinking clouded by the new mythology, not only failed to offer a counter vision but also were unable to grasp the fact that the regime's constant invocation of martyrdom and glorification of the past in sacred terms were as much reflective and constitutive of the new culture as they were part of its program to manufacture consent and legitimacy. Shielded by the effective ritualization of martyrdom, Eritrea's guerrilla politicians, as sole inheritors of the history of liberation and the Platonic custodians of the post-liberation order, had been able to build a fire wall between themselves and potential critics. The massification of the nation's intellectuals has been the veritable concomitant of a frozen political culture. To be sure, if Eritrea's leaders followed the classic road traveled by other African leaders, Eritrea's intellectuals have certainly emulated their African counterparts. Here we find ourselves in agreement with George Ayittey's (1998) acerbic denunciation of African intellectuals as party to the political crisis of the continent.

By refraining from openly criticizing the EPLF of its excesses, international friends of the Eritrean cause may have also contributed in some ways to the political deformity in Eritrea. Because the Eritrean liberators were the underdog in the bitter struggle of epic proportions, whose ability to hold their own against extraordinary odds was always in doubt, international public intellectuals and supporters of the Front implicitly accepted the Front's harsh measures against dissidents as the necessary price to pay in order to insure survival of the liberation struggle. But that blunder has fully come to light now, and has come to haunt Africa's newest state as the inherited democratic deficit has become insurmountable.

In part, this is a reflection of the tendency in all of us to ignore lessons learned elsewhere in the hope that Eritrea would be different. Hoping against hope, many students of Eritrean history and politics thought, in retrospect of course erroneously, that the EPLF was different and thus it would not follow the Angolan or Vietnamese or Nicaraguan examples. By no means do we exonerate ourselves from this blame, professionally or otherwise. In fact, in one crucial respect, the undertaking of this project on our part is not only to explore the failings of the Eritrean leadership and the structural limits of the country but also to examine the shortcomings of our own understanding of the causes for the fatal failure of the Eritrean experiment. We take to heart Hannah's Arendt's admonition: "The task of the mind is to understand what happened and this understanding … is man's way of reconciling himself with reality" (Arendt, 1954: 8).

If seen in light of what we have indicated in the foregoing pages, the idiographic imperative makes sense because the attributes of the Eritrean political order and its concomitant effects can be understood in their own terms. The idiographic approach, however, leaves a number of questions unanswered. The failure of African leadership, for example, while important, does not fully explain the African crisis. Widespread failure of leadership that has characterized African countries does not occur in a vacuum. As Cabral notes, given the internal conditions inherited from colonialism and the hostile external environment their countries continue to face, African leaders face more difficult structural conditions than most of their counterparts in other parts of the world. Perhaps, African leaders need nothing less than committing "class suicide" in order to succeed in transforming their countries.

The more common failure of African leadership thus takes place within a certain structural context. What structural determinants account for the Eritrean leadership betraying the great promise it held out for a bright future? Were there factors which Eritrea's international friends and writers missed when they hailed the country as Africa's bright spot? Why did Eritrea produce a type of leadership similar to those found in other African countries and, for that matter, throughout the developing world? Such questions cannot be answered satisfactorily without the search for general patterns that point to the commonality of leadership types, on the one hand, and the preconditions and precipitants that give rise to those leadership types throughout Africa, on the other. Therefore, a nomothetic approach, looking for general patterns of behavior and structural factors, may offer better answers and predictive insights. After all, there are interesting parallels as well as historical, ideological and experiential antecedents which Eritrea shares with many countries in the developing world, such as Mozambique, Angola, Vietnam and Nicaragua. Those of us whose interest had long been intertwined with the history of the Eritrean struggle and the evolution of the post-liberation political order could and should have anticipated a potential drift of the Eritrean system toward authoritarianism by placing the study of the country within a larger comparative canvass. If history teaches us anything, it is the fact that no liberation or revolutionary movement ever produced a democratic order in the twentieth century. It also teaches us that African leaders, revolutionary or not, have not yet crafted states that are organically connected with their constituents and are committed to the advancement of the social interests of their citizens. As a creation of the colonial state, the post-independence African state has essentially remained beyond the control of its citizens and largely detached from the social interests, cultural values and institutions of citizens.

What follows from these general observations is another simple fact that we could have reasonably predicted: the likelihood that Eritrea would follow the path of previous movements. Of course, such an extrapolation does not suggest an empirical demonstration of hypotheses but rather points to the pertinence of historical illustrations to draw insightful pedagogical lessons from the experiences of states that have traveled a similar road. To the extent that the species of states to which Eritrea belongs are similar in their antecedent conditions, experiences, internal compositions and present levels of development, they should be expected to be proximate to each other structurally, functionally and behaviorally. This observation offers a partial explanation of why African states have more or less uniformly failed to securely anchor democratic governance, make sustained economic progress and prevent internal fragmentation and interstate conflicts before they became the continent's trademarks. The life of a nation, like all historical entities, is profoundly influenced and continually conditioned by objective structural determinants, conjunctural factors and temporal contingencies. Whether these determinants, factors and contingencies move in tandem or not is what makes states more or less similar or different. A juxtaposition of developing states of which Eritrea is a part and western democracies should provide an important historical illustration of the point we are trying to establish as a prefatory proposition to our undertaking. Because western democracies are the living model in which developing countries, like Eritrea, see their own future image, a word or two on how the former historically evolved into being is in order.

The absence among African countries of developed institutions that curtail the tendencies of those who control state power to subvert social interests in favor of private interests is among the critical differences between developed western democracies and African states. If democracy is about the general population controlling public policy on an ongoing basis (Beetham, 1992), democracy requires the presence of a private space outside of the government from which citizens can wage their activities to control the state. In advanced countries the presence of a developed market system and a private economic space empower citizens to have relative independence from the state and provide them the institutional arrangement that would enable them to organize and engage in controlling those in power. In the absence of a developed private sector, citizens to a large extent depend on the state for their livelihood, as often is the case in African countries. Under such conditions the ability of citizens to organize in order to control the activities of the state is limited.

As Robert Heilbroner (1993) cogently observed, to date democracy has empirically demonstrated itself only in countries where markets are fully developed. However, the relationship between markets and democracies is rather complex and not linear. The market system together with an independent class of bourgeoisie does certainly form the requisite condition for the delineation between the state and civil society or the portioning off of the public realm from the private sphere (Heilbroner, 1993). Yet having a capitalist mode of production with an advanced market and a class of capitalists alone is not a sufficient condition for democracy to establish itself securely. Moreover, as Dahl (1993), Lindblom (1982) and Macpherson (1966) note, democracy is also threatened when the market-based private sector overwhelms the public sector. In circumstances of transition, the capitalist class may also become party to a regressive gambit by joining the military and agrarian interests to thwart the democratic option as happened in many developing countries (O'Donnell, 1973 and 1978).

Although capitalism and democracy are intrinsically linked both in diachronic and synchronic terms (Huber and Stephens, 1999), the transition to and consolidation of democracy in the long run hinge on a sufficient degree of social differentiation and the resulting social equilibrium and class compromise. As capitalist development expands and deepens, conditions favorable to the rise and strengthening of civil society are created, permitting private civic associations, labor organizations and programmatic political parties increasingly to assert themselves to create and defend their autonomous spaces, and to challenge the appearance of anti-democratic styles of governance and tendencies as well (Huber and Stephens, 1999). According to Linz and Stepan (1996), a functioning modern democracy requires at least five essentials, including a well ordered state, a functioning market economy, the existence of a robust civil society, an autonomous political society that is fully conversant with and respectful of the procedures of governance and legality and constitutionalism. This conceptualization is particularly useful to the extent that it accurately reflects the reality that democracy is not reducible to one or two variables. As the transition to democracy spirally moves through a wearisome process in a continuum from persistence to consolidation and then to habituation (Khagram, 1993), a number of things can happen; the process may march forward with minor snags or it may produce a partially malformed system or it may even become completely derailed before reaching its logical terminus. The key to the problem of transition depends on a thorough understanding of the complex and dialectical relationship between structure and agency.

In any case, the absence of institutions such as the market in addition to the historical conditions under which the African state was created have resulted in qualitative differences in the nature of the African state from those in the advanced countries. One veritable consequence of the inability of developing states, like Eritrea, to crown themselves with fully developed markets is that the boundaries between the public and private spheres remain undifferentiated. Instead of the private sphere leading the way in matters of economic determination, the state for the most part becomes the provider of goods and services, allocator of resources and determiner of policies and strategic directions. The danger inherent in such an objective reality is that the state itself becomes the creator, accumulator and distributor of wealth, and those who wield state power along with their immediate relatives, friends and loyal clients disproportionately benefit from such an arrangement. Because transparency, accounting, and public scrutiny are inimical to the preservation of such an arrangement, the temptation to construct authoritarian architectures of coercion and control becomes unavoidable. So long as the state is instrumentally used by its holders to create personal wealth, formation of democratic governance cannot be the prospect. This objective reality is further complicated by the fact that most public officials do not know how to create personal wealth outside the public sphere. After all, there is a powerful economic rationale behind staying in power; stealing or embezzling public property is cheap, requires no particular skills and takes no effort; the only crucial requirement to be successful in public corruption is moral bankruptcy or moral turpitude.

The character and composition of the Eritrean leadership illustrates this point. The president and all his lieutenants are veterans of the liberation struggle, who spent between twenty and thirty years of their lives in the field. Almost all of them are military commanders, politburo and central committee members or political commissars. Hence, when they entered Asmara in victory, they were incurably habituated to issuing orders from above; politico-military specialization was their certified trade. Under these circumstances, engagement in alternative activity in the private sector was beyond the scope of their imagination as the public sphere became their home, their source of income, status and professional security. Their becoming jealously protective of the state and their place in it was not out of the ordinary, for this is the classic path which all liberation movement leaders before them followed. In light of this fact, our view is that, in the context of the history and existential security needs of the leadership, the Eritrean state was destined to be more the norm than the exception in its authoritarian proclivity and corrupt practices. Just as African elites created a large sector of parastatals, theoretically autonomous economic bodies which they placed under state or party control, the Eritrean elites transformed this inherited example into an art form by creating a state sector and a party sector in the economy, something that is dealt with in depth in chapter three of this book.

As elsewhere in Africa, the ideological dimension of the Front's history also was a contributing factor to the prospect for authoritarianism. With the adoption of the National Democratic Program in 1977, the EPLF proclaimed itself as the vanguard of the working class, guided by the Leninist principle of democratic centralism. Despite the oxymoronic amalgam of the phrase, democratic centralism in practice connoted the dictatorship of the leadership. Marxism in the Eritrean context, as elsewhere, was used more as an ideology of justification and mobilization than an ideology of emancipation. Notwithstanding public renunciation of Marxism since independence, there has never been a clean break with the past in terms of leadership since the same "vanguard" politicians who led the front now rule the country. Indeed, the symmetry between past acts and present actions is remarkable when one considers the political excesses exhibited then and now.

To end our introductory remarks, we return to the epistemological and methodological presuppositions sketched in this chapter and we add a clarification. In our view, the boundary between the idiographic and nomothetic approaches is one defined by mutual permeability. If nomothetic approaches provide insights into the general laws of social motion, contexts and patterns, idiographic approaches furnish the details of the script or text. Without diminishing the significance and peculiarities of Eritrea's experience, we believe that we can write the text of its experience within a larger context and keep the latter largely in the background. Hence, in developing our historical, analytical and theoretical reflection in this work, we consciously shy away from reductionist models; we avoid indulging in determinist presuppositions about Eritrea's inherited structures; we offer neither a broad psycho-analytic diagnosis of the leadership nor a voluntarist prescription for how to cure Eritrea's ills. Where historical processes and structural conditions appear to be prohibitive, we give them their due weight, and where the crisis of legitimacy appears to be a function of leadership, we state so. When we argue that, in addition to sharing the many political and ideological properties of leadership with African states, Eritrea shares with them the analogous situations in history, structures, internal compositions and place in the contemporary international division of labor, we are not suggesting the inevitability of Eritrea repeating the same processes through which other African states passed; we are simply describing the structural impediments and superstructural difficulties that Eritrea has had to overcome in order to make the transition to normal democracy.

We have structured our work in ways that capture four interrelated themes that are explored in the core chapters of the book. First, like all African colonial state, Eritrea was the direct product of the 19th century European scramble for Africa. What the Italians put in place in Eritrea, using a top-down approach to governance, were essentially authoritarian institutions, which by design left the entire indigenous population outside the realm of freedom and material progress. The cultural infrastructure laid down in the service of the colonial state could not have been anything but correspondent to the authoritarian nature of the colonial state. Education to native Eritreans was severely restricted and Italian investments were limited to sectors of immediate necessities and agro-commercial plantations. Controlled colonial development substantially retarded the modernization of native forces of production and thwarted the emergence of civil society. British and Ethiopian occupation of Eritrea made no substantial modifications on existing conditions either. In essence, what the Eritrean liberators inherited from the colonizers was an authoritarian political infrastructure steeped in an authoritarian political culture. Hence, the prospects for forging a regime of democratic governance in Eritrea were dimmer than we always tended to assert. But again, this is something that Eritrea shares with African colonial states, something that is reflected in the character of its transition: the line of reasoning in our second chapter, reviewing the impact of historical processes and structures on the birth and growth of the Eritrean struggle and the intra-liberation contradictions that emanated therefrom. The chapter also previews major themes to be developed in chapters three and four.

Despite the introduction of the capitalist mode of production into Eritrea, the country remains essentially condemned to specialization in the production of a small basket of primary commodities and extractive resources. This division of labor makes the Eritrean economy globally uncompetitive and significantly limits the possibility of promoting internal economic integration and consequent social differentiation, which dampens the prospect for creating the requisite conditions of democracy. Again, this is something Eritrea shares with its African counterparts. Focusing on the agrarian mode of interest articulation and the leadership's tampering with the traditional methods of agrarian governance, on the one hand, and the compartmentalization of the industrial economy into three distinct sectors under state supervision, on the other, chapter three provides a full account of how economic constraints hobble the effort of the state to put in place an economy with predictable prospect for growth and development. The chapter shows how the regime's policy of economic governance has in practice impeded mobilization of native capital, and by extension how it has interfered with the democratic option.

Intra-country heterogeneity is a crucial dimension of politics that complicates the process of transition. Like all sub-Saharan African states, Eritrea is multiethnic and multi-religious in character and composition. What makes this objective reality particularly salient in the African context is that the economic linkages among the constituent groups of African societies are fragile at best, thereby making cooperative interdependence exceedingly difficult to forge. In circumstances of no democratic alternative, this makes politics primarily antagonistic since groups are likely to seek to control the levers of power in order to improve their respective positions in society. Unable to meet growing demands from competing groups, which may use ethnicity and/or religion as the organizing principle of politics, the elites in control of state power increasingly resort to methods of coercion and repression. In turn, unable to obtain what they perceive to be their fair share within the established order, disaffected groups seek refuge in centrifugalism. This gives the ruling elites reason or justification to curtail or abolish constitutional means of governance. Precisely such a dynamic is the subject of chapter four. It provides an in-depth analysis of how the Eritrean regime has opted for a unitary conception of politics and how this conception is given constitutional expression to cope with the presumed vulnerability of the nation to ethnic and religious fragmentation. The chapter also assesses the long range implication of the regime's constitutionalism for the democratic option.

Not surprisingly, the post-independence Eritrean state resembles other African states in its external orientations and relations. A frequent argument is that, given their historical limitations, internal political fragmentation and economic weaknesses, the ability of African states to influence their external environment is severely curtailed. In fact, they become vulnerable to external manipulations as their leaders seek international patrons to subsidize their internal repression or execute wars of aggression against neighbors or to defend themselves against aggression from neighbors in exchange for the provision of proxy services to their external patrons. Moreover, the exteriorization of internal difficulties provides the pretext for postponing political reforms, on the one hand, and creates the circumstances that distort the prospect for economic development as crucial resources are diverted to war-making capability, on the other. This preliminary description aptly captures the external character and behavior of the Eritrean state. Chapters five and six take up this issue and explore the extent to which Eritrea's external relations have short-circuited both constitutional governance and economic development.

Finally, in chapter seven, we pull together the various threads of our historical disquisitions, economic analyses, constitutional probes and foreign policy discussions as well as the elements of our pedagogical understandings and theoretical speculation to give a full picture of Eritrea's post-independence politics, economics and foreign policy. We conclude our intellectual journey by reviewing the current challenges facing the country and previewing its future prospects.

In conclusion, we acknowledge that the quality of the text we have produced in this book is as good as the materials we have gathered and the sources we have consulted. There were two limitations to our research effort. The first involved the iron wall of secrecy that the EPLF built around itself, something that continued into the post-liberation period. There are limited archival materials that are readily accessible by the researcher. The scarcity of documents pertaining to the decision-making process is such that one wonders if the Front ever put in writing the multifarious decisions taken over the decades. The second problem is related to the first one. Our interviews with the participants in the armed struggle or in the government now did not yield results to our satisfaction. The problem in part lies in the fact that the use of a diary to document what is observed, one's experiences or impressions is not customary in the Eritrean context. Even if there were some actors who might have recorded certain events, the culture of secrecy was never conducive to such practice; one would unnecessarily cast suspicion on himself or herself. Given this reality, our interviewees had to reconstruct their answers to our questions from memory. However, human memory is notoriously unreliable. Moreover, there is always the human tendency to exaggerate some events, belittle other acts, embellish facts that support one's own position and denigrate other aspects to present the other side in bad light. Despite these limitations, however, we have carefully selected our materials and scrupulously rejected other materials that we thought did not contribute to the text of our findings.

CHAPTER TWO

HISTORY AND ANATOMY OF
A POPULIST AUTHORITARIAN STATE

In a short decade since liberation in 1991, Eritrea passed through two contradictory images. The first image presented Eritrea as the triumph or beacon of hope. This positive imagery was a continuation of the international reputation the Eritrean liberators earned during the bitter war with the Soviet-backed Ethiopian regime of Mengistu Hailemariam. Despite the Soviets pouring billions of dollars into Ethiopia to bolster the fighting capacity of the Ethiopian army, the Eritrean liberators shattered Ethiopia's war machine with unprecedented tenacity and resilience. What Eritrea demonstrated during the decades of struggle was not only its ability to fight but also its ability to do so on the basis of indigenously fashioned self-reliance. The confidence placed by Eritrean liberators in their own self-reliance gave many observers the hope that the experience in independent struggle would carry over to the building of economic and political democracy in post-conflict Eritrea. However, the exuberant hopes and expectations of Eritreans and their international supporters came to naught within a few years of independence as the country slouched towards dictatorship. This raises the fundamental question as to whether the Eritrean slide to authoritarianism was unavoidable. The position taken here is that the material and cultural conditions and historical experiences of the country were more favorable to the formation of an authoritarian political order than to the emergence of a democratic governance. Fundamental errors in economic and foreign policy, as well as the diplomatic fiasco which the country experienced since liberation, seem unavoidable given the nature of the regime. The overarching purpose of this chapter is not to offer fresh insight into the political history of Eritrea but rather to establish a historical framework within which the present authoritarian political formation must be analyzed and understood.

The Movement That Never Was

Karl Marx wrote in *The 18th Brummier* that men make their history not under conditions of their own choosing but in circumstances chosen for them by the unfolding of material forces (Marx, 1969). Nowhere does this poignant observation have more bearing than on the Eritrean experience. The formation of the Eritrean state was profoundly shaped by the pre-colonial and colonial experiences of the country. In the pre-colonial period, various communities were differentiated from one another by their social morphology and their sharply contrasting material determinants. Structurally, these communities subsisted under different modes of production. In the lowland regions of the country, pastoralism and agro-pastoralism defined the social existence of the inhabitants while sedentary agricultural settlements defined the mode of production in highland Eritrea.

Superstructurally, variations in the mode of production in the lowland and highland regions were contextualized by differences in religious and ethnic markers. Whereas Tigrigna-speaking highlanders professed Christianity, Eritrean lowlanders not only professed Islam but also belonged to different ethnic formations. Compounding the structural determinants and the differences in their superstructural markers were their divergent external experiences. Lowlanders interacted more with their Islamic neighbors to the north and east, while highlanders interacted more with their neighbors to the south. It was these structurally and socially morphological and experientially divergent communities that Italy assembled to construct a colonial state in 1890.

Bringing together the various ethnic and religious formations, Italy created the requisite conditions for inter-communal migrations and interactions that were to leaven Eritrean nationalism. As elsewhere, Italian colonialism provided the necessary elements for the rise of prototype Eritrean nationalism as well as the building blocks for Eritrean nationalism. However, in addition to the fact that the benefits of colonialism were uneven between regions, the colonial impacts on the pre-existing modes of production were ineffective in obliterating the historically inherited conditions of primordialism that expressed themselves in religious, ethnic and regional terms. Moreover, whatever contribution Italy made to the development of Eritrea, it was largely limited to the highland region of the country. For example, as part of its feverish preparation for the war against Ethiopia in the 1930s, Italy undertook a wide range of industrial activities and infrastructure development in highland Eritrea. These actions resulted in accentuating the distinctiveness of the highland region from the rest of Eritrea. The inhabitants of Asmara, for instance, rose sharply from 15,000 in 1935 to 120,000 in 1941(Pool, 2001). By contrast, Italian undertakings in the lowlands focused primarily on the provision of veterinary services to livestock herders and a handful of owners of agro-commercial plantations. Even in the 1950s, there were only five primary schools in the lowland district of Aqordat. These five schools attempted to serve 365 pupils with only eleven teachers. Furthermore, there was only one clinic in the entire district, which was administered by a single nurse (Pool, 2001).

The disparities in the distribution of colonial benefits were made worse in the 1940s when the British Military

Administration found ethnic and religious polarization in the country instrumentally beneficial to the perpetuation of British imperial interest in the area. As the empire builders in London sought to partition Eritrea between the Sudan and Ethiopia, the division was viewed as a facilitator of their aims. The enduring legacy of such exterior machinations was that the use of religion, ethnicity and region as the organizing principles of politics became integral to the evolution of Eritrea's political culture. To be sure, the insufficient structural transformation of the Eritrean economy under colonialism and the stubborn persistence of the primordial conditions of social existence, aggravated by the machinations of external empire builders and internal power seekers, continued to plague Eritrean politics in which the foundations of the present dictatorship are based. The early rivalry between the Eritrean Liberation Movement (ELM) and the Eritrean Liberation Front (ELF) should illustrate the above observation.

When the United States engineered a federal arrangement between Eritrea and Ethiopia, using the United Nations as a front, Eritreans grudgingly accepted the federal formula as an inescapable condition from which they would create the most ideal situation possible. However, the imperial Ethiopian regime proceeded in earnest to draw down the substance of the federal relationship by subverting Eritrea's separate constitutional identity, political pluralism, freedom of speech and organization. In addition, Ethiopia's language, educational system, civil and penal codes and labor law were introduced into Eritrea and, finally, the Eritrean flag was lowered and the emblems of the Eritrean government were altered. Ethiopia's policy to devitalize Eritrea's economy in order to break up the trade unions also led to mass immigration, including 30,000 workers to Saudi Arabia and 20,000 workers to Sudan (Halliday, 1971; Lobban, 1976). In response to these developments, Eritrean students and workers took to the streets with remarkable regularity to halt the erosion of Eritrean autonomy. The civic opposition to Ethiopia's policy of annexation took an organizational form when five Eritrean students, led by Mohammed Said Nawid, created the ELM in November 1958 in Port Sudan (Markakis, 1987). The formation of the ELM was crucial in the sense that its founders displayed a remarkably progressive outlook. Because Mohammed Said Nawid was a member of the Sudanese Communist Youth League, the secularization of Eritrean politics appeared to be an encouraging prospect. Inside Eritrea, Nawid and his comrades demonstrated their secular and progressive vision when they tapped into the growing alienation of Christians, including former unionists, by aggressively recruiting them for the anti-Ethiopian cause. The preamble to the ELM manifesto, for example, stated, "Moslems and Christians are brothers; their unity makes Eritrea one nation" (Markakis, 1987: 105).

As part of a comprehensive plan to mobilize and organize Eritreans inside and outside Eritrea, the ELM leaders also decided to make a political foray into the Eritrean emigre community in Cairo. Cairo was particularly seen by the organizers as a highly prized destination for two reasons. First, there was a large Eritrean community that included over 300 university students. Second, Cairo was the home for many anti-colonial and anti-imperial liberation organizations because of the generous provision of material, diplomatic and moral support by Gamal Abdel Nasser. In order to use this seemingly favorable political climate, ELM leaders dispatched a delegation to Cairo in 1959 and again in 1960 to begin mobilizing the Eritrean community for the nationalist cause. On both occasions, however, the ELM effort was rebuffed by veteran Eritrean politicians who had by this time instituted powerful influence in Cairo. Idris Mohammed Adem, in particular, displayed extreme hostility towards the formation of the ELM. Notably, Idris was a well-known conservative politician from the Beni Amer community in the Barka region. In the late

1940s, he took a group of Moslem lowlanders out of the Moslem League (ML), headed by Ibrahim Sultan Ali, because the League and its leader possessed progressive ideologies with which Idris disagreed. Having eliminated his group from the ML, Idris allied himself with the pro-Ethiopian Unionist Party (Markakis, 1987; Sherman, 1980). This opportunistic maneuvering enabled Idris to become president of the unionist-dominated Eritrean parliament. His realization of the inevitable demise of the federal relationship with Ethiopia and his political fate caused Idris to follow Woldeab Woldemariam and Ibrahim Sultan Ali to Cairo. Once in Cairo, Idris separated himself from the towering figures of Eritrean politics and began to create his own political future. He also simultaneously launched a vitriolic campaign against ELM and its leaders. Threatened by the youthful and secular orientation of the ELM leadership and by Idris Nawid's early affiliation with the Sudanese Communist Party, Idris Adem roused Eritrean nationalists against the ELM (Markakis, 1987; Sherman, 1980). Idris was further aggravated by the fact that Woldeab Woldemariam welcomed the formation of the ELM and offered his services to further its cause. In addition to pushing for progressive politics, Woldeab was a Christian highlander, which appalled Idris.

In the furtherance of sectarian politics, Idris led the creation of a new organization, known as the ELF in 1960. Using religion and ethnicity, Idris recruited a number of Eritreans from the diaspora, notable among whom were Idris Osman Geladewos and Osman Saleh Sabbe. Together, they imposed their overlordship on the ELF. Without ideological clarity, political program and organizational accountability, the three ELF leaders began to lead an armed struggle by remote control from Cairo. The object of their political and armed campaigns was not only Ethiopia but also the ELM. As John Markakis correctly noted, there were three characteristics of the ELM that openly vitiated the sectarian politics of the ELF leadership.

40

First, the ELM was primarily urban centered with particular focus on Asmara and Massawa for fresh recruits. The induction of Christians into the nationalist movement, including former unionists, strongly militated against sectarian politics. Second, the original founders of the ELM came from the regions of Sahel and Keren, whereas Idris Adem and his political clients came from the Barka area. Hence, the conflict between the ELM leadership and the ELF patrons had regional dimensions. Third, the secular orientation of the ELM leadership was equally threatening to the sectarian agenda of the ELF leadership. In fact, the ELF leadership focused extensively on Nawid's early connection with Sudanese Communists in a way that was calculated to vitiate the rising fortune of the ELM. Indeed, the ELF presented ELM leaders as "outsiders with Communist connections and ulterior motives, atheists, and possibly agents of Ethiopia" (Markakis, 1987: 107).

Continually cornered, the ELM leaders finally decided to establish a military presence in Eritrea to advance the cause of Eritrean nationalism under conditions of secular politics. In 1962, the ELM leadership was able to convince thirty policemen to leave their posts with their weapons in order to form the nucleus of the armed struggle. However, they were quickly encircled by the Ethiopian security forces and their effort was extinguished. Another attempt was made in 1965 when the ELM leadership dispatched a force of 50 armed men to Sahel to begin the process of building a national liberation army. In their still naive understanding of politics, the ELM leadership erroneously provided advance notice to ELF forces regarding their military plan in the hope of inducing a unity conference. Fully equipped with advance information, an armed contingent from the ELF force surrounded the arriving ELM elements and disarmed them, but only after six were killed (Markakis, 1987; Sherman, 1980). This marked the beginning of the bloody civil war in Eritrea that was going to haunt the nation for decades. Moreover, the ascendance of the ELF leadership represented the triumph of sectarian politics over secular forces.

Having first weakened and then removed the ELM altogether from the liberation landscape, Idris Adem, Idris Geladewos and Osman Saleh Sabbe proceeded to construct the liberation army on the basis of sectarian criteria of religion, region and ethnicity. Mimicking the Algerian zonal military construction, the ELF leadership created four zonal military forces. All four commanders of the zonal divisions were not only Moslems but were also tied to their political overlords by a system of patronage, which was watered by region, religion and ethnicity. The ELF's unmistakable drift towards religion, ethnicity and region not only retarded the progressive evolution of liberation politics but also worsened inter-communal relations as ELF units took sides in civic disputes between Christian peasants and Moslem pastoralists. By grounding liberation politics in religious and ethnic cleavages, the ELF leadership sowed the first seeds of an authoritarian political formation in Eritrea. In consequence, the precious seminal moment that presented itself in favor of a democratic liberation governance was wastefully squandered.

Formation of the Eritrean People's Liberation Front (EPLF)

After long resistance to the induction of Christian nationalists into the liberation struggle, ELF leaders were eventually forced to accommodate the integration of Christian nationalists into the movement under controlled conditions. As the influx of Christian activists increased, the leadership created a fifth zonal division primarily comprised of Christian fighters under a Christian commander. However, the growing presence of Christians began to unravel the internal contradictions of the front. In addition to the differences in religious, ethnic and regional markers between the lowland and highland fighters, the secular disposition and radical political outlook of the highlanders became problematic from the perspective of the ELF leadership. The inherited Moslem suspicion of Christian highlanders as having been pro-integration continued to put in context the leadership's hostility towards Christian nationalists. In 1967 Ethiopia launched a number of highly coordinated campaigns of encirclement and suppression against the Front's highly disjointed military structure, and Christians were particularly blamed for the poor performance of the Front's fighting force and the military setbacks from which they suffered. For example, a certain Osman Hishal, Geladewos' protégé and Moslem deputy commander of the fifth zonal division, summarily executed twenty-seven Christian fighters on alleged poor performance. The deputy commander was able to take such draconian measures because Wolday Kahsai, the Christian commander of the fifth division, happened to be in the Sudan. This prompted Wolday to surrender to Ethiopia together with nineteen fighters, which the ELF leadership interpreted as confirmation of Christian untrustworthiness (Markakis, 1987; Sherman, 1980).

Another negative feature of the history of the ELF was the mistreatment of three hundred Christian fighters, who were at the time referred to as *"Sriya Addis Abeba"* because most of them came from Addis Abeba. On mere suspicion of being Ethiopian agents alone, these fighters were made to endure unbearable torture at the hands of ELF interrogators; a large number of them were also summarily executed. By some accounts, between two hundred and three hundred Christian fighters and fifty Christian peasants were executed at the behest of ELF leadership (Pool, 2001; Sherman, 1980).

In the end, however, the saliency of sectarian politics brought the viability of the Front into serious question. The Front had to either break up into pieces or reform itself along multiethnic, secular and democratic lines. In 1968 the clash between the peddlers in sectarian politics and the secular elements became unavoidable. The position of the secular forces appears to have been strengthened by two factors. In the first instance, the forty-three ELF cadres sent to China and Cuba for training had returned to Eritrea and took their positions as political commissars or commanders within the liberation army. Notable among the returnees were Ramadan Mohammed Nur and Isaias Afeworki, who became political commissars of the 4th and 5th zones respectively. The shared experiences the two developed within the ELF and in China would be crucial in shaping the character of the EPLF later.

The second factor militating in favor of reform was the growing influx of Christian highlanders into the Front, who were armed with the radical imagery of how a liberation front should be structured. Invigorated by their own experiences and the addition of recruits, the secular forces within the ELF now called for the radical overhaul of the Front by abolishing the zonal military configuration, establishing a political leadership within Eritrea and centralizing the Front's supply networks.

Although the reformers initially appeared to have succeeded in their primary objectives, ultimately they lost it to the sectarian forces and the Front fractured into pieces. The Ala group, made up of Christian highlanders, the Popular Liberation Forces, made up of fighters from the Massawa and Sahel areas and a group of Obelians from the Barka region, broke away from the ELF and began roaming parts of Eritrea in search of liberation space and identity.

Eventually, the declaration of war by the ELF on the three breakaway factions prompted them to close ranks and form a union, leading to the formation of the EPLF. The ELF leadership claimed that the Eritrean field was too small to accommodate several liberation forces and leadership, therefore justifying their declaration of war on the separated factions. In effect, this anticipated the EPLF's reasoning in the early 1980s when EPLF forces militarily evicted the ELF from Eritrea.

In any case, having acquired organizational distinctness, the EPLF crafted a secular vision for both itself and for Eritrea. However, the secular vision it articulated was fraught with contradictions and complications that completed the authoritarianization of the country's political culture. First, it seems that the EPLF leadership succumbed to pressure from the Ethiopian left to go beyond nationalism in embracing Marxism in order to recognize the EPLF as an authentic and credible anti-imperialist and progressive force of the age. Second, the returnees from China and Cuba seemed to have indiscriminately internalized what they observed and learned about political organization, which could not have been formulated from anything but Stalinist ideology. Nasserist and Baathist influences on the political thinking of certain elements within the EPLF could not have been precluded either. Third, the broader cultural environment within which the fighters were brought up could not be excluded from factors that influenced the formation of EPLF ideology and organization. Ethiopia's political culture was largely based on brute force; coercion was central to the exercise of control. Thus, when the nationalists trickled to the field, they could not have completely discarded their conception of coercive authority. Moreover, the experiences of the leading founders of the EPLF within the ELF shaped their general disposition towards the value of control, cohesion, discipline and secrecy. The cumulative effect of these influences probably led to the articulation of an ideology of justification of the end, embedded in a unitary conception of liberation organization. The means employed to further the unitary conception of liberation were justified by reference to the achievement of authoritarian efficiency as critical to internal cohesion and external impenetrability (Pool, 2001; Sherman, 1980).

The internal contradictions that emerged within the EPLF reinforced the totalizing tendency within the front. This tendency expressed itself in the struggle between those who migrated from the ELF to the EPLF and those who joined the EPLF after its formation in the early 1970s. It is useful to recall that, beginning in 1968, the Ethiopian student movement decidedly moved leftward on the basis of an ideology of nationalism and anti-imperialism, embellished by an amalgam of Stalinist, Maoist, Guevaraist and Castrite inclinations. Eritrean students were influenced by the same principles that were highly active in campus politics in Addis Abeba and developed a good working relationship with their Ethiopian comrades on the basis of shared ideological vision. With the formation of the Ala group, many of the campus politicians flocked into the new liberation forces. However, the optimism of the new recruits for a full-blown socialist revolution was bound to clash with the political priority of older fighters who were still motivated by unpleasant experiences under an authoritarian culture in the ELF. The new recruits, led by Mussie Tesfamichael and Yohannes Sebhatu, political commissar and director of propaganda respectively, brought the Front's entire structure of governance into question. By so doing, they initiated a power struggle between themselves and the older fighters, who were led by Isaias Afeworki. The followers of Isaias gave the opposition the pejorative name *Menkaa*, from the Tigrinya word for bat, suggesting that the challengers were ultra-leftists devoted to hatching plots under the cover of darkness. In a nutshell, what the challengers raised were questions of leadership, political education, democracy both within the Front and between the Front and the civilian population, and the nature of the struggle. The *Menkaa* group saw the prevalence of poor coordination among the fighting units, slow movements or inadequate provisions of supplies, direct physical abuse of fighters by Isaias that included beating or striking, mistreatment of civilians by fighters, censorship of publications and Isaias' compulsive intrusion into the autonomy of cadres as fatal errors (Markakis, 1987; Pool, 2001). To rectify these flaws, the challengers called for the

46

formation of a "people's administration," guarded by supervisory bodies, the promotion of democratic transparency and accountability by means of power sharing, the establishment of a popular committee to scrutinize the decisions and monitor the actions of the leadership and the election of unit leaders by their unit members. In this view, administrative decentralization and the diffusion of responsibilities among the Front's entities could insure the promotion of a democratic order within the Front and the general populace at large (Pool, 2001; Markakis, 1987).

In contrast, by presenting the EPLF as above the individual, Isaias envisioned a corporatist political structure embedded in Leninist-Stalinist values. As David Pool noted, to Isaias the centrality and continuity of political leadership and "controlled participation" were critical to the cohesion, efficacy and success of the Front. In keeping with this corporatist vision, it was incumbent on the leadership to discover what the real needs and desires of the masses were, whereupon the leadership would fashion realistic decisions to solve the problems facing the front and its popular constituencies; the decisions were then to be vertically channeled to those responsible to implement them. Moreover, the leadership was politically answerable to the Front only to the extent that it was under a formal obligation to receive critical feedback from enforcement mechanisms of the front (Pool, 2001).

Several EPLF cadres who were present at the creation of the power struggle have recounted (to us) that the challengers were initially in ascendance as they were able to rally the majority of the fighters to their side. According to their account, over 80% of the fighters were receptive to the challengers' reasoning and vision. Even Solomon Woldemariam, who was then the Front's security chief, told a small group in Khartoum in the summer of 1976 that up to one thousand fighters were participants in the *Menkaa* movement. In spite of popular support, however, the challengers appear to have lost the struggle due to a combination of their own tactically fatal errors and Isaias' superior tactical maneuvering.

First, early on the challengers displayed their tactical immaturity by taking for granted the substantial amount of support they received from the rank and file fighters. Moreover, according to our informants, the challengers were reckless in their political activity by treating the field as if it were a university campus. In their exercise of immature politics, some elements within the *Menkaa* group used soccer as a metaphor to rouse support; using the megaphone at night they assigned points to the nation's provinces; the higher the points a province got, the greater the support that province presumably gave to the cause of the challengers. In effect, the challengers were insensitive to the differentiating regional and religious markers among the fighters.

Second, the challengers' primary focus of political agitation was the highlanders. Immersed in their own hyper-revolutionary jargon, the challengers failed to connect with the Moslem lowlanders by using more ordinary language of politics. They disregarded the importance of the Ramadan group to the outcome of the struggle, therefore allowing Isaias to retaliate against the challengers by utilizing his former relationship with Ramadan. Through Ramadan, Isaias effectively mobilized Moslem lowlanders against the challengers. Another informant told us that Isaias was extremely shrewd in his surreptitious use of regional and religious differences to advance his political ambition while appearing to stay above the fray in parochial politics. Using regionalism as a fodder of politics, for example, he astutely played Solomon Woldemariam and Tewolde Eyob against each other. By some accounts, Solomon and Tewolde were two ambitious rivals with equally strong regionalist proclivity. While Isaias fueled the rivalry between the two, he appeared publicly to be against such divisive rivalry. Incidentally, both Solomon and Tewolde were the only two original members of the *Ala* leadership who were sympathetic toward the "*Menkaa*" group, not necessarily out of ideological conviction but rather out of political ambition. Tewolde was among the first batch of *Menkaa* elements executed, and Solomon would be executed five years later.

Finally, Isaias pulled an EPLF unit from the highland region to Sahel in the hope of capitalizing on the unit's nonparticipation in the power struggle. Not privy to what went on in Sahel, the unit cast its support for the Isaias group, perhaps sealing the fate of the challengers (Markakis, 1987).

Having secured the upper hand, Isaias then adroitly engineered the formation of a committee to investigate the episode. Packed with pro-Isaias elements, the committee had no difficulty in recommending a jury to try those who participated in the *Menkaa* movement. The challengers were found guilty of crimes against the Front in particular and the struggle in general. A cadre told us that one of the charges secretly produced before the jury, cleverly crafted to prejudice the outcome of the proceedings, was that the challengers buried badly needed arms in places where the Ethiopian army could easily find them. The informant added that the Isaias group deliberately spread the rumor that there were up to one hundred and fifty CIA spies within the Front whom the challengers handled.

Although there is no official EPLF counting of those executed, some writers give the number of those executed around eleven (Pool, 2001; Connell, 2000). Others, however, assess the figure to be significantly higher. In fact, in the summer of 1976, Solomon Woldemariam dismissed the above-mentioned number of those executed for having led or participated in the *Menkaa* movement as too small, suggesting that the number was much larger. Solomon added that around one thousand fighters who participated in the movement were rehabilitated after undergoing serious political indoctrination and self-criticism. Moreover, the purge of the *Menkaa* group was not a single act but rather a sequence of events that continued over an extended period of time. In fact, *Menkaa* became a widely used term of opprobrium, a short-hand for demonizing any opponent as a prelude to his or her physical elimination. Moreover, an informant recounted to us that the term "*Menkaa*" served a useful function of socialization to produce unquestioning collective minds, because the mere insinuation of invoking the term against anyone who dared to raise questions about even mundane matters would terrify him or her into sheepish silence.

It is worth recalling that Teklay Aden, an EPLF security chief who defected to the Ethiopian regime in 1981, revealed that three thousand fighters were physically liquidated by the Front between the start of the internal power struggle and the time of his defection. Because of his defection, many observers (including us) have called his credibility into question. In recent years, however, some of our interviewees have seemed to support Teklay's claim without necessarily accepting the three thousand figure as wholly accurate. One informant said that the number of fighters physically eliminated by the Front between 1973 and the liberation of Eritrea in 1991 could range between three thousand and five thousand if those fighters who disappeared under mysterious circumstances are included. A caveat must be noted here: in the absence of documentary evidence, the reported numbers of fighters executed by the Front for political reasons must be taken with a healthy dose of skepticism until a thorough and complete study or a meticulous compilation of the various pieces of the puzzle is made. None of the persons we interviewed was privy to all the circumstances surrounding the executions and disappearances of fighters. However, one fact is clear. A large number of fighters were eliminated for political reasons. Moreover, it was common to send potentially troublesome fighters to frontlines where pitched battles with the Ethiopian army were anticipated so that they would perish by Ethiopian bullets. The fate of some former ELF fighters at the battle of

Massawa illustrates Isaias' expedient stratagem. When the ELF internally fractured, a group of democratic fighters, numbering around two thousand, broke away from the front in 1977 and tried to create their own liberation space. Pursued by the "mother" front, however, they were unable to establish themselves as a viable and independent force, and they were prompted to join the EPLF. Simple commonsense dictates that the EPLF leadership would have integrated these democrats by spreading them around the front's various entities. Instead, the Isaias leadership deployed them as a group to the Massawa front where a fierce battle was raging between the Eritrean liberators and the Ethiopian army, the latter heavily supported by air and navy. Massawa was where the former ELF democrats perished without enough survivors to tell their story. The working hypothesis of the time was that Isaias did not want their integration into the general EPLF structure lest they infected EPLF units with the democratic germ— questioning the Front's method of governance, absence of open debate and over-centralization.

In any event, apart from the tragic elimination of many fighters under false charges of association with the alleged "ultra-leftist" tendency, the enduring legacy of the power struggle that plagued the EPLF in the 1970s was the negative contribution it made to the totalizing process of authoritarianization within the Front. One lasting effect of the power struggle was the anti-intellectual culture that developed within the EPLF, carried over to post-liberation Eritrea.

Beneath the veneer of the ideo-political struggle between the challengers and Isaias, there were deep clashes of ambition and personality. According to some accounts, Isaias was never comfortable with the new arrivals from Addis Abeba, especially with Mussie and Yohannes. Before their departure for the Eritrean field, Mussie and Yohannes were fast rising stars within the Eritrean and Ethiopian student population. Moreover, both were among the seven students who highjacked an Ethiopian passenger airliner on their way to the field, and such Guevaraist adventurism was seen as a mark of revolutionary virtue of the age which aided in the rise of their ideo-political currency. In addition, Mussie, Yohannes and their followers were reputed to have been colorful debaters. By contrast, Isaias was said to hate open ideological debate. His style was to use frequented cliches to disparage the ideas and arguments of his opponents. He would withdraw pouting or use physical force to intimidate his opponents during open discussions. One informant told us that Isaias was unforgiving, vengeful and ruthless towards anyone who challenged him intellectually, ideologically and politically. Against this backdrop Isaias began to view fresh educated recruits with suspicion. In due course, heavy political indoctrination, perpetual surveillance of intellectuals and continually assigning them to different positions and different places became Isaias' methods of containment and preemption. Promotion of distrust among potential rivals, humiliating them through hard labor, freezing them without explanation and imprisonment were used meticulously. Secrecy was central to the maintenance of discipline and subservience. Even punishments were meted out in secrecy. In most cases, only the victims and the enforcers of the reprimand would know the reasons and nature of the punishments. It was strictly prohibited to hold discussion regarding incarceration and punishment with anyone (Pool, 2001).

The power struggle between the *Menkaa* challengers and Isaias was a watershed event in an even more crucial respect. Irrespective of the merits of the competing visions, the manner in which the internal contradictions were resolved represented the triumph of the Stalinist centralization of the entire structure of liberation governance. The ruthless liquidation of the challengers heralded the rise of Isaias as the central figure and led to the creation of the Eritrean People's Revolutionary Party

(EPRP) in 1973. This guaranteed the ubiquity of internal repression of dissent, unmistakably putting the trajectory of the liberation struggle on the classic road to dictatorship. The EPRP, clandestinely intended to provide Marxist ideological vision and political direction to the national struggle, was placed at the center of the totalizing process. Henceforth, any step taken by the Front was to be defended by reference to the ossified dogma of democratic centralism. Discipline, national unity, organizational cohesion and containment of sectarian tendencies (Connell, 1996) became the buzz phrases fostering conformism and stifling creative thinking. Political indoctrination was critical to attaining these subjective goals. The standard bearers of the indoctrinating enterprise were carefully selected and trained partisan cadres who were placed in charge of the ideological mission of the Front. Between 1979 and 1982 alone the Front trained four hundred political indoctrinators, which was a sharp rise in the generation of cadres when compared with the two hundred sixty-six political operatives the Front produced between 1975 and 1979 (Connell, 1996). By 1977 the Stalinist regimentation of the EPLF was completed when the Marxist leadership marketed the EPLF as a nationalist front under "proletarian" leadership. When necessary, the nationalist character of the front was emphasized particularly in the Middle East and on other occasions the "proletarian" aspect of the front was highlighted when dealing with Socialist countries. In retrospect, the front settled for territorial liberation without political emancipation, something that predetermined the character of the post-liberation regime.

A dictatorial regime, securely embedded in authoritarian political culture, was born and nursed to maturity in the next two decades. That the EPLF was internally abusive was well known to many Eritreans and to international supporters of the Eritrean cause. Its abuses were tolerated in the temporal context within which the Eritrean struggle faced the largest enemy army in Africa, fully supported, trained and armed by both superpowers. Martin Plaut recently stated it best when he wrote: "Fighting a successful campaign under such conditions required the EPLF to take some fairly draconian measures to insure its internal and external survival. But it was widely assumed that these were only temporary phenomena, necessitated by the exigencies of the moment" (Plaut, 2002). However, the problem was that, once the mechanics of dictatorship were put in place, it was very unlikely to undo them as they would naturally acquire their own logic of permanence.

The Long March to Dictatorship

By the time the EPLF held its first congress in January 1977, preceded in the previous year by the party's congress that produced the list of candidates for the central committee and politburo, the Front's popularity had reached its high water mark. The military prowess that EPLF units demonstrated against the Ethiopian army unavoidably elevated the political credibility of the EPLF both nationally and internationally. Many observers mistakenly associated the military successes of the Front with its leadership quality. At any rate, the political capital of the EPLF rose significantly over the years, while that of the ELF diminished appreciably.

In its 1971 and 1975 congressional resolutions, the ELF leadership had tried to mimic the secular drift of the EPLF and its socialist orientation as well. However, ELF resolutions remained a mere articulation of vision and orientation; the socialist agenda was to be realized only by a post-liberation Eritrean government. The agrarian question and gender issues were matters that had to wait for the post-independence order to handle. Moreover, despite the official abandonment of parochial and sectarian politics, the ELF leadership remained predominantly Islamic and lowland. For example, of the thirteen member top ELF leadership that was chosen by the first congress, only one Christian highlander, Hirouy Tedla Bayru, was included. As a result, the highland/lowland and Christian/Moslem divide continued to define the political configuration of the ELF. This divide grossly hampered the ELF leadership's ability to centralize information, power and control. As more and more Christian highlanders with a secular vision flocked into the Front following the Ethiopian revolution, the ELF leadership's ability to provide a new direction and vision increasingly diminished. The result was that competing tendencies began to pull the ELF in different directions. As the contradictions between the new fighters seeking greater democracy and the old leadership clinging to the antiquated methods sharpened, the ELF splintered into factions. Lack of supplies and safe zones left the ELF unable to stand on their own and caused many ELF fighters to join the EPLF. Buffeted by internal dissension and depleted by defection, the ELF now appeared vulnerable to EPLF machinations. By the late 1970s, the number of ELF forces had dropped to as low as 7,000 while EPLF could count on 30,000 highly trained and well-armed liberators (Sherman, 1980; Halliday and Molyneux, 1981). Isaias and his group resorted to the old ELF argument that Eritrea could not support more than one liberation front as justification in unleashing EPLF's war machine on the sisterly front. Ironically, until 1977, the EPLF poignantly argued that secondary contradictions could not and should not be resolved by armed means, suggesting that political dialogue and ideological competition were the proper methods of handling inter-liberation differences and conflicts. But this was when the EPLF was militarily weak relative to its rival. Capitalizing on the shift in the balance of forces between the ELF and itself, however, the EPLF leadership chose to use armed forces to resolve secondary contradictions, claiming that the now sharpened class contradictions in Eritrea called for such action.

With the physical elimination of the ELF, the prospect of totalizing the process of authoritarian politics became inescapable. Without countervailing pressure from a rival front, universalizing the Front's political mode of operation inside Eritrea and embellishing its external imagery proceeded hand in hand. Employing a top-down approach, the Front segmented the civilian population in liberated areas by using social or occupational criteria which were already in operation in the Sahel and Senhit regions. Upon liberating Keren in 1977, for example, the Front compartmentalized the area into six political and administrative zones, each zone in turn compartmented into six associations on the basis of gender, occupation and class. There was even an association for the petty bourgeoisie (Houtart, 1980). The associations were subjected to fifty weekly sessions to receive political education from the Front's political cadres (Houtart, 1980). The political curriculum was developed by the Front's ideological school without input of any kind from the mass organizations. The political education, supposedly allowing the masses to differentiate between their friends and enemies, amounted to no more than sheer indoctrination of the broad masses; uniformity of thought, not diversity of views or critical thinking, was the ultimate purpose of the Front's political education. Blind loyalty to and absolute trust in the Front were treated as the only political virtues of anyone worthy of joining the EPLF. In effect, by developing the mass associations into means of mobilization and a mere transmission belt of control, the Front effectively thwarted the prospect for creating competing democratic spaces from below.

Externally, the EPLF marketed itself as the sole representative of the Eritrean people and many outside the country accepted it. By fiat, the EPLF leadership appropriated the entire liberation history of the country; the ELF was not only physically evicted from Eritrea but also the role it played in the liberation struggle was erased from the consciousness of fighters and masses alike. Hence, both objectively and subjectively, the EPLF leadership was well-positioned without an internally legitimate and externally recognized opposition to establishment of a monopoly control on the country's political landscape. A byproduct of these circumstances with far-reaching implications for democracy was the grand illusion that developed about the Front's future ability to perpetuate itself in power without partners or rivals in legitimating national discourse.

The coincidence of Eritrea's liberation with the fall of Soviet Communism and the consequent expectation of a new era of emerging democratization offered a glimpse of a bright future for Eritrea. The early moves of the provisional regime in the direction of greater centralization, however, sent ominous signals. For example, having begun a dialogue with one faction of the ELF, namely the Eritrean Liberation Front-Revolutionary Command (ELF-RC), the provisional regime capriciously suspended the discussion on the eve when the ELF-RC delegation was due in Asmara to finalize the outcome of the exchange. This was in open defiance of the basic principle of good faith and trust as well as to the notion of political pluralism. Cushioned by the huge political capital the Front had accumulated, the unquestioning popular support it had amassed and by the promise of American patronage, Isaias felt secure enough to defy any intimation at political democracy. Whenever subdued inquiries were made with regard to the Front's political vision and future plans, Isaias used the "tortoise walk" as a metaphor to scoff at those who implied pluralism by such inquiries. Economic reconstruction, not political democracy, became the all-explaining mantra of the regime. Isaias's determination to perpetuate a dictatorial order became even clearer when he used the Front's Third Congress in February 1994 to transform the EPLF into the Popular Front for Democracy and Justice (PFDJ) as the single ruling party. The congress adopted a national charter ostensibly to guide the party and the regime until a constitution was drafted and ratified. No one dared to ask the question at the time why a national charter was needed when a constitutional commission was already established to draft a national constitution, nor did anyone grasp the apparent incongruity between the adoption of the national charter and formation of the single ruling party, on the one hand, and the establishment of the constitutional commission, on the other.

In any event, the national charter is lucidly revealing of the single party's intentions and plans. The document is fraught with contradictions, clichés, redundancies and platitudes. What was drawn out in thirty-three pages could have been easily presented in three to five pages. In a nutshell, the new party manifesto promised the promotion of "cultural democracy," "economic democracy" and "political democracy" as central to the mission of the party and the regime. These broad categories of democracy were to express themselves in the operational understanding and practical demonstration of national unity, gender and ethnic equality, popular participation, social justice, self-reliance and collective leadership. In the balance of this chapter we will examine whether the regime's normative pledges matched its practices.

The Fallacy of "Cultural Democracy"

On its face, the recognition of "cultural democracy" as central to the progressive evolution of the Eritrean society is sound. In view of the ethnic and religious heterogeneity of the country, the construction of a cultural framework to combat ethnic chauvinism and religious bigotry is certainly warranted. Hence, given the multiethnic and multi-religious character as well as the structural underdevelopment of the country, a strong case could be made for a larger role for the state in creating the requisite conditions of primitive cultural accumulation. The implantation, evolution and universalization of norms of reciprocity, trust and civic solidarity (or social capital in the parlance of the age), which were still in their infancy in Eritrea, would certainly favor the agency of the state. To the extent that these values were a function of the emergence of dense networks of economic relationships, they could only be created over time and under conditions of sustained economic transformation and democratic governance. No doubt, the liberation of the country presented an opportune situation for the various ethnic and religious communities to redefine or reconfigure their perceived beliefs, values and practices under new sets of discursive communication and constitutive cultural representation. In other words, norms of reciprocity, trust and civic orientation could only result from the complex interaction between contestation and approbation taking place within a legitimating national discourse. The anticipated role of the government thus became to use the state as the agent in creating the conducive environment for the cultural reconfiguration and renewal to take place from below.

Upon deconstruction, however, it is extremely difficult to interpret the regime's articulation of "cultural democracy" policy as integral to its overall goals. In one breath, the framers of the manifesto contended that critical to effectuating the policy was to vigorously combat divisive tendencies that were to manifest themselves in the forms of religion, ethnicity and region. The party and regime could determine what constituted divisive tendencies. On the other hand, the party manifesto pledged that the state would do everything in its capacity to assist in the development, promotion and popularization of cultural diversity, the cultivation of minority languages and the protection of minority group rights (PFDJ Charter, 1994). Moreover, the party manifesto particularized Eritrean culture by asserting that this culture was developed and tested during the liberation years, which in effect suggested there was a single Eritrean culture in the field and negated the initial premise relative to the existence of cultural diversity in the country. Furthermore, by presenting Eritrean culture as uniquely rooted in self-reliance, the authors of the document seemed to reject the existence of universal cultural norms. In any case, the aim of the cultural policy seemed more to provide a central channel of corporatist control than to create an environment within which the indigenous communities could develop, promote and popularize their own cultural forms of existence. Before assessing the outcomes of the regime's policy, a word or so on the paradigmatic framework must be said.

In the early 1970s, Augustin Girard, head of the cultural research unit within the French Ministry of Cultures, popularized "democratization of culture" and "cultural democracy" as two contrasting approaches to the policy of developing, promoting and popularizing core cultural values under the stewardship of the state (Everald, 1997; Langsted, 1990). The "democratization of culture" policy presupposes the existence of one national culture. In this view, the problem is that the national culture is not accessible to the disadvantaged, underprivileged and poorly educated common man. The solution to the problem of access then becomes one of developing a cultural infrastructure that will democratically distribute cultural commodities and disseminate information about available cultural values and choices.

By contrast, "cultural democracy" presupposes the existence of multiple layers of cultural values, norms, choices and products, requiring their discovery and satisfaction by pursuing a policy that creates the conditions for multiple forms of self-assertion, self-expression and self-development. "[A] model of 'cultural democracy' may be defined as one founded on free individual choice, in which the role of a cultural policy is not to interfere with the preferences expressed by citizen-consumers but to support the choices made by individuals or social groups through a regulatory policy applied to the distribution of information or the structures of supply, as happens in other types of markets" (Averald, 1997: 167-175). Thus, "cultural democracy" signifies the creation of requisite conditions under which individuals and groups are able to cultivate themselves in the arts, literature, philosophy, aesthetics and ethics. The purpose is to unleash the critical minds and energies of all cultural forces to actively engage in the creation, production and administration of a wide variety of cultural goods and services, which is viewed as essential to nurturing progress.

On the general level, the authors of the PFDJ manifesto were not even close to understanding the ordinary definition of "cultural democracy," much less to implementing it. Their description of the concept was embedded in the presumption that there was a single Eritrean culture that was incubated, hatched and developed in the field and grounded in self-reliance, which had to be applied to all communities in the country. In this sense, the members of the political class actually meant "democratization of culture" when they unconsciously or unknowingly slipped the notion of "cultural democracy" into the manifesto. The political result of the regime's cultural policy affirmed this conclusion. By monopolizing the flow of information, education and the cultural grid itself, the regime stifled critical thinking and thwarted the emergence and flowering of pluralist cultural tendencies and creativities. By actively promoting a culture that looked to the past—past heroism, past martyrdom, past sacrifices—it effectively blocked the emergence of a forward thinking and progressive cultural milieu.

On the micro level, the regime's cultural policy has not to date fostered cultural diversity either. By imposing a unitary conception of culture on the various ethnic, religious and regional formations in the country, the regime has effectively arrested the search for cultural autonomy, authenticity and particularity. For example, intended to weaken the saliency of cultural particularity and ethnic identity, the regime has reconfigured the territorial markers of the country so that ethnic groups would not associate identity with territory on the basis of which they might claim cultural autonomy and authenticity. In addition, the regime's language policy is one that has discouraged the blossoming of "cultural democracy." In theory, the ethnic groups in the country are allowed to learn in their vernacular. In practice, however, the policy is far from intellectually empowering group members. Allowing an ethnic community to count from one to ten in the native tongue or allowing it to have its own alphabet does not constitute cultural development. Language democracy includes enabling a community to create the requisite conditions for a literate community, capable of writing poetry, developing literature, and producing works in economics, politics, philosophy, jurisprudence and the like in their mother tongue. Moreover, the regime's language policy has in effect preempted ethnic communities from choosing a language that they prefer to use. One commonly heard complaint from such ethnic groups as the Saho and Afar communities is that the regime has forced them to learn in their local languages in primary schools for fear that the common use of Arabic language would unify the several ethnic groups and make them defiant of the corporatist stratagem of containment. Regardless whether the complaint has merits, the point is that, by substituting its own cultural preferences for community choices, the regime has demonstrably hindered the development of "cultural democracy." From the regime's standpoint, the use of Arabic by various ethnic groups appears to be interfering with the secular process of nation-building. Only one (Rashayda) out of the nine ethnic groups in the country could legitimately claim to have Arabic heritage in terms of culture and language, but members of the Rashayda community represent a mere two percent of the total population in the country. In addition to the geopolitical dimension, the religious connotation of Arabic and hence its use by non-Arab ethnic communities is problematic for the regime since it could potentially dilute the search for a non-Arab and secular Eritrean identity. The communities which demand that the Arabic language be given a national and constitutional standing want it not because they are Arabs but because they are Moslems. In any event, the regime's language policy has failed to resonate with the ethnic groups either because the regime is unable to overcome the gap between the objective markers of the groups and their subjective understandings of those markers or because the regime's top-down approach to social communication is resented by the ethnic groups.

The regime's obsequious promotion of regionalism is another dimension of the problem. At the official level, the regime bemoans the reappearance of regionalist tendencies in Eritrean politics in the wake of the current power struggle among the old liberators themselves. However, the regime appears to be the chief promoter of regionalism, intending to undercut the opposition's ability to mount a united front against the regime. According to our informants, by orchestrating the association of the undertakers of parochialism with the province of Akele Guzai, Isaias tried to recast the recent political struggle in regional terms. This time, however, the political reformers appear to have held together, foiling the regionalist machination. The fact that the eleven senior government officials who have been in jail since September 2001 represent almost all regions of the country illustrates the ineffectiveness of the divide and contain strategem. It is useful to recall that the application of regionalism as a stratagem of containment began by Isaias himself during his struggle with the *Menkaa* group in the 1970s. Assisted by his political operatives, Isaias orchestrated the rumor that the "*Menkaa* plotters" were exclusively from Akele Guzai, which eye witnesses regard as patently untrue. Regionalism in the context of Eritrean politics usually refers to rivalry between the three Christian and Tigrinya-speaking highland provinces of the country. Even if applying this narrower definition of regionalism, one could surely argue that the *Menkaa* movement was multi-regional in composition since members of the group came from all three highland provinces. Yet because Mussie and Yohannes were from Akele Guzai and because they were widely popular, eclipsing Isaias' inflated sense of self-importance to the movement, he was partially successful in brainwashing a large number of his political operatives that the opposition was an Akele Guzai undertaking. One of us has interviewed both Eritrean and Ethiopian contemporaries who closely knew Mussie and Yohannes and none accused them of narrow nationalism or regionalism. If anything, Mussie and Yohannes were too internationalist in their outlook so as not to blindly fall into regionalist trappings. After all, such prominent liberators like Petros Solomon and Sebhat Ephraim, who were not from Akele Guzai and who held various ministerial portfolios after independence, were active in the *Menkaa* movement. Some veteran fighters told one of us that by establishing a connection between the widespread recognition of Yohannes and Mussie and the province from which they came, Isaias found regionalism conveniently effective to isolate and eliminate the *Menkaa* group.

Lest the above characterization might be interpreted that Isaias is regionalist, a cautionary note is warranted here. Those who know Isaias told us that he does not have any regionalist impulse at all, which is his greatest strength. An urbane Asmaran without distinct ties to the traditional provinces of Eritrea, Isaias could not have displayed regionalist predilections. His use of regionalism as a political means of divide and contain is purely utilitarian without preference for a particular region or religion. To Isaias' corporatist vision, the region and religion of his loyalists are immaterial; only when the loyalists fall out of favor with him do their origins or religions become expedient for political exploitation in order to protect the corporatist unity and direction of his agenda. Moreover, Isaias could not manufacture regionalism out of thin air; regionalism did and does exist as a raw material in

Eritrean society as one of the manifestations of the absence of structural integration. In the context of sharpening political struggles, all contenders for power could not but resort to processing existing political raw materials to better their positions in the struggles. In this sense, Isaias could not have been an exception; no one could deny that there were regionalist divisions during and after liberation either.

The emancipation of women from all forms of degradation was also noted in the PFDJ manifesto as the centerpiece of cultural democracy. The participation of women in the armed struggle—constituting a third of the fighting force—was the most cherished trademark of the Front. However, although women were highly visible on the frontline in health, administration, transport, metal and electrical workshops, their conspicuous absence, not by choice but by exclusion, from the commanding heights of the Front's politics, power and responsibility did not portend well for the future of women in post-liberation Eritrea. Like all developing countries, Eritrea has unhealthy, inherited traditions and customs that degrade the humanity, integrity and dignity of women. Through the perpetuation of "functional and utilitarian socialization" of gender roles (Stefanos,1997), Eritrean women have hitherto been relegated to second class status, discriminated against in education, employment and ownership of land, worsened by their subjection to inhumane treatments at the hands of their husbands in particular and society in general. Noting the centrality of women to the struggle, the 1977 EPLF "National Democratic Program" pledged to provide a national context for the "Fight to eradicate prostitution" and "Respect the right of women not to engage in work harmful to their health." The 1994 PFDJ manifesto also pledged to push forward female emancipation by taking comprehensive programs that would promote the education and skills of women as well as the protection of their social rights and equality (PFDJ Charter 1994). However, the regime has been long on rhetoric and short on implementation of the promises pertaining to the status of women both in the economy and the polity. The regime is utterly unable to go beyond rhetoric to fighting the cultural conditions that continue to foster the perpetuation of female degradation. As Asgedet Stefanos has splendidly summarized: "[T]he government has been highly cautious in the area of sexual practices that oppress women. It has only tentatively and sporadically questioned customs, such as female seclusion, polygamy and female circumcision.... There are no educational campaigns to pressure, enlighten or teach skills to men so that they can perform more household tasks, care effectively for children, or gain new appreciation for daughters" (Stefanos, 1997: 658-688).

Noteworthy is that one of the cardinal pledges the EPLF made in 1977 was to fight prostitution. However, after liberation, rather than dismantling the inherited domain of prostitution, the political operatives of the new state became the principal consumers of prostitution. In fact, an Eritrean intellectual found himself dumbfounded in 1994 after he discovered that government ministers, generals and other high-ranking officials were helping promote concubinage as they "appropriated" for themselves the top female bar and tavern owners. In consequence, instead of shrinking, prostitution in post-liberation Eritrea blossomed into a chief industry. Moreover, one of the regime's first acts after liberation was to export Eritrean women to the Arab gulf region. In 1993 the regime subjected women fighters who joined the Front since 1990 to an exasperating experience when they were asked to participate in lottery drawings in the towns and cities of the country for indentured work in Kuwait.

Perhaps it was not surprising that the regime backtracked on the issue of female emancipation if one carefully scrutinized the Front's gender policy. In the 1987 second EPLF Congress, a woman was for the first time included in the Central Committee of the Front, but only twelve women were selected to the 75-member Central Committee of the PFDJ in 1994 (Markakis, 1995). Although blaming received traditions and culture was fashionable for the degraded status of women, members of the regime and the fighting forces were the first after liberation to attempt to turn the clock back on women by divorcing their veteran wives and marrying new brides, who were much younger than they and, for the most part, "virgin" (Connell, 1998). Moreover, in 1992 misogynist men set up clandestine committees to block the distribution of land to women which the regime dismantled only after women marched to the Office of the President demanding action (Connell, 1998).

The utter failure of the regime's gender policy was attested to by the rise of female organizations outside the corporatist framework of officialdom within four short years after liberation. By presenting women as a single homogenous block, the regime created the National Union of Eritrean Women (NUEW) as a corporatist appendage to PFDJ. The aim was control, not emancipation of women. NUEW leaders were hand-chosen and simply echoed official policy rather than championing the cause of female emancipation. Dan Connell (2002), for example, noted a striking symmetry between the views of the official government and NUEW leaders on the untimeliness and impropriety of discussing female circumcision at this stage of cultural development. Furthermore, as veteran fighters reclaimed their male privileges in public and private spaces, NUEW continued to watch from the sideline the growth of male dominance (Connell, 2002). When female trade unionists set up a child daycare center as a pilot project with contributions from workers and factory managers, government officials scoffed at the very idea of child care "as a luxury" enterprise (Connell, 2002). The PFDJ also obsequiously used the NUEW to discourage the rise of autonomous women initiatives. For example, in March 1996, when female trade unionists approached NUEW with the suggestion that the National Confederation of Eritrean Workers (NCEW) and NUEW celebrate international women's day together, NUEW leaders scoffed at the idea. In the same year when the NCEW kindly invited the NUEW to co-sponsor a gender forum with representatives from governmental agencies and non-governmental organizations, the NUEW rejected the idea outright (Connell, 2002). The aim of the NUEW in turning down such invitations was of course designed to prevent displays of public and legitimate support for independent initiatives.

Bemoaning corporatist centralism, a veteran woman who rescinded her membership in the NUEW told Dan Connell, "Women's concerns are so diverse that we need a wide variety of organizational forms—issue oriented organizations, perhaps affiliated with the national union but autonomous. We need to have lots of democracy" (Connell, 2002: 120). However, the creation of the NUEW as the sole representative organization of women was precisely to thwart the emergence of "lots of democracy" expressed through autonomous entities. In the context of the fact that women were unable to carve out for themselves a niche in the prevailing order, many demobilized women fighters chose not to join the government-controlled women's association, and many others who had joined later revoked their membership, arguing that the official women's association did not champion their cause. Determined to improve their own status and the future of other women veterans as well, many veteran women fighters organized themselves on private lines.

One of the well-known self-help share companies was Bana, formed in 1995 by six demobilized women who pooled their demobilization allowances from the government to launch a self-help business undertaking. By 1997 Bana's membership reached over one thousand (*Women's International Network News,* Spring 1997). Bana's guiding principle was the recognition that women's emancipation could be realized only through economic empowerment, and the means to it were self-employment, self-education and self-training. To this end, Bana began setting up a chain of small cooperative businesses, such as a bakery, a carpentry service, a fish market, and a truck driving service. Indeed, by early 1997, the company was training seventy-one women in carpentry and another thirty-nine of them in truck driving (*Women's International Network News*, Spring 1997). To assist in the training of members, Bana created a satellite wing as an NGO in 1996 to raise funds from domestic and international sources. The NGO soon began to receive substantial amounts of foreign grants and contributions, which attracted the regime's jealous attention. The Office of the President then ordered Bana's NGO closed, claiming that the company could not operate as both a business and nonprofit entity; the regime added that Bana's receipt of substantial amounts of foreign assistance was incompatible with the official policy of self-reliance (Pool, 2001). However, the real reason for the order to close was the regime's fear that the success of Bana might set an example for other independent business organizations and private voluntary associations to rise and compete to create their own spaces, undermining the monopolistic hold of the PFDJ and its satellite associations on both public and private spaces. After all, PFDJ-affiliated associations were well known as untiring solicitors to the Eritrean diaspora-community and the international humanitarian aid regime. Bana was not the only one affected by the anti-women policy; the regime had already shut down another women's self-help group and a regional human rights center after both civic groups attracted large scale foreign grants and contributions.

To be sure, after a decade since liberation, Eritrea's ethnic minorities and the nation's female population have yet to see signs of cultural democracy. In fact, some ethnic groups, such as the Kunama and the Afars, have formed their own ethno-political movements to fight for their rights by all means.

Women are also becoming increasingly alienated from the corporatist women's association. Like the ethnic minorities, Eritrea's women appear to be initiating their own struggle to create their own space and defend their rights. This sentiment is expressed by none other than a veteran woman who told Dan Connell (2002: 123), "There is so much potential for the women's movement here— women who have come out of the liberation struggle, women who lived under occupation, women who have come back from abroad, women with a lot of experience. This potential can either be provided with the ground to develop into something or it can be stifled. If it is stifled, it will be a great loss to the country."

The Fallacy of Economic Democracy

Perhaps the most advertised trademark of the Eritrean regime was the policy of self-reliance, something that was ill-conceptualized in the post-liberation period. According to the regime, the foundations of "economic democracy" were Proclamations No. 58/1994 and No. 59/1994, dealing with agriculture and industry respectively. As a first step toward the promotion of rural democracy, the land proclamation transformed the state into the only landlord in the country, owning all urban and rural lands. In total possession of arable land, the state could give usufruct right to anyone who chose to make a living by farming. Several considerations drove the concentration of land ownership in the state. First, like her neighbors, Eritrea historically has been vulnerable to the vagaries of nature expressed in cycles of drought, famine and the invasion of locusts, compounded by war and massive deforestation, which all contributed to soil erosion, nutrient depletion and aridity. In the 1920s, for example, 30% of Eritrea was under forest cover, which dropped to a trifling 1% at independence (Negash, 1999). As a result, the country's food security always precariously hung in the balance. In 1993, for example, 80% of the country's harvest was lost to drought and locusts; consequently total grain production precipitously plummeted from 260,000 tons in 1992 to 86,000 tons in 1993, making two-thirds of the population dependent on international food aid (*Africa Report,* January 1994). Even during years of good harvest, Eritrea's structural food deficit always stood around 50%, since its annual food need on average is between 450,000 tons and 600,000 tons (Makki, 1996). Given this reality, the primary aim of the agrarian proclamation was to overcome the vagaries of nature with assistance of and through the intermediation of the state in the modernization of agriculture. In other words, promotion of national food security was at the heart of the agrarian initiative, which could presumably be achieved by the state.

Second, at independence there were 700,000 Eritreans living in refugee camps in the Sudan or working in the Gulf Arab states. The regime was also making preparations to demobilize up to 60,000 of the defense force (Sutton, 1994). Substantial numbers of repatriated refugees and demobilized fighters were expected to be integrated into rural society. Furthermore, there was the urgency to democratize land ownership by including women in the allocation of landed property. Since land was the only source of livelihood, controlled by private farmers or communities, the new arrivals could have access to cultivable plots only if all land was placed at the disposal of the state (Rock, 2000).

Third, blending the collectivization of legal ownership of land with the actual privatization of agrarian production was supposed to stimulate innovation, avoid the traditionally vexing intra-village and inter-village conflicts over land arising from legal ambiguities and promote uniform regulation of land disputes. In addition, because the agrarian proclamation presupposed lifetime occupancy, individual farmers were expected to make major investment in their possessions, which they could bequeath to their children if they chose farming as an occupation (Joireman, 1996; Wilson, 1999; Rock, 2000).

The new agrarian policy had several admirable virtues. First, the egalitarian character of the policy was certainly revolutionary. Under the new plan, every Eritrean irrespective of ethnicity, religion and gender would receive from the state as a matter of right the same size of cultivable land. Even more revolutionary was the empowerment of women for the first time to cultivate their own land, making them economically independent, especially in the event of divorce or if they chose to remain single beyond the age of eighteen. The second advantage of the plan was conflict abatement and/or orderly resolution of land disputes since the relationship of every farmer would now be directly with the state.

In the long run, however, the drawbacks of the agrarian policy would outweigh the benefits. First, the proclamation completely glossed over the place of pastoralism in the new agrarian economy of the country. Since the means of livelihood of 40% of the rural population in the country is based on pastoralism and agro-pastoralism, the issue was not something that could have been brushed aside without considering its long range ramifications. To the extent that grazing space and access to water are the defining characteristics of a pastoral economy, the continual enclosure of land for purposes of settling new arrivals or commercial production would unavoidably undermine the basic infrastructure of the pastoral economy. The problem would loom even larger if and when the pastoralists increased livestock production in order to raise their living standard; increasing the livestock population would certainly require more grazing space and access to more water (Joireman, 1996; Wilson, 1999; Rock, 2000). In the Eritrean context, both the agrarian and pastoral economies could not have been seen apart from the social morphology and geography of the country. While sedentary agriculture remains the dominant mode of production in highland Eritrea, pastoral economy predominates in the lowlands. The cruel historical irony is that the majority of the land available for distribution by the state is in the lowland. The pastoral lowlanders are distinct in their religious and ethnic markers from the Christian and Tigrigna-speaking highlanders. Thus the new mode of agrarian distribution as envisaged by the land proclamation could easily invite social and religious cleavages with long range implications for social cohesion and internal stability. After all, the presumption that pastoralism was a dying species of political economy was inherently undemocratic. For certain, the pastoralists would not leave the new agrarian order unchallenged when they found their freedom to move around in search of pasture and water constricted. What was equally undemocratic about the whole exercise was the fact that the planners never even contemplated the possibility of fashioning some sort of transitional framework to mitigate the effects of enclosure on the pastoral mode of existence as well as to ease the transition of the pastoralists to whatever the state considered a better alternative. Sandra Joireman's (1996) notation in this regard is right on the mark: "That there is in the proclamation no justification for the disregard of pastoral interests is telling. It emphasizes the fact that this government has not concerned itself with understanding the interests—either social or economic—of the pastoralist lowlanders" .

The second drawback of the agrarian policy was the presumptive supremacy of state bureaucracy in insuring democratic allocation of land and adjudication of land disputes. Given the history of post-liberation bureaucracies elsewhere, there was always the temptation for land allocators and dispute adjudicators to fall back on personal and familial predilections and social connections in executing their administrative functions in ways that would distort the democratic implementation of the proclamation. There was even greater danger in the proportion of landed property the state could allocate to itself for purposes of mining, timber harvesting and agro-commercial development. According to the provisions of the proclamation, the state reserved the right to set aside any amount of land—whose magnitude and location could be determined by state bureaucrats—for purposes of leasing to large investors, whether foreign or domestic (Rock, 2000; Joireman, 1996; Wilson, 1999). This meant that big capital could potentially drive out the small land holders as happened before in other post-liberation orders. Given the natural tendency of capital to look for not only size but also quality, the state could end up granting big agro-businesses better land, defined in terms of superior quality of soil, hydrological conditions and proximity to dense networks of commerce and communication. Moreover, since the proclamation did not make any distinction between national capital and international concerns, foreign entities with mega-capital could potentially penetrate and in effect dominate the modern agrarian sector of the country. Thus a close scrutiny of the agrarian model supplied by the proclamation was neither new nor self-reliant in content and practical implications.

The agrarian model was simply a duplication of what African states had adopted and then abandoned thirty years ago. Sandra Joireman (1996) has rightly observed, "One of the most surprising facets of the Eritrean land reform is its seeming revival of modernization theory in its agricultural applications. Two questions of the land reform give evidence to the paradigmatic retreat: the seeming lack of understanding of the value of pastoralism as a mode of production and the emphasis on external investment as a key factor in developing the countryside." To be sure, the resurrection of "modernization theory" in the garb of neoliberal developmentalism won for the Eritrean elite the grace of The World Bank and the International Monetary Fund (IMF) in the 1990s. The elite's full embrace of neoliberal developmentalism was also an important lubricant in the U.S.-Eritrean relations.

Proclamation No. 59/1994—supposed to guide the industrialization process—was hardly different from the agrarian policy construction in its content. The proclamation was neoliberal through and through, readily endorsing the presumptive sovereignty of the market and resting on the mobilization of domestic and foreign resources (Negash, 1999). In the minds of the framers of the proclamation, the industrial model was the least understood Singaporean paradigm, reliant on the injection of massive foreign capital. In keeping with the catechism of "modernization theory," the framers thought that Eritrea's industrial development could be accomplished only through the infusion of external capital, which would presumably stimulate the prompt utilization of the country's natural resources, the creation of an import-substituting and exporting sector and the introduction of modern technology while readily lending itself to production efficiency and ultimately generating the necessary conditions for national capital accumulation and full employment. The mellifluent enticement to corporate capital was presented in the form of exemptions from taxation on exports and imports of capital goods and raw materials and a guarantee of full repatriation of capital, profits and interests (Markakis, 1994; *Business America*, August 1997).

However, two important events should illustrate the limits of external capital—whether public or private—in the development of Eritrea. In December 1992, The World Bank sponsored a donor's conference to raise capital in the form of official development aid. The conference, however, only generated a pitiful sum of $140 million, for a country which was in desperate need of $2 billion to jump start its devastated economy (Gauch, 1993). For its part, the U.N. High Commissioner for Refugees (UNHCR) assembled representatives of potential donor countries in July 1994 to raise $262 million in order to repatriate the half a million or so Eritrean refugees still languishing under abject conditions in the Sudan; but the conference managed to raise only $32.5 million and half of that was in the form of food aid (Sutton, 1994; Rock, 1999). Even though the refugee repatriation program was meant to be completed by January 1997, there were over 165,000 refugees still awaiting resettlement when the war with Ethiopia resumed in May 1998 (Baringaber, 2001).

In retrospect, even though the war with Ethiopia supplied an easy excuse as to why both the agrarian and industrial proclamations are not implemented as of this writing, the macro-economic orientation of the regime was flawed conceptually and practically. In its practical implications, the neoliberal macro-economic policy promised not the defense and the further enrichment of self-reliance but the total integration of the Eritrean economy into global capitalism. There were three essentials which the Eritrean framers of the industrial proclamation failed to internalize.

First, in the present context of late capitalism, the Singaporean model cannot be emulated or replicated. The relative success of the East Asian model was a function of a propitious confluence of factors, including specific cultural and temporal conditions, geography and history, and the dynamics of Cold War politics, none of which are presently available to Eritrea (Leonard, 1992). The premium that Singapore and its neighbors placed on the quality of basic education and the centrality of technocracy to economic progress must be particularly noted here. To illustrate the strategic importance of technocracy in development, Paul Kennedy (1993) noted that in 1989 twelve of the fourteen ministers in Taiwan's government had Ph.D. degrees from top American and British universities. The result of the importance of early emphasis on education is today empirically shown by the fact that Taiwan annually graduates 50,000 engineers, as 45% of its high-school graduates go on to acquire university education. South Korea's college population dramatically rose from 142,000 in 1965 to 1.4 million by the late 1980s. By the same token, Singapore's workforce is today rated the best in the world (Lairson and Skidmore, 2003). This is something not captured by the Eritrean president's operational understanding of the Singaporean model, which he held up for imitation. Indeed, he shocked many observers in August 2002 when he was asked if he was concerned over the brain drain that Eritrea had been experiencing since many educated citizens were leaving the country for better prospects abroad. In an answer not worthy of a president, Isaias said: "Globalization is equalizer. If there is money, there is no problem. You can import people. In the past, we looked for and could not find laborers and construction workers; we imported them from Sri Lanka, the Philippines and India. Yesterday, we were looking for five architects and we imported them from the Philippines. If we cannot find a professor, we go to India and import him. So, if one says, 'I want to go to America,' let him try it" (The Awate Team, Sept. 1, 2002).

Second, the ambition to begin and then accelerate the modernization of Eritrea's political economy by transforming the country into a post-modern citadel of multinational corporations was a loser from the start. Given the micro-segmented nature of global production, driven by knowledge-based product innovation and the electronic revolution, location is no longer decisively relevant to global corporations. After all, contrary to what the Eritrean elite perceives of itself, the political order prevailing in Eritrea today could scarcely inspire confidence in the managers of late capitalism. As a member of a regional subsystem defined by political uncertainties, social and ethnic cleavages and interstate conflicts, Eritrea is not well positioned to become the new citadel of global corporations anymore than its immediate neighbors are.

Third, the ambition to achieve big before attaining small was flawed both conceptually and macro-economically. The basic tenet of self-reliance as a strategy of development is for any government to create the requisite conditions where small producers emerge and flourish, conditions that would allow small producers to unleash their latent energies and creativity.

The state could play an important role in the economy not by placing itself at the center of the accumulation process but by providing infrastructure, information services and pursuing predictable and transparent fiscal and monetary policies. Beyond this, the state could create conditions that would promote synergy and complimentarity of the various compartments of the nation's political economy. The pursuit of such goals would of course require the presence of enlightened leaders in power: leaders who would have demonstrable capacity for approaching the new forces of globalization with an authoritative lucidity of perception, understanding and analysis. Adhering to an antiquated mode of governance and reproducing outdated models of development will not work. A momentary focus on one project, the Asmara Intercontinental Hotel, should illustrate the above observation.

Meant to meet the needs of high-powered managers of global corporations, international dignitaries and affluent tourists, the Asmara Intercontinental Hotel was conceived in the mid-nineties at the cost of $25 million; but when it was completed in November 1999, the cost overrun reached $40 million. This "white elephant" hotel invites two questions as to whether the cost was justified and even whether this kind of luxury hotel was needed in the first place. As one critic pointed out, using the traditional method of calculating the cost of construction, the cost per room of the Asmara Intercontinental Hotel was $223,000, and this was without including the value of the land which was free. By comparison, to build a luxury hotel in New York, considered the most expensive place in the United States, would range between $104,000 and $121,000 per room, including the value of the land; this meant that the cost to build a luxury hotel in Asmara was twice as expensive as in New York (Yosef, 2001). The opportunity cost of the giant hotel was very high. With the amount of money spent on it, a good size garment industry

78

could have been started in Asmara, using the labor of thousands of Eritrean women who were treated as export commodities to the Arab world or condemned to dehumanizing prostitution.

The Rise of a Central Figure as the Negation of Political Democracy

If the economic policy of the Eritrean elite is a poor imitation of what the African elite had discarded a quarter of a century ago, Eritrea's political model is equally a flawed duplication of African political systems of yesteryear. During the liberation years, the EPLF had earned the admiration of friend and foe alike, not only for the remarkable fighting capability it displayed but also for the great promises it held out; the implantation of a self-reliant order and the empowerment of women were among its potential trademarks. Like many of its kind before, however, the EPLF has fallen victim too soon to post-liberation sclerosis, which has come to eat the country inside out. Many friends of Eritrea today are startled by the lightning speed with which the post-liberation order in Eritrea has deteriorated into an overt dictatorship. Hence, the debate among analysts a decade after liberation is not over whether the Eritrean regime is democratic or not, but rather over how to politically characterize it.

Over many decades now, a host of scholars have attempted to construct empirical political structures that approximate Max Weber's ideal types. Weber articulated that all political systems could roughly be categorized either into traditional, charismatic or bureaucratic rule, each being a legitimated domination. In traditional systems, the legitimation of domination is grounded in patriarchal or patrimonial habits, precepts and rules, whereas a system based on the charisma of a single figure rests on the sheer personality and peculiar qualities of a leader. A modern version of charismatic domination can be exercised by an outright demagogue or a political party boss. On the other hand, bureaucratic domination finds its inner justification in the rationalization of competencies and statutory obligations, routinization of impersonal rules and procedures and the rotation of administrative functions and responsibilities among competent bureaucrats (Weber, 1954).

The fundamental question here is to which of these ideal types does political order in Eritrea since liberation approximate. Confusion can naturally arise from the way post-liberation regimes mimic the characteristics and qualities of the modern state, endlessly invoking the ghost of democracy. On the surface, the post-liberation Eritrean political order, like many post-liberation orders, appears to approximate a system based on charismatic domination because in the post-liberation Eritrean context things are over-centralized around a single figure in order to insure control of events and developments. As we will show later, however, the presumed charisma of the Eritrean leader is not natural, but politically forged by extolling his invented virtues and debasing the qualities of his partners and actual or potential rivals. In this sense, the Eritrean political order may be best characterized as one based on populist authoritarianism, resting on the centrality of a single figure and corporatist strategies of mass mobilization rather than on charismatic domination. For example, consider the political anomaly that is inherent in the Eritrean political order whereas the party boss is simultaneously head of state and government, chairman of the national assembly and in effect head of the judiciary since he can dismiss the chief justice of the Supreme Court at will, as he did in August 2001, simply because the chief justice complained about undue intrusions into his sphere of competence by the office of the president. It thus stands to reason that the Eritrean leader represents the continued African pattern of centralization of authority, anchored in a blend of populism and patrimonial politics.

The extensive concentration of power in the hands of the central figure could be explained in historical terms. The traumatic effects of the bloody feuds within and between the Eritrean fronts in conjunction with Ethiopia's military assaults on the liberators did create circumstances that indubitably produced collective and personal disorientation, confusion and disorganization. Such conditions tend to impel individuals and groups to place their trust in a central figure as part of the effort to energize one another in order to achieve coherence of purpose and mission and overcome the seemingly insurmountable difficulties facing them (Coleman, 1990). In this sense, a powerfully central leader may not necessarily be a product of his sheer personality or peculiar qualities but rather of other social circumstances. Here we agree with James Coleman that the objective characteristics of a situation in combination with the characteristics of the individuals and groups who place their trust in a leader as a way of coping with their disorienting circumstances may offer invaluable insights into leadership formation (Coleman, 1990). A close investigation of the circumstances under which the Eritrean central figure rose to power and his behavior since liberation would support the latter interpretation, a point which will be further explored below.

The "national charter," which the third Congress of EPLF produced, defined "political democracy" as consisting of "patriotism, national unity, secularism and social justice" (*PFDJ Charter*, 1994). The identification of these values as integral components of "political democracy" is uncontroversial. But how were these values going to be nested in a predictable institutional framework? *The National Charter*—distinguished more by its ambiguity than by its clarity—is silent on the mechanisms of institutionalizing the values of democracy. In practice, though, the PFDJ remains crowned as the custodian of "political democracy" since it is the sole political party, claiming the membership of 600,000 Eritreans inside and

81

outside the country. All social groups considered relevant are classified into three satellite associations, namely, the National Confederation of Eritrean Workers which claims 20,000 members, the National Union of Eritrean Women, which claims the membership of 200,000 female members, and the National Union of Eritrean Students and Youth, which claims to represent 130,000 members between the ages of 16 and 35 (Connell, 2000). These associations are sponsored by and are supposed to revolve permanently around the PFDJ; the preclusion of other voluntary civic associations is presumed. To insure the associations' subordination and the flow of partisan orders within the political constellation, the presidents of NUEW and NUESY are made members of PFDJ's Executive Committee. Limiting the number of occupational and gender associations is meant to give vertical coherence to what the president of the country calls "controlled democracy" (Zarenbo, 1995). This corporatist vision of control was what Isaias articulated during his confrontation with the *Menkaa* group twenty years earlier. Since deconcentration of democratic values was deemed incompatible with "controlled democracy," the president was also formally placed by the third Congress in charge of all major arteries of the body politic; that is, the Congress conferred on him all the reins of power of the presidency, parliament, the judiciary and the armed forces. He was even made chancellor of the University of Asmara. The delegates to the Congress, captivated by the exuberant euphoria of the moment, placed their trust in the benevolence of the central figure without realizing the long range consequences of their collective decision on the evolution of the political order in the country. Given these anomalies inherent in the political structure which the third Congress sanctioned, it was inevitable for a crisis of legitimation to become veritable. In effect, though, what the third Congress did was simply formalize the *de facto* supremacy of the leader that had already been in place.

One of the early manifestations of the post-liberation political stagnation was the fact that the Front fell back on a kind of liberation fundamentalism, which led the central leader to develop a stunted view of the world, without the capacity to appreciate the fact that the Eritrean national struggle was a tiny footnote in the evolution of human history. Some of the symptomatic manifestations of this incapacity were an inflated sense of self-importance that the leader developed and the exaggerated perception he has had of Eritrea's ability to influence regional and international politics.

In the first place, the Eritrean leader with the aid of his political operatives constructed the mythology of "warrior-patriot" culture in which only those who carried weapons in the armed struggle were entitled to assuming positions of power; past loyalty to the Front, not present competence or administrative skills, became the basis for recruiting the members of the new class, resulting in the *de facto* exclusion of qualified and educated Eritreans from the diaspora community or those who happened to have been under Ethiopian-controlled regions. Apparently, the central figure felt that without his exclusive leadership and his political operatives both the gains and promises of the revolution would be betrayed and consequently Eritrea would break asunder. The leader treated the nation's class of intellectuals as immature followers incapable of even properly managing functional agencies, much less running the affairs of the nation. Instead, 12,000 veteran fighters were immediately inducted into the state to staff and run the various state bureaucracies (Makki, 1996). The official practice of recruiting, selecting and placing administrators and managers openly negated what was pledged in the PFDJ manifesto. The manifesto promised not only "a collective leadership" but also a "periodic change of leadership and infusion of new blood into leadership" as critical to effectuating the transition to a democratic order (*PFDJ Charter*, 1994).

83

Second, the political order that was slouching toward a dictatorship had to *ipso facto* give birth to a central figure that would be endowed with the vision and ability to fashion Eritrea's future in terms of both its internal reconstruction and external relations. The net result was that every decision pertaining to any issue, whether domestic or international, small or big, had to be made by himself without national deliberation and public scrutiny. Moreover, because he began to distrust the judgment and loyalty of his ministers, he developed the impulse to represent Eritrea in person in all bilateral, regional and international conferences, including even those which required representation by minor officials, making Eritrea's political figure the most traveled leader of the 1990s.

The way the central figure distributed political resources was another expression of a system that had gone awry. Not only did he appoint ministers, judges, governors and diplomats at will without regard to competence and qualifications and without parliamentary consent and oversight, but he also constantly shuffled them around like dominos. If he was dissatisfied with a minister or a diplomat, the central figure would simply freeze the official. To win back the favor or grace of the leader, the victim had to display utmost patience coupled with a sense of humiliation; seeking explanation or asking questions about one's status would only worsen the situation. In fact, the freezing of officials became so commonplace that people in Asmara nicknamed the victims of freezing "street sweepers" because of the manner they spent their days loitering on the sidewalks as they visited one tavern or one cappuccino house after another.

Corollary to this practice was subjecting officials to trials under trumped up charges. "Corruption" was the all-purpose charge that fitted all categories. In 1996, the central figure gave an institutional expression to this practice when he ordered the creation of a special court to try officials charged with alleged crimes of corruption. The court was given sweeping powers to hear evidence and try anyone in secrecy, and its verdicts were unappealable. The first victim of the court was a certain Ermias Debbesai, once Isaias' trusted confidant and Eritrea's ambassador to China. The cited crime of corruption in this instance was that he embezzled public funds intended for the purchase of arms. No outside person or group witnessed the proceedings, making it virtually impossible for anyone to render an objective evaluation of the merit of the case or the seven year imprisonment that the court imposed on Ermias. Sources familiar with the circumstances, however, maintained that the defendant was tried not for embezzling public funds but for raising an objection to the dispatch of Eritrean troops to Rwanda and the Congo to help African dictators (Plaut, 2002). Indeed, the primary mission of the extrajudicial court was political, pure and simple. Otherwise a court committed to fighting public corruption would make transparency and openness the hallmark of its existence. By bringing all alleged crimes of corruption into the open air, the regime could teach the general public valuable lessons about open governance, the purpose of deterrence would be served, and the regime could accumulate important capital in the form of credibility and respect for the rule of law. However, since the court's mission was political, opponents could be handled to the satisfaction of the leader only under conditions of secrecy, which represented an atrocious negation of due process.

There were other factors that manifested themselves in the drift toward dictatorship. Ever since the liberation of Eritrea from Ethiopia in 1991, the central figure systematically proceeded to construct a political order, which in practice negated the utility of pluralism. The presumption was that the multi-religious and poly-ethnic character of Eritrea coupled with the presumed political immaturity of the Eritrean people was not conducive to participatory political democracy. Despite redundant enumerations of the fundamental rights of citizens in the new *PFDJ Charter*, repetitiously arranged in keeping with the Maoist political glossary, the Eritrean leader continued to assert that advocacy for pluralist institutions "would amount to moving the institutions of the formerly colonialist States to different societies" (*EIU 1st Quarter*, 1994: 24).

In this view, politics and democracy were articles of luxury, which Eritrea could dispense with until the nation's unity was securely anchored and the economic reconstruction of the country was completed. But nothing was new in this orientation; the champions of the first wave of African politics had said the same thing in the 1960s and 1970s by using ethnic heterogeneity and religious diversity as justifications for the postponement of political development. At any rate, in keeping with his basic orientation, the central figure publicly repudiated the legitimate existence of divergent political opinions or political groups inside or outside Eritrea and re-baptized the EPLF as the PFDJ, making it not only the sole legal political party in the country but also the richest entity in the country. Anticipating open criticism from friends and adversaries alike, the PFDJ contended that its notion of democracy was different from what was practiced elsewhere. As the manifesto put it,

> Democracy is sometimes narrowly viewed in terms of political parties and whether regular elections are held.... democracy means the existence of a society governed by democratic principles and procedures, the existence of democratic institutions and culture, broad public participation in decision making and a government that is accountable to the people.... In the context of our society, democracy is dependent not on the number of political parties and on regular elections but on the actual participation of people in the decision making

process at community and national levels" (*PFDJ Charter*, 1994).

On first reading, this statement seems to suggest the Eritrean political system must be judged not by its form but by its content. However, such presentation is grossly misleading precisely because content cannot exist without form and principles cannot express themselves without procedures. After all, what do such pairs in the cited passage as "democratic principles and procedures" and "democratic institutions and culture" suggest? Pluralism of content and form as well as the diversity of institutions and culture? Isn't it through regular elections and multiple parties that people make their differentiated choices known and express their participation in the process to affirm or negate the content of any policy? The framers of the manifesto did not seem to have been aware of the dilemma into which they put themselves. The kernel of their intention was, in fact, embedded in their statement's last sentence. The Eritrean people were supposed to participate in the political process through channels provided for them by the government and the single party. But this was nothing but a corporatist machination of containment and preemption. Yet form without content can exist in politics when governments suppress content by thwarting the emergence of pluralist institutions and changing the outcomes of regular elections. Content can exist only when elections change governments. More importantly, the notion of democracy is embedded in the recognition of secular reasoning and pluralism as the cardinal sources of political legitimacy. Herein alone resides a legitimating democratic discourse.

Further evidence of the totalizing nature of the Eritrean political order was the absence or the suppression of free press. On April 25, 1997, for example, security forces arbitrarily took Ruth Simon, a local reporter for the French news agency AFP, into custody. Her cardinal "sin" was that she quoted the

Eritrean leader as saying that "Eritrean casualties were the price to pay for advancing and establishing the peace, which is so badly needed" (*EIU 3rd quarter*, 1997: 20). The leader apparently gave the speech in private to his political cadres in a seminar, where he admitted for the first time that Eritrean troops were actually participating alongside armed Sudanese dissidents in military engagement against Sudanese troops. Apparently, he was offended by Ruth's temerity to report on his private speech rather than by her actually reporting of Eritrea's military participation in the Sudan since reports on mutual armed incursions by the two countries into each other's territory were rampant elsewhere. To be sure, Ruth's long detention without trial was yet another lucid manifestation of a political system in a totalizing process.

The noxious effects of this political system were not limited to independent political initiatives. Even humanitarian organizations, both national and foreign, had already become casualties of the authoritarianization process. The regime displayed its contempt for private civic organization in May 1993 when the security forces invaded the office of the Regional Center for Human Rights (RCHR) and ordered it closed after freezing the center's bank holdings, sequestering its files and abrogating the director's travel permit. The RCHR was seen as a threat to the evolving order on two counts. First, the mission of the center implicitly challenged the drift towards an authoritarian order, since the elements of the center's mission included monitoring the evolution of constitutional governance, assisting in the promotion of freedom of expression, helping in the promotion of electoral transparency, advocacy for environmental governance and fostering the growth of a cluster of humanitarian organizations (Connell, 2000). Second, the regime was perturbed by the center's spectacular success in garnishing $1 million as seed money from foreign donors to carry out its stated mission. From the regime's standpoint, money of this magnitude was supposed to flow directly to the coffers of the PFDJ and its satellite entities. Moreover, as increasing numbers of private entities might potentially compete for foreign sources of funding, the regime's ability to centralize the financial arteries that connected Eritrea to the international community in general and the Eritrean diaspora-community in particular would be severely undercut. The rise of pluralist private entities and the ties that they might cultivate with foreign counterparts would have also politically vitiated the regime's ability to enforce its unitary conception of state and society.

Beginning in 1994, the regime also tightened the leash on foreign humanitarian organizations. Foreign NGOs that could not carry on their operations on less than 10% of their resources had to close and leave the country or run their projects from their home countries, monitoring progress of their projects by visiting Eritrea as needed (Connell, 2000). In a concerted effort to force the voluntary withdrawal of foreign non-governmental organizations from Eritrea, the Eritrean Ministry of finance informed these humanitarian entities that their expatriate workers were required to pay 38% in income tax. Furthermore, the government declared that all NGOs must work on projects only in collaboration with government-designated agencies and that all foreign aid must henceforth be funneled through the ministries of education and health (Weissman, 1996; *EIU 2nd quarter,* 1997). The net result of this heavy-handed policy was that many foreign non-governmental organizations packed up and left. Those which ignored the regime's call to voluntarily evacuate were told by the government to leave; a host of charges were labeled against them ranging from recurrent interventions in Eritrean internal affairs to spying (*EIU 2nd quarter,* 1997). The immediate result of their expulsion was that many local projects came to a screeching halt for lack of operating funds and expertise. The irony of ironies was that a year later the regime had to literally beg the expelled foreign NGOs to return to the country to help cope with the horrific consequences of the war with Ethiopia as the regime's Rehabilitation Commission began pleading with Western NGOs to come back. In so doing, the regime exposed its own inner limits and outer vulnerabilities.

The Crisis of Legitimation

Based on our previous analysis, three broad generalizations emerge. First, the exceptionalist notion of the Eritrean experience is fatally flawed. The manner in which Eritrea's post-independence political order has slouched into what writers may variously characterize as "one man rule," "presidential monarchy" or "authoritarian rule" is remarkably analogous to the post-colonial orders prevailing in the rest of the African continent. The explanation for this symmetry, of course, inheres in the complex tangle of structural, conjunctural and temporal factors that Eritrea shares with other African states.

Second, the complex set of political, ideological and personal motivations and ambitions of actors cannot be understood in isolation from the dynamic interactions of history, economics and politics. The plausible deduction here is that, if Eritrea produced a leadership similar to those in other African states in terms of ambitions, motivations and vulnerabilities to the seduction of power, Eritrea must share the essential causal determinants and attributes of the same social evolution.

Third, given the above two conditions, the likelihood is that Eritrea would experience the same crisis of legitimation as the rest of post-colonial African states. If we failed as trained observers to sense soon enough the sign posts of a crisis that had been simmering beneath the façade of orderliness and stability in the country, it says more about the shortcomings of our own scholarship than about the exceptional character of the Eritrean experience. Like other members of civil society, scholars can have minds colored by the atmospherics of the moment. In a presentation on the prospects of democracy in

Africa before a group of academics and professionals, for example, a distinguished international scholar who attended a constitutional symposium in Asmara in January, 1995, organized by the Eritrean Constitutional Commission, buoyantly heralded the democratization process in Eritrea as having been built on a solid ground. His chastened optimism in part stemmed from the manner in which the Eritrean leader displayed himself at the symposium. The Eritrean leader, whom the scholar described to the audience as charismatically simple, plain and unpretentious, came to the conference unattended by security forces and in his field outfit. The speaker added that the Eritrean leader drove a badly beaten Toyota around the city by himself without a chauffeur as a striking demonstration of his simplicity and ordinariness. This is a good illustration of how even highly versed scholars may on occasions substitute fleeting impressions about the atmospherics of events for complete understandings of deeply embedded forces, which may lay seemingly dormant for the moment.

In any event, given the above generalizations and supported by the narrative of this chapter, we should have anticipated the likelihood of the present crisis of legitimation in Eritrea occurring by monitoring how the various aspects of the political system progressed. In fact, the unsavory conclusion one must reach is that the trajectory of Eritrea's progress was off its track long before liberation. The latest Ethio-Eritrean war simply brought out the structural anomalies inherent in the Eritrean political system. Following Eritrea's less than stellar military performance during Ethiopia's third offensive in 2000, a large section of veteran fighters attempted to use the crisis as an opportunity to rectify things before they got out of hand. Unable to manage the crisis of legitimation by the familiar means of co-optation or liquidation, the president responded to the demands by cunningly conceding the necessity of implementing the already ratified constitution coupled with a promise to hold national elections in December 2001. A renaissance of freedom appeared to be on the horizon as ordinary citizens began for the first time to criticize the government openly. The nascent private newspapers and magazines increasingly grew assertive in questioning the regime's overall performance. In the words of *The Economist*, "The newspaper sellers in Asmara have never had it so good. They are selling out everyday and selling out of reprints, too. In the letters columns, ordinary members of the public are furiously venting their opinions. After ten years of one-party rule under a popular dictator, Eritrea is experiencing its first political crisis. It is not completely unexpected" (*The Economist*, May 20, 2001). The press and the political reformers thought that they had won an important victory, but the Eritrean leader was buying time. Just three months before the supposed elections were to take place, he threw the reformers in jail together with a slew of journalists and students. Taking advantage of the international preoccupation with the terrorist attacks on the United States, the Eritrean leader resorted with impunity to the best method he knew to contain the internal contradictions that had been simmering beneath the surface for a while. He ordered a nationwide clampdown on his opponents, whom he viewed as journalists and students. On September 18, 2001, the regime arrested eleven veteran liberators who were also members of the national assembly and the executive council of the ruling party. Sweeping arrests of their followers, university students and journalists and closure of all private newspapers and magazines followed in short order. The alleged crimes of the political reformers—as they came to be called—were that they defiantly challenged one-man rule, complained that Eritrea's external relations were poorly managed and that the war with Ethiopia was ill-led. In order to rectify the misfortunes of governance and to put the original trajectory of the Eritrean struggle back on its track, the reformers demanded the convocation of both the National

Assembly and the Executive Council of the ruling party to deliberate on how to overhaul the political system and democratize state institutions. However, the Eritrean leader, having initially conceded the demands, outmaneuvered the reformers and annulled the concessions he promised. December came and quietly went without the regime having shown even a modicum of decency to tell the Eritrean people that the scheduled elections were postponed or cancelled. The Eritrean leader's actions were so sweeping that they invited this comment from a long watcher of Eritrean politics: "It is certainly a tragedy that so many men and women who had worked all their lives for the liberation of their country now find themselves at odds with the movement that they served for so many years. It also denies Eritrea of the skills and energies of some of its most talented and dedicated citizens" (Plaut, 2002).

Eritrea is today showing all the signposts that Rotberg (2002) associated with failed states. According to Rotberg, the first signposts to look at on the economic side of the ledger are when living standards of the populace precipitously plummet, shortages of foreign exchanges and fuels run rampant, a food crisis looms large and the regime drastically slashes public spending on such essentials as educational, medical and logistical services. Such deterioration in the basic conditions of life becomes aggravated by growing rampant corruption as members of the political class compete to divide up the ever shrinking resources. To insure the loyalty of his quiescent clients, whose membership diminishes in proportion to the deterioration of the economy, the central leader must squander the few remaining resources on dispensing privileges and rewards. On the political side, Rotberg argues, a leader facing a deepening crisis of legitimation increasingly resorts to coercive measures in a desperate hope to contain the crisis and prolong his stay in power. National legislators, judges and bureaucrats are intimidated into sheepish submission as the leader tightens his grips on the security and defense forces.

In the final phase, the erosion of state legitimacy becomes veritable as stark poverty, gross underpayment and growing political repression compel protesters to take matters into their own hands. The inherent danger in such a scenario is that the resistance to a delegitimized regime can take ethnic, linguistic and religious forms. "Because small arms and even more formidable weapons are cheap and easy to find, because historical grievances are readily remembered or manufactured, and because the spoils of separation, autonomy or a total take-over are attractive, the potential for violent conflict grows exponentially as the state's power and legitimacy recede" (Rotberg, 2000).

Does Eritrea display these signposts of a deepening crisis at the beginning of the first decade of the new century, entitling her to the dubious distinction of a failed state? Unfortunately, this question is something that cannot be evaded by simply hoping against hope. Since 1998 the Eritrean economy has been mired in stagnation; the nation's currency has lost most of its purchasing power, accentuating the poor living standard of urbanite and peasant alike; the food crisis in the country is looming larger by the day, compounded by unprecedented drought and dislocation; unemployment is such that it is easier to count the employed than to statistically configure the national unemployment rate. In fact, anticipating a potential convulsion from returning soldiers, in the summer of 2002, the Eritrean leader ordered the postponement of demobilization of the defense forces. Instead, the regime manufactured a preemption plan and dubbed it "the national strategy of development," intended to direct the 200,000 armed soldiers away from the cities and towns for two years in various projects, such as construction, road building, digging wells and working on plantations owned by the ruling party.

Politically, too, the Eritrean state appears to be teetering on the edges of the cliff. The regime has increasingly resorted to deplorable measures of repression. The U.S. Department of State, Amnesty International and other human rights organizations have continued issuing scathing statements on the worsening human rights violations in Eritrea. With twenty-five journalists reported as either imprisoned or missing by the end of 2002, Eritrea enjoys the dubious distinction of becoming the worst place for journalists in the world. When nine journalists went on hunger strike in late March 2002, demanding that they be tried or released, the regime dispatched them to an unknown place where they have been held incommunicado ever since. Reports have continued to surface that the security forces have continued to use physical torture and beating against prisoners or detainees and are authorized to shoot army deserters on first sight. Tying the feet and hands of draft evaders and then exposing them to 103 degrees Fahrenheit in the sun for an extended period of time have become a common occurrence. We should note that in August 2001, two thousand university students were arrested in mass by the security forces and driven to one of the hottest places in the world, between Massawa and Assab, where they were exposed to 113 degree heat. Two of the students died from heat stroke and many more were hospitalized.

Furthermore, restrictions on freedom of movement, arbitrary arrests and detentions, and forced labor have seemingly become permanent fixtures in the political system. Local and international human rights groups are repeatedly denied visitation to prisoners and detainees (U.S. Department of State, 2002; Amnesty International, 2002).

Finally, as the economic and political predicament of the Eritrean people worsened and the heavy-handedness of the regime has taken on even uglier dimensions, all the nation's top generals, legislators and bureaucrats appear to be reduced to sheepish agents of internal repression and execution. In the summer of 2002, the Eritrean leader divided the country into four security zones, each headed by a general, in effect imposing an undeclared martial law on the nation. Under this arrangement, civil administrators must report to the general in charge of the designated security zone. Lamentably, the once gallant Eritrean liberation army has been reduced to a ragtag army of internal repression. On the opposition side, thirteen or fourteen political fragments have gathered themselves under the Eritrean National Alliance (ENA), vowing to topple the Eritrean leader. The fact that the ENA has been supported by Ethiopia and Sudan does not augur well. Because the ENA is presently headed by figures with shadowy and checkered pasts, it is hard to tell how such a collection of political fragments could provide a promising alternative to the PFDJ regime. Some of the internal reformers who escaped arrest by Isaias have also organized themselves into the Eritrean Democratic Party (EDP). However, they too have thus far been unable to inspire the diaspora community into action. To be sure, the prospect for further political fragmentation on ethnic and religious lines and armed clashes between and among Eritrean forces appears to be in the making unless all contending parties find alternative modes of struggle and conflict management.

In 1994 the ruling party declared to the world that, "...unless peace, justice and prosperity prevail in Eritrea, the independence we won with heavy sacrifices will be meaningless. That is to say, if we do not lift people out of poverty and depravation, safeguard their human and democratic rights and improve their material, cultural and spiritual lives, attaining independence will not amount to anything" (*PFDJ Charter,* 1994). Sadly, what the Eritrean people have experienced in the decade since independence is anything but "peace, justice and prosperity." Misery, injustice, war and violations of basic rights have continued to haunt them. Hence, at the beginning of the first decade of the new century, Eritrea's future does not look any brighter than it was in 1961, the year the Eritrean armed struggle began.

96

CHAPTER THREE

POST-LIBERATION ERITREA'S DYSFUNCTIONAL ECONOMIC STRATEGY

Eritrea's economy, like the economies of most other post-colonial African countries, faces many fundamental problems, including a lack of capable and selfless leaders, a shortage of a skilled workforce, internal economic and social fragmentation, political instability, poor institutional infrastructure, a lack of adequate transportation and communication networks, asymmetrical trade relations and debilitating debt. Additionally, the country's economy is beset by structural problems emanating mainly from three ill-conceived policy measures, comprising the ruling party's engagement in business activities, state control of the country's human resources and the country's land tenure system. This chapter examines how the combined effects of these policy measures, in conjunction with the border war with Ethiopia and reoccurring droughts, have stifled the country's socioeconomic development, and the democratization of its political system.

The Party Sector

For a brief period following independence (1991-1998), notable rehabilitation of the Eritrean economy took place, largely as a peace dividend. The economy's average annual real growth rate for the period between 1991 and 1996 was a respectable 4% and in 1997 the rate of growth jumped to 7% (IMF, 1998). Despite this promising performance, the structural problems of the country's economy and their impacts were evident even during this initial period of recovery.

At the time of the country's independence in 1991, the Eritrean People's Liberation Front (EPLF) inherited an economic system characterized by a state sector and a private sector. Both sectors were in dismal condition, due to a number of factors, including the protracted war of liberation, an oppressive political system, neglect by Ethiopia's military government (the Derg) and the Derg's poorly conceived socialist economic policy. The state sector mainly consisted of small manufacturing plants in the areas of textiles, leather and shoes, cement and limestone, beverages and bottling, tobacco, the oil refinery at Assab and some hotels (IMF, 1998). Most of these concerns were poorly maintained and operated using old machinery. At the time of the country's independence, the EPLF, perhaps influenced by global developments that transpired at the end of the Cold War, including the crisis of socialism and the shift in global ideological orientation, seemed to change its long held socialist orientation by officially adopting a macro-economic policy that promised to foster a free enterprise market system. The EPLF also privatized some of the state owned establishments and closed down others while a few were modestly revamped (IMF, 1998).

The Front, however, kept the economic assets, which it had built as a liberation front separate from the assets of the state, creating a ruling party sector, as a third leg of the country's economy. Unlike most economies, which are characterized by a mixture of varying proportions of a private sector and a state (public) sector, Eritrea's economy was founded on three sectors. The Front's business ventures range from retail of consumer goods, including alcoholic beverages to import-export business, tourism, land and marine transportation, mining, export-oriented commercial agriculture, banking, currency exchange and furniture and construction industries. In some areas, such as the construction industry, import-export and tourism, the PFDJ, for all practical purposes, has established a near monopoly control. The party's mass organizations, such as the National Union of Eritrean Women, the National Union of Eritrean Workers and the National Union of Eritrean Students and Youth also control significant economic assets in a number of areas, including fisheries.

The two-year border war with Ethiopia along with hostilities with Sudan has had a devastating impact on the Eritrean economy. About 80% of Eritrea's exports went to Ethiopia and the Sudan before the war. These markets have essentially been lost since the start of the war with Ethiopia and the escalation of tensions with the Sudan. The country has also, for all practical purposes, lost the bulk of its supply of raw materials. The impacts of the war are discussed in greater detail in chapter six. Here we only note that the condition in the aftermath of the war led to a shift in the government's economic policy towards a more centralized economic system as a strategy of recovery. Continued expansion of the party sector of the economy, despite growing tensions with the private sector, is one indication of the shift in policy. Control of the workforce through the Warsay-Yikeallo development campaign (WY campaign) that the government waged at the end of the two-year border war is another. The land policy, which gives the state control of all land, has also remained unchanged.

The last several decades have revealed the inherent problems of centrally planned economies under undemocratic regimes. These economies have generally been characterized by gross inefficiencies in the resource allocation process and lack of incentive mechanisms and flexibility. The state and party sectors of Eritrea's economy share many of the characteristics of statist economies, such as the incentive problems and inefficiency in allocation of resources. The long milk lines in Asmara and the amount of time it takes to buy products, such as construction materials, from the state and party distribution centers are among the obvious manifestations of how poorly these sectors distribute products to consumers. More importantly, the dominant role of the party sector, along with the government's control over human and financial resources and land, has hampered the growth of the private sector in various ways and has placed the direction of the Eritrean economy in a flux.

The party sector has crowded out resources from the private sector. Access to foreign exchange for private businesses that compete against the party's firms has been made difficult while the party's firms have first access to these scarce resources. The party's firms have free and speedy access to land which is not the case with private firms and citizens, as will be shown in the last section of this chapter. The WY campaign has also created a severe labor shortage in the private sector driving wages up while the party's and the state's firms obtain access to free labor.

The party's engagement in business activities which brings it in direct competition with the private sector has also made it impossible to establish partnership between the government and the private sector, which is crucial for developing the country's economy. The government often blames the private sector, in general and merchants in particular, for many of the country's economic ills, including price instability. Rapid increases in the prices of locally produced goods that are directly supplied by producers to consumers, however, reveal that the problem of inflation that the country is presently facing is not merely due to mischief of merchants that would be solved by stricter government control over trade, as the Minister of Trade recently claimed (*ERNA News*, August 20, 2004). Yet, the government continues to intensify its regulatory mechanisms.

In the summer of 2004 even bakeries were instructed by government bureaucrats what kinds of bread to bake.

The party sector, in conjunction with excessive regulatory measures by the state and the existing governance structures, which allow the executive branch of the government to change policies and regulations at whim and with little control by an independent legislature or judiciary, have placed the Eritrean economy in a precarious situation. Sudden policy changes, for example, discourage investments by increasing the risks of uncertainly. Governments that do what they wish without subjecting themselves to the rule of law often face the problem that is known as the "sovereign's paradox" (Bates, 2000). Such governments are generally perceived by investors, foreign and domestic, to pose high investment risk, as their unbridled power allows them to rapidly and unexpectedly change policies or even to seize resources from the private sector. The Eritrean government's September 7, 2004 decision to stop gold exploration by Northern Mining Resources Ltd., Nevsun Resources Ltd., Sanu Resources Ltd, and Sunridge Gold Corp. is a case in point. The government may have legitimate reasons for wanting to renegotiate terms with the identified corporations. Oftentimes small and poor countries lack the capacity to safeguard their interests in negotiating terms with mining corporations. When the need to renegotiate terms arises, however, the more transparently governments make their case the better because they often have justifiable causes, which may be supported by international law. More importantly transparency would help reassure other corporations that government policies are not hostile to foreign investment. Sudden and arbitrary decisions made with little or no public explanation, as is done in Eritrea, are likely to make investors think hard before they decide to invest in the country.

The party sector has also created critical political problems. In most African countries the distinction between governments and ruling parties is not very clear. The PFDJ's engagement in business activities makes the distinction between the two even more obscure, especially since high ranking members of the bureaucracy are often members of the party. There is no institutional mechanism, for instance, to safeguard public assets or interests from the party, when such interests are in competition with the party's interests. There is also no mechanism to ensure the public's interest when the party's firms are providing service to the government. There isn't even a clear audit system to ensure that the party's concerns pay the appropriate rate of taxes.

Another serious political problem created by the ruling party's engagement in business relates to the PFDJ's monopoly of political power. Entry of new political parties into the political arena and meaningful political competition is highly unlikely when the PFDJ maintains its economic power. Considering that opposition parties are bound to challenge its participation in business activities, the PFDJ is very likely to continue to rule out legalization of political parties. Even if it legalizes them, the country is destined to remain under a *de facto* single party rule, as long as the PFDJ's economic power remains intact. The party's ability to deny opponents an economic basis ensures its continued hegemony. It can deny its critics access to economic opportunities through its licensing mechanism or it can destroy their businesses through the competitive power of its firms. The party can also use its economic power to create a system of patronage that rewards its supporters. As the principal employer in the country, by virtue of its control of the party and state sectors, it can even make political support a covert criteria for access to jobs.

The party's engagement in economic activity also makes repressive rule inescapable since the PFDJ cannot maintain its present economic and political dominance under a democratic political system. One of the reasons why the PFDJ has not been able to implement the constitution, which was ratified in May 1997, is because a constitutional government would not enable it to preserve its present economic and political privileges. This issue will be explored further in chapter 4.

The Warsay-Yikeallo Campaign

The second major policy problem the economy faces is the government's control over the country's human resources. The WY campaign is the most obvious manifestation of this problem. The campaign requires people between the ages of eighteen and forty to extend their national military service and to work for a nominal wage in public projects, such as road building, or projects run by firms that are owned by the PFDJ. For a country to require national service from its citizens is not unusual. Many countries impose such obligations. The duration of the national service, which is nominally eighteen months is also reasonable. However, since the border war broke out the government has extended the duration of the service indefinitely. At the time of writing demobilization of those who have served several years beyond the eighteen months has yet to take place. A large portion of Eritrea's work force has, thus, been tied up in military camps for the last seven years. High school students are also required to do public service (*Maetot*) in the summer months when school is not in session.

According to its official declaration, the government expects the WY campaign to bring about rehabilitation of the country's economy after the devastation caused by the 1998-2000 war. It is highly doubtful, however, that the campaign would lead to rehabilitation of the economy. The campaigners are not always placed in areas where they are engaged in productive work after their military training. Even when they are, the campaign removes large segments of the country's work force from areas of voluntary and gainful employment to an area of involuntary work in the public and party sectors of the economy. In extensive travels in Eritrea's rural areas, we observed many young men flocking to the hills to spend nights in hiding from the frequent round-ups the government undertakes to recruit for the WY campaign. Many others continue to flee the country partly to avoid the campaign and partly due to lack of political freedom. In an attempt to control the ranks of those who dodge the WY campaign, the government has relocated all twelfth grade classes in the country to the military training camp at Sawa. Obtaining a high school completion certificate or securing admission to the country's only university or to vocational training colleges now require enrollment in the WY campaign. We are unable to confirm the magnitude of the problem, however, many female students are said to drop out of school after completing eleventh grade rather than do the national service, at least, in part, due to reports that rapes are widespread in the camps.

The government's primary intentions in waging the WY campaign might be to extend the military service necessitated by the continued hostilities the country faces from its neighbors in general and the uncertainty about the border problem with Ethiopia in particular. The economic considerations of the campaign might be secondary. The Eritrean society, which has paid so dearly in achieving its independence and maintaining its sovereignty, would clearly support a system of compulsory military service to secure the country. Eritreans did not expect payment to fight the long liberation war or the two-year border war. Conversations with many ordinary people in both urban and rural areas also revealed that, given the security threats the country faces, the population would be supportive of military service, even an extended one if it was managed properly. Among the commonly expressed views are that the nature of the service be clearly defined, and those who complete their service be demobilized promptly and kept as reserves to be recalled to active duty if and when needed. Instead, the government has simply extended the duration of the military service for an indefinite duration and turned the service into unpaid labor. Such extension of the national service has caused a major disruption of the country's system of production, contributed to a rapidly rising inflation and resulted in extreme hardship for some segments of the population. Many families, especially old people and children, are often left with no one to support them or care for them, as the government simply rounds up people within the specified age bracket and sends them to the service for years without looking into situations that might merit exemptions. While traveling on foot in the southern part of the country in July 2003, one of the authors took shelter from a heavy late afternoon rain in a WY military camp. When it was getting dark and the tent was flooded the author remarked to the group of men in the tent that their situation was rough. With a clear sense of frustration, one of the men replied, "the situation of our children is worse."

Needless to say, the campaign has generated widespread discontent. It has also deprived the private sector, especially in rural areas, of its labor force. Consequently, the rural household as an economic unit has been crippled. In July 2002 an aging farmer aptly articulated the situation in rural areas when he lamented, "they [the government] have taken away those who are strong enough to farm. We are too old to till our land and even our plough-oxen do not respect us when we try."

As noted in chapter two, Eritrea frequently faces droughts and was ravaged by several wars in the twentieth century. Yet the Eritrean society generally managed to avoid severe starvation and to remain largely self-reliant in the past, mainly due to the tenacity of its work force. Rural Eritrea is now engulfed by severe food shortages and, deprived of its' work force, is largely at the mercy of external intervention to ward off widespread starvation. Even when demobilization of troops takes place, many of the young people in the service are unlikely to return to the villages to become farmers. The shortage of labor in the traditional agricultural sector, thus, may be permanent, and the country is facing a crisis of transition not only in terms of economic production but also in terms of retaining its traditional institutions. Rural Eritrea is now largely inhabited by people who are either too old or too young to sustain basic production and to uphold their fundamental institutions of governing themselves. It has now become common for villages to appoint old men in their 70s to guard village crops, trees and pasture reserved for plough-oxen.

Another side effect of the campaign is the rapid spread of HIV/AIDS. The socially conservative Eritrean society, which traditionally censured pre-marital and extra-marital sex through various means, is now unable to control individual behavior in the camps. As a result, the spread of HIV infections and unwanted pregnancies has reached alarming rates. The government's conservative estimate is that 4.6% of the country's men and women in the military are HIV positive compared to a 2.4% infection rate among the general population (UNAIDS, 2002). Soon these higher rates within the military will likely spill to the general population. Many parents are also said to be prematurely marrying off their daughters to avoid sending them to the national service or the Warsay-Yikeallo campaign, even though the government warns that dodging the national service and the campaign results in loss of certain rights awarded to citizens.

As a small country with limited natural resources, Eritrea's success in development depends on its efficient management of its human resources. The campaign represents a serious mismanagement of the country's human resources in several respects. The long war of liberation deprived a generation of Eritreans of access to education as thousands of young people joined the liberation struggle, which left the country in dire shortage of trained personnel. Years of military service under the WY campaign have extended the deprivation of young people of access to education and skill training. The country's ability to operate in the knowledge-based global economic system, thus, continues to be undermined. In the early 1990s the government attempted to address the country's shortage of skilled man-power by sending scores of students abroad for training. With the growing unpopularity of the WY campaign and the government's failure to liberalize the political system, many foreign trained Eritreans chose not to return to their country. A growing number of young Eritreans have also begun to flee the country. In response, the government has resorted to restricting the number of students going abroad for training. It has prevented students from leaving privately, drastically reduced the number of those it sponsors to study abroad, and even requires guarantees from those it allows to go to ensure their return. At one point the University of Asmara announced that each student would have to deposit a sum of $15,000 as collateral in order to be allowed to go abroad (*BBC News*, 13 February, 2001). Obviously, few Eritreans could be expected to be able to deposit such an amount as a guarantee and the plan was scrapped following an outcry by students. One of the authors, who visited the President of the University of Asmara, the country's only university, in July 2002, was amazed to see a note posted on the door of the President's office stating that the country has suspended issuing exit visas to students, who privately secure scholarships to go abroad for further training. The government's reaction is ill-advised, and it is strange that the university's president would take charge of screening exit visas.

African countries face a serious problem of brain drain. A report by the Pollution Research Group at Natal University in South Africa, for example, claims that the continent has lost a third of its skilled professionals in recent decades at a cost of $4 billion a year to replace them with expatriates (*BBC News*, October 17, 2001). The factors causing the brain drain are complex, involving pushes by political insecurity at home and pulls by economic opportunities abroad. Like many other African countries, Eritrea has faced its share of brain drain, which has been intensified by the border war and the WY campaign.

The problem is difficult to deal with since African countries do not have the resources to compete against the advanced countries in terms of providing the economic opportunities to their skilled personnel. But African countries can reduce the push factors by democratizing their political systems and respecting individual liberties. The Eritrean government can try to address the problem of brain drain by creating more inviting conditions for the foreign-trained citizens to come back instead of resorting to draconian measures of preventing students from leaving the country for advanced training, when the needed training is not available in the country and when the training is crucial for the country's development. That about 85% of Eritrean students sent abroad for training returned to their country before the institution of the WY campaign is indicative that the rate of return would be high when conducive political conditions exist (*BBC News*, 13 February, 2001). Of course, some of those who go abroad for training will not come back, but they too will support their country through various means, as Eritreans in the diaspora have done over many years. Diaspora populations have become important sources of resources to their home countries through remittances, foreign investment and technology transfer. For instance, Eritrea received roughly 35% of its annual GDP from remittances from its diaspora population between 1995 and 2002 (The World Bank, 2004)

Another important factor that adversely affects the development of the country's human resources is the country's educational system. At 1.4% of GDP, the country's expenditures on education rank among the lowest in Africa (The World Bank, 2002). The country's only university has also not admitted new students for the last two years. The government's rigid control of the workforce along with the poor educational policy are likely to have a serious impact on productivity of the workforce and on the development of the country's human resources for years to come.

Eritrea's Land Policy

Another serious policy obstacle to Eritrea's economic development is the government's land policy. A brief description of the country's land tenure system is provided in order to give context to the problems the land policy poses.

The land tenure system in Eritrea is rather complex, varying from one locality to another. Nevertheless, three types of land tenure systems are predominant. These are: *diessa* (village ownership), *risti* (kinship and family ownership) and *demaniale* (public land). In the *diessa* system arable land is periodically (usually every seven years) redistributed relatively equally among all households in the village. At marriage every household is entitled to a *gibri* (a share of arable land). In cases of divorce, the household's land is divided equally between the two parties. If one of them remarries, however, the new household is given a new full *gibri* from the village land. Single widows/widowers, spinsters and orphans are also entitled to one-half of a *gibri* from the village land while females married outside the village obtain a *gibri* in the husband's village.

In order to ensure some degree of fairness, the village land is categorized into fertile, semi-fertile and poor lands, and each household gets a plot from each kind. Pastureland is left for communal use. Land is not sold or inherited, although in peri-urban areas, especially around Asmara, some villages privatized certain parts of their land, most of which was subsequently sold to developers and city dwellers in the 1960s and 1970s.

The second type of land tenure in Eritrea is the *risti* (kinship ownership) system. There are several types of *risti* often with minor variations. In the *tselmi*, the most common type of *risti*, ultimate ownership of arable land resides in the extended family of remote ancestors, who are believed to have pioneered the settlement in the area. In the *tselmi* tenure system land is generally divided among the male members of the kinship. Individual *tselmi* holders often require the consent of the extended family in order to sell or give away as a gift any portion of their share.

As in the village tenure system, pasture land is communally used in most of the *risti* systems. For these reasons, the *risti* system also can be regarded as communal at least in part. The *risti* system was predominant in the province of Seraye (now part of the South Region) before the tenure system in that region was converted to *diessa* by the Ethiopian government in the early 1980s. At the time of the country's independence *risti* was found primarily in pockets in the northeastern and western lowlands of the country.

The third tenure system is the *demaniale* (public land). This is land which was appropriated by the Italian colonial state (1890-1941) and retained as state land by subsequent governments. *Demaniale* is predominant in the lowlands, but pockets of it are found throughout Eritrea. Despite its legal control, the state in the past rarely restricted access to such lands. Peasants, for the most part, had almost open access to these lands for grazing their animals and in most cases even for farming. For all practical purposes, *demaniale* land can also be regarded as communal land. Following Eritrea's independence in 1991, peasants in some areas have laid claim to these lands on the grounds that these lands were forcibly taken away from them by the Italian colonial state and that these lands remained under nominal state control only because the successive (British and Ethiopian) colonial states failed to hear their pleas.

Several advantages are attributable to the country's communal land tenure systems. All three tenure systems prevent the problem of landlessness, although inequalities of holdings between villages and kinships are common in the *diessa* and *risti* systems. However, both systems maintain relative equality within villages and kinships. As a result, they promote a relatively egalitarian community. The tenure system also allows the sustainability of traditional institutions that foster a highly decentralized and democratic system of local governance throughout the country's rural areas, but especially in the highlands.

Despite these benefits, the communal tenure system generates a number of disadvantages. The periodic rotation of village land discourages long term investments. Communal ownership in concert with recurring droughts, a rapid population growth and the breakdown of traditional conservation measures, mostly due to the protracted war of liberation, has also culminated in land shortages, fragmentation, overgrazing, deforestation and severe land degradation. Growing demand for charcoal and fuel wood in the urban areas has exacerbated the rapid land degradation, as trees have been cut to supply charcoal and firewood for urban areas. Most rural areas have faced a sharp decline in crop yield. In many parts of the country, the depletion of the top soil by erosion and loss of grass seeds have resulted in barren land. As a result, the population of livestock in the country has declined significantly (University of Asmara, 1996).

The Land Reform Proclamation and Its Implications

In an attempt to respond to these challenges, the government proclaimed a rather ambitious land tenure reform in August 1994. Among the key components of the proposed reform decree are that (1) ultimate ownership of land rests with the state, (2) the state determines the allocation and use of land, (3) in rural areas, farm land and land for building dwellings are to be redistributed to private users (farmers) and developers who will have permanent usufructuary rights, (4) every Eritrean over 18 years of age is entitled to a plot of land for housing and those who want to live by farming are entitled to land use rights with no regard to ethnic, religious, and gender differences, (5) the existing village, district, and regional boundaries are to be disregarded in the redistribution of arable land, and (6) that the state reserves the right to take land deemed essential for national development from its holders by paying due compensation (Proclamation No. 58/1994).

As noted, the traditional land tenure systems had several problems that necessitated reforms. However, many aspects of the proposed reform are simply unrealistic and others create problems that are worse than the once they were intended to solve. Replacing the *diessa* and *risti* tenure systems by permanent usufructuary rights may perhaps be able to reduce the problems of land mismanagement, continued fragmentation of holdings, and encourage long term investments on land. A 1992 small sample survey by one of the authors revealed that there is evidence that periodic rotation of holdings does indeed impede permanent investments. Some farmers interviewed for the survey, especially those who had holdings suitable for irrigation, indicated that it discourages them from making permanent improvements on their holdings (Mengisteab, 1988). In some areas farmers had even resisted new rotations because they had made permanent investments on their holdings. In other areas, however, peasants have developed a system of compensation for permanent investments at the time of land rotation. Peasants in villages, such as Terra Emni, in Seraye, for example, have devised ways of compensating owners of water wells and other investments.

Yet the survey also showed that periodic rotation of land holdings remains very popular among the overwhelming majority of farmers in the *diessa* land tenure areas. A 1969 survey by the Ethiopian Ministry of Land Reform and Administration also found that a great majority of the farmers wanted to maintain the communal ownership against the option of privatization of land. A popular traditional tenure system is not necessarily the most suitable for development. Peasant farmers, however, attribute two important benefits to the *diessa* system. One is its ability to maintain equality of access to land among all members of the village. The system's ability to provide land to new households by taking land away from holders that moved away permanently or from deceased holders and by dividing holdings into smaller plots when an increase in the number of households occurs is another reason why the *diessa* tenure system remains popular.

In company with strict regulation of cutting of trees and aggressive reforestation measures, the proposed land tenure reform has the potential to reverse land degradation. Some steps were initiated in reforestation before they were disrupted by the 1998-2000 border war. In concert with policies that provide affordable alternative forms of energy and affordable building materials, the proposed land reform has the potential to reduce and even to reverse the deforestation process. Continued reliance on firewood as a source of fuel for cooking and for construction of the traditional housing in highland Eritrea, the *hidmo*, are no longer sustainable. Unfortunately, alternative sources of energy, including natural gas, remain inaccessible for much of the population.

The reform has not been fully implemented since the country does not have any reliable land surveys or agro-ecological zoning. In the absence of such information, the proclamation could not be implemented as the size of land to be allocated to each holder could not be determined. The proclamation is also unrealistic in many respects. For example, how future land-seekers obtain land after the initial redistribution, unless such claimants are expected to abandon the rural areas and migrate to urban areas remains uncertain. One of the merits of the communal tenure system is that it allows people to stay in agriculture until more attractive employment alternatives are created. It has a mechanism that regulates rural-urban migration and unemployment, although it generates underemployment in densely populated villages. The proclamation, by contrast, creates a condition for the emergence of a class of landless peasants who would be forced to flock to urban areas.

Issuing land to eighteen-year-olds instead of to households may also worsen land fragmentation and may even have detrimental effects on the family. The intention of the proclamation may be to ensure gender equality in access to land, which is noble. However, the traditional communal tenure system gives land to households. As noted, spouses divide their share of land equally in cases of divorce. Single-person households and orphans also obtain a half share irrespective of their gender. Giving land to eighteen-year-olds creates the problem of what happens to the land when the youngsters marry to people from distant villages and have to move since such couples cannot sell or trade the land. Since marriages can not be confined to take place within same villages, the proclamation's practicality and implications on the family are, at best, uncertain.

Implications to Nomadic Areas
Another major problem with the land proclamation relates to its implications for nomadic people. Given the existing shortage of arable land in the highlands, granting usufractory rights to land to all adults over eighteen years of age is certain to lead to marked encroachment on grazing lands. Additionally, the proposed tenure system encourages the development of large scale commercial farming by allowing the government to grant land concessions to commercial farmers. A number of commercial farms have already sprouted in the lowlands. The PFDJ itself has actively participated in establishing commercial farms. Such developments in themselves would be positive in that commercial farming might help alleviate food shortages in the country and may even generate some foreign exchange earnings from the exports of fruits and vegetables. However,

there is no mechanism put in place to protect the interests of nomadic people.

Some observers have cautioned that the failure of the proclamation to protect grazing and nomadic areas from encroachment by farmers would lead to conflict and serious political instability in the country. For example, Joireman (1996) regards the lack of protection of nomadic areas as a "minefield." Markakis (1995) also warns that "little thought seems to have been given to the obvious impact of such development on the pastoralist mode of production, and to the reaction of people in what are politically sensitive regions." One observer attributes ethnic politics to the land policy by claiming that the EPLF confiscates land from the Kunama to settle "tigreans" (highland Eritreans) in the Kunama's agro-pastoral lands in the Gash and Setit (Gilkes, 2005:236).

There is no evidence to support Gilke's unscrupulous claim. However, as noted earlier, the state lands are predominant in the eastern and western lowlands. The largely nomadic inhabitants in these regions are likely to suffer the most from encroachment on grazing areas. They may also be the most likely to resist encroachment on state lands, which they regard as their own. However, neither pastoralism nor the adverse impacts of the land policy are limited to the lowlands. Considerable numbers of peasants in the highlands practice mixed farming and roughly 40% of the livestock population in the country is found in the highlands (University of Asmara, 1996). Many of the highlanders move their livestock to the lowlands for pasture during the period between November and May when it is dry season in the highlands. Many lowlanders also move their livestock to the highlands during the dry season in the lowlands, June through October. The land reform simply does not appreciate and take into account this vital interdependence between the inhabitants of the two ecological zones.

The vision of the government might be to settle the nomads and transform the nomadic mode of production. The process of transforming nomads, however, cannot begin with encroachment on lands they customarily use and exposing them to more hardship before undertaking concrete measures to first attract and integrate them into a different mode of production that offers them a better way of life. So far, while commercial farms have encroached on nomadic areas, the government has not taken any notable measures that would facilitate the transformation of pastoralists.

Implications for Urban Development

Perhaps the most immediate impact of the government's land policy, so far, has been on urban development. Unlike the traditional tenure system, the land reform proclamation does not allow privatization of semi-urban land and thus precludes the development of a free urban land market. Instead it vests ownership of land on the state and promises to provide every Eritrean the right to land for dwelling as well as for business operations on lease basis for a nominal fee. In 1997, the lease fee for residential land ranged from 0.10 *bir* to 0.25 *bir* per square meter annually while the fee for land for business operations ranged from 0.20 *bir* to 0.25 *bir* per square meter annually (Proclamation 31/1997). The exchange rate at the time was 7.50 *bir* = US$1.00.

With these low rates, and given the country's low population density, the proclamation would seem to enable many Eritreans to own their homes relatively inexpensively and that the country would alleviate housing problems. In reality, however, the proclamation has led to a number of serious problems, including housing crisis in urban areas.

One serious problem is that the government has not been able to distribute land effectively. Fourteen years after assuming power, the PFDJ has not been able to develop a credible mechanism of distribution of urban land. This critical failure

116

in conjunction with the effects of long wars and the *Derg's* failed socialist policies has left the country's urban areas in a serious housing crisis. In reaction to the crisis, the population has resorted to underground land market which has driven housing prices beyond the reach of Eritreans, other than the very wealthy or those in the diaspora. The government has, in fact, privileged people in the diaspora in the distribution of urban land. Scores of Eritreans in the diaspora have paid for land in hard currency although the proclamation promises all Eritrean citizens free access to urban land.

Another problem is that it has victimized peasants in peri-urban areas as the government has engaged in repossessing land from them without paying any compensation, in stark contradiction to the proclamation, which guarantees compensations either in the form of land or in cash to be paid to peasants whose holdings are appropriated. In the absence of a land market to determine what constitutes a fair compensation is difficult. More importantly, since land is declared state property, it is unlikely that peasants in semi-urban areas will have a legal basis for claiming compensation for land the government takes away from them for urban development. The rate of expropriation of semi-urban land is likely to increase as rural-urban migration intensifies and urban expansion takes place.

A third problem with the proclamation is that it discriminates against the poor. One of the government's stated goals prohibiting a market allocation of land was to ensure access to urban land for the poor. However, obtaining land through the bureaucratic mechanism has been a slow and arduous process that the poor can ill afford. Moreover, people who obtain land risk losing it if they fail to start building on the land within a given time frame (nominally six months) after obtaining the land. Facing the threat of losing the land they obtain, many who do not have the means to build on the land have devised creative ways of getting around the legal restrictions. One common practice has been to get into a contractual agreement with a developer who builds on the land and then buys the property from the person who obtained the land at a discounted price. Another common practice is for the land recipient to exchange half of the land for a building on the remaining half. Through these creative arrangements the poor have attempted to benefit from the proclamation since it is legal to sell and buy buildings but not the land they are built on. Such underground markets, of course, have raised transaction costs undermining urban development. More importantly, the government has recently declared such transactions illegal (Ertra.com/2004/News_May 24). If the government acts against the underground transactions, access to urban land for the poorer segments of the population would be severely curtailed.

In a country where the government tries hard to project a corruption free image, the land proclamation has also created structural conditions that facilitate corruption. Obtaining a plot of land in a location of one's choice or even in any location through the bureaucracy is a very arduous process that encourages corruption. The government clamps down on corruption periodically. These are, however, exercises in futility since the government, as a matter of policy, has used land as a means of creating a system of patronage. The government has established criteria for determining who obtains land first. Justifiably veterans of the war of liberation and people who have completed their national service are given priority in the distribution of land. There is, however, little convincing explanation why firms, including PFDJ firms, have easy access to land while the general population is facing severe housing shortage due to lack of access to land. Also unclear is why the government sells access to land to people in the diaspora in a manner that appears to be in violation of the land proclamation. In any case, absence of clearly defined property rights has created various problems, including raising transaction costs as people are forced to rely on bribery and various underground or indirect measures to conduct land related transactions.

Implications for Traditional Institutions

Yet another adverse implication of the land policy is its ramifications on the traditional institutions of governance in the country's rural areas. To understand why these institutions are relevant for the governance of contemporary Eritrean society and how they are undermined by the proposed land policy, requires a brief description of the key aspects of the traditional institutions, especially the role of the Eritrean village *baito* (assembly) in local governance.

Like many African societies, Eritrea has a rich tradition of political, economic and social institutions that deal with allocation of resources, law-making and social control. Traditional African institutions, of course, vary from place to place. Well before the advent of colonialism some parts of Africa had developed centralized systems of governance with kings and chiefs. Often times, as in the case of the Ashanti kings of Ghana, the power of these rulers were restricted by various arrangements, including the institution of councils (Beattie, 1967). In other cases, such as Abyssinia and Rwanda, the rulers enjoyed more absolute power. Yet in most parts of Africa, political tasks such as social control were not carried out by a centralized state. They were highly decentralized and under the control of local entities, such as ethnic groupings and village communities. Eritrea's traditional institutions of governance belong to the latter category.

One characteristic that is common among many of the decentralized African political systems is a consensual system of decision-making in the areas of public concern, such as resource allocation, law-making and social control. Settlement of differences and disputes in such a consensual scheme of decision-making involves the narrowing of differences through negotiations rather than through adversarial procedures that produce winners and losers. The Igbo village assembly in Eastern Nigeria, the *kgotla* in Botswana and the *gada* system of the Oromo in Ethiopia and Kenya are among well known examples where decisions are made in a consensual manner. The Eritrean village *baito* is another well known institution of a consensual system of decision-making.

Other common characteristics we find among many traditional African institutions of governance, especially those in the decentralized political systems, are respect for ancestors, elders, rights of individuals and community norms. A decision-making system that requires unanimous consent of all the participants, as the Eritrean village *baito* does, is inherently built on respect for the rights and opinions of all individuals.

African societies in the decentralized systems rarely had an executive branch of governance with police forces that penetrate communities to enforce laws and rules of society. Members of the community observed the rules and norms of their communities primarily because they were party to their making through the consensual decision-making process and partly due to various mechanisms of community censure, including social isolation. The system in such societies rarely created a permanent separation between makers and enforcers of rules.

Undoubtedly the decentralized traditional African institutions of governance, such as the Eritrean village *baito*, have many limitations. One glaring limitation is the fact that women rarely participate in such institutions, although they are not formally excluded. Also unlikely is that the traditional institutions in their old form would be applicable to the more complex modern way of life. Nevertheless, these institutions have many characteristics that can serve as foundations for building culturally-relevant modern institutions of democratic governance in contemporary Africa. The decentralization and devolution of power and the values of respect of individual rights, which are critical components of many of these institutions are, for example, essential to the development of democratic institutions in contemporary Africa. Since the continent is plagued with problems of undemocratic governance and crisis of state building, which are manifested by ethnic and regional strife, the consensual nature of decision-making and settlement of disputes through mechanisms of narrowing of differences is also likely to be relevant in today's Africa.

Roles of the Eritrean Village *Baito*

A village in highland Eritrea would typically have a *chiqa* or *dagna* roughly translated as judge, and *shimagle* (elders or those who arbitrate). Often the *shimagle* consists of three men representing different kinship groups in the village. Each kinship selects its' *shimagle* usually through a system of rotation among the elders within the kinship. The *chiqa,* who is generally a widely respected village elder, is appointed by the district administrator. It is a non-paying appointment without a term limit. The *shimagle* generally serve for one year and they too serve without compensation. The *chiqa* calls the village *baito* to discuss village issues as needed and presides over litigations conducted in front of an assembly consisting of village elders and other adult males of the village. Disputes are generally resolved on the basis of a consensus that emerges in the assembly with the *chiqa* pronouncing the consensus. One or both parties to the dispute can decline to accept the *baito*'s consensus verdict and appeal to the district court or to higher courts. Appeals are, however, extremely rare and are invoked only when the dispute is over a very important issue.

Rules governing the village are also established by unanimous consensus in the *baito*. Decisions on land for grazing, land for building houses, land for cultivation and land to be kept fallow are all decided by the *baito*. Conservation measures including the protection of trees are also made in the same manner. The village also ensures the protection of its members from both internal and external harm. It resolves disputes among members, as well as with outsiders, mostly through mediation by elders and by imposing *kahsa* (compensation) upon the guilty party. *Kahsa* is rarely taken, however.

Another key role of the village *baito* deals with resource allocation and land is the most important resource. As noted, in the communal tenure system arable land is periodically redistributed (usually every seven years) relatively equally among all households in the village. The *baito* establishes a committee that is representative of all kinship groups in the village to execute the redistribution of land. Households have full control over what they do with the share of land they hold between rotations, and there is no restriction over the size of livestock village members can raise. Income distribution among villagers is thus by no means egalitarian. Many factors, including the distribution of labor, skill and level of hard work and differences in livestock size account for income inequalities. Village norms encourage individual responsibility among households. Successful households are generally well-respected. However, the village provides some safety net through equal distribution of land and, in many cases, supports the old and the sick in plowing their plots and harvesting their produce when close relatives fail to provide adequate assistance.

Village norms are observed by individuals through the *baito*'s conflict resolution measures and through other various mechanisms of social pressure, including fear of isolation and fear of curse by elders. Rapes, adultery and premarital sex are, for example, strongly censured. Shaming transgressors is one of the deterrent mechanisms used.

Relevance of the Village Institutions

As the foregoing brief description reveals, the village *baito* performs important administrative, economic and social functions. One crucial characteristic of its administrative function is the consensual decision-making system. Countries that are still facing significant challenges in their state building process can draw an important lesson from this arrangement, which mitigates conflict between different entities and majority and minority segments of the village population by preventing the majority from imposing its will upon the minority. By requiring unanimous agreement for passing resolutions, the *baito* respects individual opinions and differences and institutionalizes the narrowing of differences through compromises. However, village norms also require that dissenting individuals respect the will of the majority and to be flexible in their positions. This way the *baito* avoids the winner-take-all type of outcomes that generally accompany modern adversarial election systems. More importantly, it prevents concentration of power in the hands of any individuals. The *baito* also prevents the emergence of a permanent divide between the governing organ and the governed (government and civil society) as decisions on the making and implementing of rules are highly decentralized and made through consensus.

Of course, the consensual system of the village cannot be expected to be operational in its present form at the state level in contemporary Eritrea. There is, however, no reason why the democratic system of governance of the traditional system cannot be adopted with some modifications. Moreover, at the state level careful constitutional arrangements can be designed to prevent conflicts between majorities and minorities not only at the level of ethnic and religious groups but also at the level of political organizations. Many practical measures can also be drawn to ensure that competitive political party systems do not exclude minority parties from the decision-making process. Such organizations, after all, are likely to have some ethnic and religious underpinnings.

Winner-take-all types of election systems have the tendency to subjugate the minority (whether they are ethnic, religious or political groups) to the tyranny of the majority. This type of adversarial election system is alien to the consensus-based traditional system of governance of the village *baito*. No doubt, elections would be essential in modern state systems but they can be modified so that they are compatible with societal values and protect minorities as the traditional institutions manage to do. Respect for differences of views and reconciling differences instead of suppressing alternative or minority views, are key lessons of the village *baito*.

Another relevant aspect of the *baito* institution is the decentralized system of decision making. Extensive decentralization together with a consensual system of decision-making, not only in the making of rules but also in their implementation, allows villagers to become masters of their own affairs. There is little disadvantage in preserving this system. It saves the country in administrative costs since the overwhelming majority of the population lives in villages and administers itself. More importantly, it empowers the population by allowing it to control decision-making that affects its own livelihood and narrows the gap between civil society and the government by preventing the government from becoming too overbearing. Again, this aspect of the traditional institutions is highly relevant to the building of a democratic system of governance in contemporary Eritrea. As a small country, Eritrea perhaps does not need some of the formal institutions of decentralization, such as a federal arrangement. However, the Eritrean traditional system of governance is highly decentralized and there is little benefit in replacing it by a centralized system that can stifle local initiatives.

Conflict resolution through mediation by *shimagle* is another traditional institution that is highly relevant. This institution is pervasive even in the country's urban areas. Various types of disputes are often settled through this mechanism and even the modern courts sanction settlements rendered by the system of *shimagle*. Again this is a valuable mechanism for resolving conflicts without resorting to violence and with minimal legal costs. When a dispute broke out in March 2001 within the Eritrean political leadership over a number of issues, including the government's failure to implement the ratified constitution and a dissident group of fifteen high ranking government officials was formed, some elders attempted to mediate between the two sides in line with the country's tradition of *shimagle*. Unfortunately, the government not only rejected the offer by the elders but also threw them into prison, along with the group of dissidents. The dispute has escalated into a political crisis since September 2001 when the dissidents who were in the country at the time were arrested. The dissidents have remained in prison without formal charges since their arrest. We will examine the conflict within the elite in more detail in chapter four.

Another aspect of the village institutions that is relevant for building a genuine democratic system is the involvement of the village population in the determination of how resources are allocated. The *baito* system of resource allocation does not stifle private initiatives or free exchange. Households are responsible for their own well being. At the same time, by ensuring that every member of the village has equal access to land, the village prevents the exclusion of any member from access to opportunities to participate in the system of production and exchange. Advanced countries can provide access to opportunities to their citizens through a system of universal primary education, a widespread access to higher education and a developed welfare system that provides citizens some safety net. In poor countries such as Eritrea, where access to education is limited and a state welfare system is non-existent, that a traditional resource allocation system, which mitigates the inequalities in access to opportunities among citizens is preserved is imperative.

In an era of free market globalization, where inequality and poverty have intensified in the African continent, the

Eritrean village *baito* system offers a very important example of how to combine private initiatives with social protection. Such a mixed economic system is essential for the success of genuine democratization, at least until the economic system is developed enough to create alternative opportunities.

Neglect of the Traditional Institutions of Governance
The foregoing analysis shows that the *baito* institution has a lot to offer to contemporary Eritrean society. The village *baito* is relevant as a mechanism of (1) decentralized democratic self-governance, (2) conflict prevention and resolution, (3) equitable access to land, (4) community-based support system that promotes collective self-reliance and (5) community policing that controls behavior that is incongruent with social norms. Yet the country's post-colonial state has made little effort to apply the country's valuable traditional institutions. Strikingly, villages that are a few kilometers away from the capital city conduct their affairs in a democratic consensual manner, while within the capital city the state operates in a very hierarchical and authoritarian manner in complete contrast to the rest of the country.

The *baito*, which survived colonial rule by different powers, ironically has faced a number of developments that threaten its viability in the post-independence era. The government's land policy is one important development that has endangered the village *baito*. With the proposed land reform, control and allocation of land has been transferred from the village to the state. The proclamation also eliminates village boundaries. Without control of land and without retaining its boundaries, the village's traditional administrative and social functions can not be maintained. With the role of the village as an administrative unit subverted, the significance of the Eritrean village *baito* would also be lost. Without its boundaries, the village is also unlikely to remain an administrative unit and a source of identity and the traditional cooperative and democratic values that the village represents are likely to disappear.

As noted, the 1994 land reform proclamation has not yet been implemented fully. However, the state has already begun enacting the decree that places all land under its control, for example, by beginning acquisition of land from villages in peri-urban areas without paying any compensation to the peasants. The government has also begun drafting master-plans for villages near Asmara, the capital city, designating land for residential areas, for farming and for grazing while disregarding the role of the village and its *baito* in these matters.

In addition, the government has instituted a policy that merges several villages together for administrative purposes. The *chiqa* and village *shimagle* have been replaced by cadres of the ruling party who allegedly are elected by the villagers. With these changes the *baito* has for all practical purposes been reduced to a conduit by which government directives are transmitted to rural people and its traditional role of providing independent local administration has been drastically reduced. Government sponsored local elections, even when conducted properly, are a poor substitute for the traditional institutions. Unlike the traditional institutions, they do not have a mechanism to enable them to maintain a careful balance between different entities of the population, including majorities and minorities.

The neglect of traditional institutions is a common phenomenon throughout Africa. There are many plausible explanations as to why the post-independence African state has neglected the traditional institutions. The nature of the African state is, however, a critical factor. As a creation of the colonial state and the imperialism of decolonization, the African state itself is largely detached from society. An extroverted state largely run by functionaries who are either self-serving or closely tied with outside interests can hardly be expected to be the custodian of the cultural roots of its constituents and their traditional institutions or to empower citizens by ensuring their ownership of these institutions. Moreover, the decentralized system of decision-making that many of the traditional institutions represent is incompatible with the centralizing tendencies of self-serving dictatorial rule.

The neglect of traditional institutions thus appears to be a symptom of the disjunction between the state and society. The post-independence African state, like the colonial state, remains largely an imposition on society and has not yet transformed itself into an overarching organization of citizens devoted to advancing broad interests of its constituency. Reconstitution of the state, i.e., democratizing it by bringing it under the control of society, would be essential for the preservation and development of relevant traditional institutions. That African societies would summarily neglect their traditional institutions under a system of democratic governance that empowers the masses is unlikely.

Conclusion

As noted at the outset, the goals of this chapter were to examine how the ruling party's active participation in business activities and the government's policies of land tenure and workforce management have affected the country's process of economic development, in general, and its democratization process, in particular. Disaggregating the economic impacts of these policy problems is difficult given that the country's economy has been ravaged by other factors, including the 1998-2000 war with Ethiopia and the ongoing drought, which started in 2002. The Eritrean economy, however, was facing serious strains from these policies even before the war. The housing crisis in the country's urban areas, for example, predates the war. The crowding out effect of the party sector on the private sector was also felt well before the war. The combined effects of these two policies along with the WY campaign, which emerged after the border war, intensified the constraints on the private sector by creating acute shortage of vital resources, including labor and foreign exchange, hampering the recovery process.

The adverse impacts of the three policy problems on the country's democratization process are also quite severe. All three policies have helped the PFDJ to create an economic and political privilege and to establish a system of patronage. By creating and maintaining such a privilege for itself, the PFDJ has removed itself from society. The post-independence Eritrean state, for all practical purposes, now resembles and behaves like the predatory colonial state with its extractive institutions. In chapter two we traced the seeds of dictatorship to the era of the liberation struggle. The government's land policy and the PFDJ's active participation in economic activity, which are part of the dictatorship formation process, were also conceived well before the country's independence. The three policies were essentially designed to establish a lasting hegemony of the EPLF on the Eritrean society. However, by denying political and economic space for civil society, these policies produced outcomes contrasting the intended goals. The EPLF, which arguably was one of the most popular fronts in the world, has been reduced into a mere shell of its old self. In less than a decade after it liberated the country, the EPLF finds itself under siege by the very population it liberated.

CHAPTER FOUR

IN DEFIANCE OF DEMOCRACY: THE PROMISE AND FAILURE OF CONSTITUTIONALISM

At the time of its formal independence in 1993, Eritrea appeared to be poised to institute a democratic system of governance. Extensive participation by the population in the drafting of the constitution was, for example, a promising step that gave Eritreans and non-Eritrean observers reason to be optimistic about the country's democratic potential (*Mail & Guardian* May 22, 2003). However, eight years after its ratification in May 1997, the Eritrean constitution has not been implemented and the country remains a one-party state devoid of political freedom. Moreover, Eritrea has now distinguished itself as the only African state without a private press and the government is widely viewed as one of Africa's most repressive regimes. According to reports by various human rights organizations, such as Amnesty International, arbitrary arrests and detentions without charges are rampant in the country. In its *2003 World Report*, Human Rights Watch described Eritrea as "a country under siege—from its own government." Reporters Without Borders (RSF) has also described Eritrea as "the world's biggest prison for journalists."

This chapter grapples with the question of what went wrong. The first part of the chapter briefly sketches the key structural impediments democratization in Africa as a whole faces. The second part examines the basis for the initial optimism about democratization in Eritrea and why the Eritrean government facilitated the involvement of the population in the drafting of the constitution, thereby raising expectations about its commitment to democratic governance, only to prevent the implementation of the constitution. The third part assesses the relevance and limitations of the Eritrean constitution. The last part explores the reasons why the government reversed course by suspending the implementation of the ratified constitution, thereby halting the democratization process.

As an overarching organization of all citizens, a state is ideally expected to have an organic relationship with the community of citizens and to be an agent for their empowerment by advancing broad social interests. Historically the formation of the state was often through coercive means and the state was rarely a promoter of broad social interests. Many states of the world have, however, been transformed through broad social struggle and have become more democratic, even though few states can claim to be fully democratic. Few African states, including those born out of popular armed struggle, have undergone a democratic transformation and such a transformation faces a number of structural impediments. The nature of the African state and its leadership and civil society's inability to reconstitute the state are among the key structural bottlenecks. The continued neocolonial grip of African countries by the advanced countries disguised as globalization is another.

In the African context, the conception of the state was reformulated by the colonial experience. For the masses the state is essentially an apparatus of exploitation and oppression. For the elite it is a source of power for control and self enrichment. A state perceived in this manner cannot be an agent for the empowerment of citizens and it cannot mobilize the general population for social development. Making the

African state relevant requires re-conceptualizing it anew to distinguish it in fundamental ways from the colonial state. Forging such a new paradigm of the state, in turn, requires establishing a system of governance with mechanisms that empower the population to safeguard its civil liberties, select its leaders and ensure that policies are coordinated with social interests. By its historic betrayal of the causes of the general population the post-independence state has utterly failed to change the conception of the state held by Africans. The post-independence African state has essentially inherited the extractive institutions of the colonial state (Acemoglu Johnson and Robinson, 2001). In most cases the inherited institutions have become mechanisms that serve the interests of a small elite of thugish dictators, who place themselves above the law and violate the rights of citizens with little restraint, in order to enrich themselves amidst the abject poverty of their populations. For the most part, therefore, the post-independence African state has remained outside the control of its citizenry and advances private interests at the expense of public interests. Indeed the "state for itself" conception proposed by Caporaso (1982) describes the African state rather well.

Independence from the influence of the citizenry has allowed many of Africa's political elites not only to engage in gross corruption but also to behave as if they own the state. Mobutu of Zaire, Idi Amin of Uganda, Bokassa of the Central African Republic, Macias Nguema of Equatorial Guinea, Mengistu of Ethiopia, Abacha of Nigeria and Taylor of Liberia are the most conspicuous examples. These dictators essentially privatized the state and used its coffers as their private bank accounts and its security forces as their private armies (*The Economist*, May 11, 2000).

Segments of the counter elite (the elite not in power), on the other hand, often saw the state as a prize to be won in order to get access to the privileges of power. Rebellions, such as those led by Savimbi in Angola and Foday Sankoh in Sierra Leone were clearly driven by a blatant drive to capture state power for self-serving purposes. Many of the military coups that took place in Africa between the late 1960s and the early 1980s were also motivated by similar, if less conspicuous, private ambitions. Leaders of opposition parties and armed rebel groups in many African countries have often been driven by the same goals. Peace plans proposed by various mediators in efforts to settle current intrastate conflicts in the continent, including those in Liberia, the Ivory Coast, the Sudan, Burundi and the Democratic Republic of the Congo are crucial. However, they largely center on power-sharing arrangements designed to incorporate rebel leaders into the power structure paying little regard for broad social interests.

Even the leaders who were not widely viewed to be self-serving, such as Kwame Nkrumah of Ghana, Jomo Kenyatta of Kenya, Kenneth Kaunda of Zambia, Sekou Toure of Guinea, Julius Nyerere of Tanzania, Leopold Senghor of Senegal and Houphouet Boigny of the Ivory Coast, did not bring the state under the control of citizens by building institutions of democratic governance. The manner in which they governed was largely an expression of their own vision and sense of benevolence rather than the expressed wishes of their populations. The unpopularity of Ujaama in Tanzania or many of Nkrumah's policies in Ghana, including the outlawing of opposition parties, are examples.

Usurpation of the state by the self-serving dictators is a major factor in producing the African predicament, which includes tragic economic conditions and the crisis of state building, manifested by the collapse of some states and widespread chronic regional, ethnic, and religious conflicts and gross violations of human rights in many others. The conditions prevailing in countries such as the Democratic Republic of the Congo, Sudan, Somalia, Burundi, the Ivory Coast and Liberia are the most obvious examples.

Failure of African leaders to reconstitute the state as an agent for the advancement of social interests by promoting democratic governance has also thwarted the development of appropriate institutions. Often institution building is undermined by leaders who cultivate the myth that they are "the souls of their countries" and, thus, irreplaceable (Gongo, *afrol.com*, Feb 4, 2003). Many such leaders supplant their personal rule for institutions and suppress the rise of alternative leadership by banning or harassing opposition parties or by rigging elections. Others, such as Togo's Eyadema, change constitutional provisions that limit terms in order to extend their tenure in power. Even when they exist, the institutions of governance are highly fragmented with the modern state largely relying on imported institutions detached from the cultural values of society while the population in rural areas largely continues to operate under traditional institutions. The failure to develop appropriate institutions is a major factor in Africa's economic crisis. Most African states have, for example, failed to develop institutions that integrate the modern enclave and the traditional sectors of their economies or to create independent central banks that would establish stable monetary systems.

Far from facilitating the transformation of the nature of the state, post-Cold War globalization has intensified the extroversion of the African state and its detachment from society, thereby further undermining the limited sovereignty that it was able to muster following decolonization in the 1960s. Debt ridden and cash strapped, African countries have been unable to resist liberalization policies imposed by the IMF, The World Bank and donor countries. As conditions for receiving loans and aid, African states have been pressured to adopt capital-friendly neo-liberal policies, including deregulation and retrenchment of state involvement in economic activity even when aspects of these policies are incompatible with African realities and the interests of their populations. Untimely trade liberalization has, for example resulted in Africa's deindustrialization by exposing African industry to globalization's hyper-competition. The neglect of social justice by the neo-liberal policies is also detrimental to African social interests, including state building, transformation of marginalized regions, ethnic groups, and social classes, including the peasantry. Yet many African states have, for all practical purposes, surrendered the responsibility of charting development strategies to technocrats in the international financial institutions, who often prescribe one failed strategy after another with little accountability. The failure of the government of the African National Congress in South Africa which, by most standards, is one of the better governments in Africa, to implement significant policies of income redistribution, including land reform, in order to rectify the gross inequalities left behind by the apartheid system is a telling example.

With globalization there has emerged a regime of economic governance with a transnational legal system and supranational world trade, finance and banking organizations. The international rules that hold together the unfolding global regime are authored, guided and dominated by powerful countries, such as those in the Group of 7 and the Organization for Economic Cooperation and Development, multinational corporations and transnational organizations, including the World Trade Organization, the International Monetary Fund, The World Bank, the Basle Committee on Banking Supervision and the International Organization of Securities Commissions. Since the influence of African countries on any of these actors is rather minimal, the more policy decisions are transferred from the state to the technocrats of these actors, the less African countries are able to chart their own strategies of development that are compatible with their realities and the interests of their populations. To claim that African economies largely remain semi-colonial economies is no exaggeration and it is difficult to conceive democracy in countries that are not free from external domination.

No doubt there are some African countries that do not comply or only partially comply with the liberalization policies. In some of these countries the elite and state functionaries continue to exercise stifling control over the private sector by sapping the energy and dynamism out of the economies of their countries. In Eritrea, for example, rigid state control co-exists with the imposed liberalization policies producing the worst of both worlds. As we saw in chapter three, the emphasis Eritrea's leadership places on the party sector has led to the stagnation of the private sector which is deprived of access to some critical resources, including labor and foreign exchange, while policy makers pretend that the country's macroeconomic policies are liberalized in line with the directives of The World Bank and the IMF.

Zimbabwe's inability to implement a meaningful land reform for over twenty years after its independence and the regime's attempt to assign blame to the west for its conspicuous failure is an example of a different sort. It represents the bankruptcy of self-serving dictators who camouflage themselves with a nationalist mantle. Unfortunately, for the scores of landless Zimbabweans the opposition party that presents itself as an alternative to Mugabe's regime does not even have a policy of land reform that would serve as an alternative to the regime's chaotic measures. Despite the different faces of African dictators, the African population, in most cases, finds itself in a double stranglehold—one by its own predatory state and another one by the exploitative global system.

Under conditions where public policy is dissociated from broad social interests due to state-society fragmentation and an external neo-colonial grip, constitutionalism and democratic governance face formidable structural obstacles. A state which is politically, economically and culturally detached from its citizens cannot be expected to be an agent of democratization and to institute a constitution that empowers citizens. An extroverted state, serving as an agent of external interests or as a private club of an elite which shares common interests with external forces, is instead more likely to reject constitutional rule altogether or to impose upon the population a constitution that projects the interests of the elite and to preserve it through authoritarian means when necessary. Neither state-building nor sustained development is likely to take place under such a state.

The global spread of democratic institutions including in Africa in the post-Cold War era appears to contradict the above analysis. Since the early 1990s most African countries have instituted multiparty political systems, conducted presidential and parliamentary elections and liberalized the mass media. However, these changes have not advanced popular influence on policy and have not translated into coordination of policy with broad social interests. Some, in fact, have characterized the democratization process in Africa as "sham" put in place to satisfy conditionality of donors (*The Economist*, 2000). The African elite has adopted economic liberalization and it is adopting political liberalization. Such political liberalization is not inconsequential since political pluralism and the civil liberties associated with it are invaluable as ends in themselves. The political liberalization measures underway in much of the continent are also not entirely in response to external pressure. The slowly emerging middle class in the continent is also a significant player. Moreover, expansion of the private sector of the economy and competition among political parties, in conjunction with a freer press, have the potentials to lead to the expansion of political and economic space for civil society and allow different civil society organizations to struggle through legal means for the narrowing of the gap between policy and social interests. The undergoing political liberalization is thus a significant improvement over the autocratic rule by self-serving dictators. However, political liberalization has rarely mobilized the African masses and it has taken place in a globalization context that undermines the sovereign control of African countries over their development strategy and within an ideological framework that has little regard for social justice. Under such conditions liberalization is unlikely to lead to genuine democratic transformation that coordinates policy with broad social interests. We now examine why the Eritrean state facilitated the involvement of the population in drafting the country's constitution only to prevent its implementation.

Democratic Promise and Undemocratic Tendencies

In March 1994, a fifty-member Constitutional Commission was established to draft a constitution for Eritrea. Soon after its formation, the Commission organized extensive instruction of the public on constitutional issues with the aid of over four hundred specially trained teachers (Habte-Selassie, 1998). During the process of the drafting of the constitution, which took three years, the commission also conducted wide-ranging public debates on various issues, including the structure of government, the level of decentralization, electoral system, political pluralism, judicial independence and human rights. To determine the extent to which the involvement of the public affected the content of the constitution is difficult. The likelihood is that it had not much impact since the nature of the population's involvement was in settings of mass meetings that are not conducive for the articulation of social interests. Absence of free press and political organizations was another major factor that limited popular influence in shaping the content of the constitution. The inclusion in the constitution of some unpopular provisions, such as those on the issues of official language and land tenure system, also suggests that input by the public had a rather limited impact. Nevertheless, the consultations that took place with the general population, even if they were mostly symbolic, were important in legitimizing the constitution and in promoting constitutionalism in the country.

The government's unwillingness to implement the constitution, however, raises the question why it allowed the involvement of the population in the making of the constitution or why it even created the constitutional commission. Answers to these questions are unclear, but there are some plausible explanations. One is related to the formative nature of the Eritrean state at the time when the constitution drafting process begun. Like most African states, Eritrea was curved out by colonialism. However, unlike most African states, the Eritrean state was not a creation of imperialism of decolonization when it was formed in 1991. Its thirty-year armed liberation struggle was waged against an African state, Ethiopia, and Eritrea's nationalist leaders did not have to strike deals with colonial powers about what kind of state they would create, at least at the time of the country's independence. Moreover, active popular participation in the armed struggle fostered the emergence of a state relatively well connected with its constituencies. At the time the constitution was drafted, the Eritrean state and the political elite were less extroverted and less detached from the general society and its cultural values and traditional institutions.

A second explanation is related to the nature of the EPLF itself. As explained in chapter two, the history of the EPLF is replete with internal struggle between democratic and authoritarian tendencies. The struggle between the forces of the two tendencies was at times violent and at other times more subtle. At the time of the drafting of the constitution, the Front's policies and policy statements were full of contradictions and projected mixed signals regarding the Front's commitment to democracy. In the National Charter, which was ratified in its 1992 Third Congress, for example, the EPLF declared that the formation of political parties should be encouraged since participation of the population could not be fully realized without political organizations. That declaration was consistent with the declarations of the Front's Second Congress held in 1987, which proclaimed the Front's commitment to a democratic governance with civil liberties, tolerance to divergent views, multiple parties, and elections. These pronouncements not withstanding, the Front's leadership was not tolerant to divergent views. As noted in chapter two, during the liberation struggle, the EPLF's harsh response to dissidents, such as the *Menkaa* is well documented (Iyob, 1995; Pool, 2001). In the post-liberation era also there are many examples that show its intolerance to different views. Its failure to allow the remnants of other liberation fronts to operate in the country as political parties, although they constituted little threat to the Front's control of power, is one example. Its response to the dissidents within its ranks, and other protests, including by university students are other examples.

The Front's governance structure as specified by Proclamation No. 23/1992 was another critical impediment to the establishment of democratic and accountable system of governance, as it lacked clarity in regards to the separation of powers within the branches of government. The proclamation created three organs of government; the judiciary, a legislative body made up of the front's the Central Committee, and a State Council, chaired by Isaias Afeworki, as the executive branch. The State Council was responsible for implementing political, economic, and social policies, and executing foreign relations and the law. In addition, the state council was entrusted to issue laws as needed intruding on the sphere of responsibility of the legislative. The Front's Secretary General, who chaired the State Council, also chaired the legislative body, blurring the separation of powers and establishing the foundation for concentration of power.

Continued expansion of the Front's business ventures was also incompatible with democratic and constitutional governance, as noted in chapter three. Despite these contradictions, there was little overt conflict within the leadership of the Front at the time of the drafting of the constitution. An undeclared common front between the proponents of the competing tendencies within the leadership, largely dictated by pragmatism during the latter years of the liberation struggle, was still holding at the time of the drafting of the constitution. The contradictory policies and lack of clarity in the separation of powers, however, suggest that the competing tendencies between democratization and authoritarian control within the Front continued to exist and that it was a matter of time before conflict between the forces of the two tendencies became overt.

A third possible explanation deals with the level of popularity the front enjoyed at the time of the drafting of the constitution. The enormous popularity of the EPLF among the population, which had endured decades of oppression under different colonial rulers, raised the level of tolerance of the population for the transgressions of the regime. The Front also had firm control over civil society organizations in the country, including women's, youth and workers associations. Such organizations were created by it and led by its cadres. Under these circumstances, the Front's leadership was confident that, in the absence of political organizations and a free press, participation by the population in the constitution drafting process would not significantly alter its agenda and that it would instead elevate its image within the international community.

In any case, the Eritrean constitution was drafted under conditions of little overt cleavage within the ruling front and between the state and society, with the exception of the excluded remnants of the ELF. There was also little overt cleavage within society as the long struggle for independence seemed to have forged unity among the different ethnic and religious segments of the population. The relative advantages Eritrea appeared to enjoy—a regime that appeared less detached from its constituency, a governing front that was relatively united and a population that was united and highly mobilized—were expected to enable the country to make a successful transition to a democratic governance.

The rare opportunity which Eritrea seemed to enjoy at the time of its independence and the drafting of its constitution, however, was not because the population had control over the state or over the governing front. Rather it was mainly due to two reasons. One is that the state-society division had not yet crystallized given the strong societal unity during the armed struggle for independence. The second reason is that the Front was successful in capturing the population through civil society organizations that operated under its directives. There were no independent civil-society organizations that could produce and sustain views different from those of the Front.

Over time, the conflicting signals of the Front and the competing tendencies within its leadership became sharper. The divergence of interests between the new elite and the population also became more apparent. As the honeymoon of independence faded, the population's level of tolerance of many of the regime's policy errors and excesses also waned. As a plurality of interests and views emerged among the Eritrean society, the Front's ability to change its top-down control and to tolerate diverse views was put to the test. A brief discussion of some of the most important shortcomings of the Eritrean constitution follows before we examine why the government has failed to implement the constitution.

Limitations of the Eritrean Constitution

A detailed analysis of the strengths and limitations of Eritrea's ratified constitution is beyond the scope of this chapter. Rather, the aim is briefly to examine the constitution on the basis of three criteria which help us assess its overall relevance. The criteria selected for this purpose are: (1) whether or not the constitution has clear mechanisms that facilitate the democratization of society by safeguarding respect for civil liberties, ensuring accountability of leaders and empowering citizens to influence if not control decision-making; (2) if the constitution facilitates socioeconomic development with social justice; and (3) if the constitution conforms with the institutions and values of society. Selection of these criteria is based on the understanding that democratization, development and building appropriate institutions that integrate fragmented societies are widely recognized to be among the most critical societal goals in contemporary Africa. Constitutions would thus have to be able, among other things, to promote these three goals in order to become relevant in addressing the prevailing conditions in Africa. Constitution making in Africa is rarely democratic and the constitutions are seldom designed to advance social interests. Rather, for the most part they are handed down by the political elite with little involvement of the population. Even when attempts are made to democratize the constitution making process, the exercise is often undermined by a failure to properly conceive democracy, how it relates to social justice and how it needs to be adapted to society's traditional institutions and cultural values to become relevant for Africa's masses.

In addition to the involvement of the public in its making, the Eritrean constitution is written in a language accessible to the general population. The constitution is also framed in a concise and general manner leaving its detailed interpretation under the sole jurisdiction of the country's High Court. However, in an attempt to be concise the framers of the constitution left the determination of many critical and contentious issues onto the government. In the context of the African political landscape, where there is little independence of the legislative and judiciary branches of the government from the executive branch, the wisdom of placing such high level of trust on the government is highly questionable.

The constitution, for example, grants citizens the right to form organizations for political, social, economic and cultural ends (Article 19 # 6). But making the laws that limit the exercise of this right, including forming political parties, is left to the legislature with little guidelines as to what type of restrictions by the government might be unconstitutional (Article 26 #1). With the resolution of the fourteenth session of the National Assembly (held in January 2002), the government officially suspended indefinitely the formation of political parties. Even if the government reverses this decision in the near future, there are no constitutional provisions that would prevent the PFDJ-dominated National Assembly from framing the laws governing party formation in a way that would make it difficult for new parties to emerge and compete effectively. Under a system where there is a well developed separation of powers, an independent judiciary would be expected to provide relief from such a danger. Eritrea, however, does not have an independent judiciary. Some of the conditions required of founders of political parties were specified in a draft law authorized by the thirteenth session of the National Assembly. The conditions set by that draft law, which was made defunct by the Assembly in its fourteenth session, were rather stringent. For example, Article 6.5 (a & b) of that draft law proposed that at least two thirds of the founders should originate from at least five ethnic entities and that followers of each of the two dominant religions in the country, Islam and Christianity, be represented by at least one third of the founders. Such conditions and others that could appear in the future may make obtaining approval to form political parties a rather arduous process that frustrates the right of citizens to form political parties. The constitution provides few safeguards to ensure political pluralism by placing some broad restrictions on what the government may or may not do in crafting the laws on the formation of political parties. Theoretically, the High Court would provide relief if the National Assembly issues laws that infringe on the rights of citizens. However, to expect the independence of courts in Eritrea's existing political landscape is unrealistic. The government's creation of a special court with powers to even review cases decided by the regular courts was a significant clue.

Another important issue on which the constitution is completely silent is the Front's engagement in business activities, which creates a number of problems, as noted in chapter three. Under the existing one-party system the boundaries between state assets and the ruling party's assets are not easy to demarcate and there is no independent agency that protects the assets and interests of the state from the party. There is also no mechanism that restrains the government from bending rules and regulations in favor of the party's business ventures at the expense of the private sector or even the state sector. In July 2001, for example, the Front's Central Committee in a meeting at Embatkala claimed that the government owed the Front $300 million for expenses incurred during the two year border war with Ethiopia (*Tirigta*, June 26, 2001). There is, however, no independent auditing mechanism, raising serious questions about the party's and the government's commitment to transparency and accountability.

The party's participation in business activities also has the potential to weaken the executive branch's need accountability for its activities. The constitution assigns control of policies on taxation, expenditures and government borrowing on the legislature (Article 32 nos. 3 and 5). Such control would enable the legislature to demand accountability form the executive branch. The party's business ventures, however, give the executive an alternative source of revenue that cannot be controlled by the legislature.

As noted in chapter three, a political party's economic dominance also creates other fundamental problems. It has the potential to make the party financially autonomous of the population. Such autonomy, in turn, may contribute to making the party unresponsive to citizens' concerns and even encourage it to cultivate a system of patronage. In other words, instead of the party relying on popular support to carry out its platform, the population would depend on the party for its economic livelihood and would be easily coerced to support the party. Under such conditions the level of control or even influence of citizens over decision-making would be severely restricted.

Surely, the framers of the constitution could not have envisioned a political system where political parties engage in business ventures. However, the constitution fails to make any reference to the party's engagement in business activities when at the time of the drafting of the constitution the need for general guidelines governing the sources of assets of political organizations was acute. Even if the PFDJ decided to divest, the constitution's silence implies that decisions on the manner and the timing of divestment are left entirely to the choosing of the PFDJ.

Article 18 of the draft law on formation of political parties and organizations, which was drafted by a committee created by the National Assembly in its thirteenth session, limits sources of assets of political parties to payments and contributions by members, contributions by Eritrean sympathizers and assistance from the government. The constitution's omission in this regard could have been corrected by this article. However, the committee that drafted that law was dismissed by the president before the draft law was ratified and the chairman of the committee along with ten other dissident members of the National Assembly and senior government officials were arrested in September 2001 and remain incarcerated without formal charges at the time of writing. As noted, in complete reversal of the legislation of the thirteenth session, the National Assembly in its fourteenth session (January 29-31, 2002) shelved indefinitely the draft electoral law and the draft law on the formation of political parties, claiming that the majority of Eritreans do not see the need for political parties at the present time.

Another important omission by the constitution relates to the land tenure issue. Since the country's independence in 1991 all land has come under state control. Absence of a land market or any other effective mechanism of allocation of urban land has severely constrained the country's housing industry (Mengisteab, 1998). Every city and town in Eritrea faces a serious housing shortage. Allocation of urban land through government officials has proved to be too slow in addressing the problem and has also created a fertile ground for corruption. Moreover, as noted in chapter three, the land the government distributes among private firms, the party's firms, commercial farmers, Eritreans in the diaspora and some urban dwellers is coming from the holdings of peasants and nomads. So far the government has not paid any compensation in the form of land or in cash to the peasants and nomads whose land it has confiscated. The government's land policy unfairly expropriates land from peasants, undermines urban development by instituting a highly ineffective system of allocation of urban land and criminalizes many urban dwellers who have built houses through underground land transactions. More importantly, the government's land policy endangers state building since certain ethnic groups in the nomadic areas suffer disproportionately from the expansion of commercial farms. Oblivious to all these glaring problems, the Constitutional Commission simply adopted the government's land policy which vests ownership of all land in the state (see Article 8, no. 3 and Article 23, no. 2 of the constitution).

The constitution defines rather well the separation of powers by correcting the ambiguities of Proclamation No. 23/1992. However, the constitution's provisions on the structure of government create a problem of a different sort. Article 32, no. 8 specifies that the president is to be elected by the National Assembly instead of by popular vote. Electing the president by popular vote may politicize ethnic and religious differences as argued by some (Ndulo, 2003). However, the provision that entrusts the National Assembly to elect the president is likely to serve as a means of perpetuation of one party-dominance given that Eritrea has a well entrenched one party system. Such a provision may also create a political system with a dominant presidency since members of the majority party are less likely to act as an effective check on the presidency and scrutinize the policies of the president who is a member of their party.

Another limitation of the constitution is its lack of linkages with the country's traditional institutions of governance. Eritrea has a wealth of traditional institutions of governance on the basis of which the country could develop modern and indigenous institutions of democratic governance. As noted in chapter three, a consensual decision-making system which safeguards minority rights and extensive decentralization of decision-making and empowers the grass-roots are among the strengths of the country's traditional institutions of governance. Despite paying lip service to the importance of traditional institutions and values, the constitution provides no tangible mechanisms to protect, revitalize and integrate the traditional institutions into the country's governance structure. For example, the constitution does nothing to override the land reform proclamation or to rectify its adverse implications on traditional institutions. Article 8 no. 3 and Article 23 no. 2 of the constitution clearly endorse the government's land policy and transfer the responsibility of land allocation in rural areas from the village to the state. This transfer of power undermines the traditional decentralized system of governance.

The constitution is thus devoid of imagination and innovation in terms of linking modern institutions with traditional institutions to make them relevant to the population. As noted, one of the major structural problems of the post-independence African state is its detachment from the values, institutions and interests of its constituency. The Eritrean constitution does little to address this crucial structural problem. Finally, the constitution did not have a provision that would put it into effect automatically upon ratification. Omission of such a provision may have contributed to the government's failure to implement it.

The foregoing analysis shows that the Eritrean constitution has significant omissions that can undermine its potential to democratize society and to facilitate development with social justice. The softness of the constitution is likely related to the weakness of civil-society in the country and to the absence of political organizations and a free press at the time of the drafting of the constitution. As noted, most of the civil-society groups, which were organized under the umbrella of the PFDJ, were not in a position to influence the Constitutional Commission to place provisions that would serve as more stringent control on the government. Another factor is the popularity of the government at the time the constitution was drafted. The Eritrean constitution was written at a time when the country's government enjoyed very high popularity and before the honeymoon of the hard won independence had faded. As a result, the constitution manifests characteristics of a prenuptial agreement written between lovers, as it leaves some important and contentious issues unattended or poorly attended to. One would expect the Constitutional Commission to be more prudent in protecting citizens from possible excesses of any future governments and not to place too much trust on the government of the day, especially given the African political landscape. However, it is also understandable why the members of the Constitutional Commission were overly influenced by the conditions of the time, although there were sufficient signals sent by the government that they could have taken clues from.

In any case, the constitution clearly has significant limitations. However, they are also flaws that can be corrected through amendments. The more difficult challenge has become implementing the constitution. We now focus on why the government has failed to implement the constitution aborting the initial promise of democratization.

Failure to Implement the Constitution

Despite internal contradictory tendencies and intolerance of divergent views, the EPLF portrayed itself, and was widely viewed by others, as a liberation front whose aim was not only to bring about the political independence of Eritrea but also to secure the freedom of the Eritrean people. The Front's failure to implement the constitution has surprised many observers. The government has not given an official explanation for suspending implementation of the constitution or for canceling the national elections, which were scheduled for December 2001. Nor has it rescheduled the elections or given any indication as to when the constitution might be implemented. The government's reasons are, however, found in various interviews by the president and high ranking officials of the party as well as in the declarations of the 14th session of the National Assembly.

Among the reasons frequently expressed in such interviews are the border war and continuing tensions with Ethiopia (U.S. Department of State, 2002). Understandably, implementing some aspects of the constitution was not feasible between May 1998, when the war with Ethiopia broke out, and December 2000, when a peace agreement was signed by the two countries ending the war. However, the decision to go to war without consultation with the National Assembly does not indicate that there was commitment to democratic procedures even before the war. We will return to this issue in chapter six. In any case, during that two year period of war safeguarding the country's independence appropriately took

151

precedence over implementing the constitution. There is, however, no explanation why the constitution was not implemented between May 1997, when the constitution was ratified, and May 1998, when the war broke out, since the outbreak of the war is said to have been unexpected. Also, four years have passed since the signing of the peace treaty. Yet it is not evident that the government is ready to implement the constitution. Undoubtedly, relations with Ethiopia have remained tense and they are likely to remain strained, at least until the border between the two countries is demarcated. However, tensions with another country hardly justify suspending the implementation of a constitution paralyzing a country's political system. Tensions with Ethiopia also did not prevent the 13th session of the National Assembly, which convened in September 2000, from drafting laws that govern elections and party formation and from scheduling elections to take place in December 2001. If the belligerent relations with Ethiopia before the signing of the peace treaty did not prevent the National Assembly from initiating the process of implementation of the constitution, it is not clear why the process would be aborted after the peace treaty was signed and U.N. peace keepers were installed. Continued tensions with Ethiopia also did not prevent the government from conducting symbolic regional elections.

Problems of internal instability caused by dissidents and the private press are also given by the government as reasons for suspending implementation of the constitution (U.S. Department of State, 2002). Following the end of the war, the government faced dissent from some members of the National Assembly, some of whom were cabinet ministers, military leaders of the liberation struggle and members of the Central Committee of the party. The dissidents, who came to be known as the Group of Fifteen (G-15), were unhappy with the way the war against Ethiopia was conducted and with the excessive concentration of decision making powers in the hands of the president. The initial demand of the dissidents, which the president rejected, was for the president to convene the 14th session of the National Assembly as was scheduled by the 13th session in order to ratify the draft laws governing party formation and elections. The broader concerns of the group, however, dealt with the problems in the country's governance structure. As noted earlier, Proclamation No. 23/1992 authorizes the executive body to issue laws as needed in addition to its task of executing the laws. This added authority enabled the president to marginalize the National Assembly, which had little mechanism to keep the president accountable to it and couldn't even meet without his authorization. The dissidents thus demanded the implementation of the constitution in order to ensure his accountability to the National Assembly.

In a system of constitutional governance with an independent judiciary such a squabble between the president and the senior members of the National Assembly, if they arise at all, would be expected to be settled by the country's High Court. Unfortunately, Eritrea does not have an independent judiciary. This was evident from the firing of the country's chief justice by the minister of justice following the chief justice's public complaint that the president's interference has undermined the independence of the country's courts. Another glaring evidence of the court's lack of independence and the absence of rule of law is the High Court's inability to force the government to bring to justice people it has detained without trial well beyond what the law authorizes. Even in Zimbabwe, a country not known for its democratic governance, the court was able to force the government to release Mugabe's main opponent, Morgan Tsvagrrai, from detention on bond in accordance with the country's law.

At the time of the outbreak of dissent by the G 15, the country's nascent private press had begun to play a critical role by serving as a medium of public expression of various views. More importantly, the concerns and views of the dissidents found outlets in the private press. On September 18, 2001 the government arrested eleven of the fifteen dissidents. Three others, who were out of the country at the time, have remained in exile and one member of the group recanted his position. The government also closed down all eight private newspapers in the country and detained eighteen journalists. Shortly thereafter the government also detained student leaders, some business leaders and several elders (*shimagle*) who attempted to mediate the dispute between the president and the detained members of the National Assembly, in accordance with the country's traditional mechanisms of conflict resolution.

The government contended that the dissidents were not arrested for criticizing the government but for treason. The country's acting Information Minister, Ali Abdu Ahmed, for example, claimed that "no person is placed under arrest because of their political views." The Minister added that "[P]eople are free to write whatever they want, they are free to express their opinions," (IRIN News, May 6, 2003). The spokesman and Director of the President's office, Yemane Gebremeskel echoed the same claim by stating, "we don't have political dissidents. No one is jailed because he has a different opinion" (IRIN, 26 May, 2005). The fourteenth session of the National Assembly, which convened ten months after its regular schedule and after the dissidents were detained, also condemned the dissidents for "crimes they committed against the people and their country" (Resolution of the fourteenth session of the National Assembly).

Regarding the private press, presidential advisor, Yemane Gebreab, laments that Eritrea's experience with the private press was negative because of the journalists' lack of professionalism, their susceptibility to intervention by the diplomatic missions in the country and the fact that they were "hijacked by the internal situation in the country" (*Agedesti*

Tsuhufat, 2002). The president also claimed that the journalists were "spies" bribed by foreign powers (Interview with Radio France Internationale, April 16, 2003). The National Assembly also accused the press of jeopardizing national unity. However, the government has not established its claims in the court of law and no formal charges have yet been leveled against the dissidents or the journalists. It would also be an incredible coincidence if all the private press journalists in the country, some of whom are veterans of the war of liberation, would be spying on their country at the same time.

Whatever the merits of the government's allegations against the dissidents and the journalists, the activities of these groups can hardly justify the government's failure to implement the constitution, especially since the essence of the demands the dissidents made peacefully and publicly was the implementation of the constitution and accountable governance. It seems highly likely that the country would have been transformed from a one-party state to political pluralism had the government followed the course set by the thirteenth session of the National Assembly and ratified the draft laws on elections and party formation and conducted national elections. Such measures would have set in motion a democratic process and have allowed the dissidents and others to form their own political parties, formulate alternative platforms and contest for power. The president, however, reversed course after he consolidated his power-base and plunged the country into a political crisis by resorting to repressive measures against the dissidents.

The displacement of large numbers of people by the war, drought and the threat of famine are also given as factors for the delay in implementing the constitution. In general this argument, which assumes a trade off between democracy and economic emergency or development, is a false argument. As Sklar (1996:29) notes, the relationship between democracy and development is a reciprocal one. Given that the absence of accountable governance has been a major factor in bringing about the African crisis, the citizenry through its elected representatives should determine how to deal with issues of famine and drought as well as how to address the development problems facing its country. Coordination of policy with social interests, which is sorely missed in Africa, can hardly be brought about and safeguarded without a democratic governance.

A fourth reason is given by the fourteenth session of the National Assembly, which condoned suspending the implementation of the constitution when it shelved the draft laws governing elections and party formation prepared by a committee formed by the thirteenth session of the National Assembly. In suspending the draft laws, the assembly declared that the overwhelming majority of Eritreans did not support the formation of political parties at the time. Presidential advisor and the PFDJ's head of Political Affairs, Yemane Gebreab, echoed the same argument when he claimed that only a minority of Eritreans are calling now for the political system to be opened up to other parties (*Asmarino.com,* March 18, 2005). In the absence of a referendum or even polls, there is little evidence to support the claim that the majority of Eritreans do not support the formation of political parties. More importantly, forming political organizations is not a policy but a right granted by the constitution and is not subject to the whim of the majority.

In addition to suppressing political opponents and journalists, the government is also widely accused by human rights watchers that it has restricted the right to worship and has persecuted religious minorities, such as the Jehovah's Witnesses and other evangelical church groups. The government disputes the accusations and claims that no groups or persons are persecuted in Eritrea for their beliefs or religion and that people are free to worship according to their wish, or to refrain from worshiping or practicing religion (Communique, Embassy of Eritrea-Washington, D.C. May 1, 2003).

Ironically, in an attempt to dispel the accusations, the government refers to Article 19 of the suspended constitution which recognizes the right of every person to practice any religion and to manifest such practice.

The reasons the government gives for suspending the implementation of the constitution are unconvincing. There is little doubt that the 1998-2000 war with Ethiopia has contributed, in at least two ways, to the abortion of the democratization process. In one respect the continued tensions between the two countries and unsettled nature of the border dispute has given the government the pretext to suspend the implementation of the constitution. In another respect, the war did not go in favor of Eritrea and it is possible that the government's suppression of the free press and other civil liberties is in part intended to prevent scrutiny of how poorly the government conducted the war.

The more plausible explanations of why the government suspended implementation of the constitution are internal to the nature of the PFDJ's leadership. They have to do with its political culture, the conflicting tendencies that have characterized the Front's leadership and the governance structure it established after liberating the country. As noted, during the war of liberation the EPLF created a highly centralized and secretive organization, which allowed little freedom to people who project different views. Once independence was attained the Front's leadership found it difficult to shed its pre-independence political culture and its highly centralized and secretive structures. These characteristics, which served it rather well during the liberation struggle, became incompatible with democratic governance, which requires open and transparent institutions. Even the circle of the leadership was kept so small that the same people who served as cabinet ministers and military leaders were also senior members of the National Assembly and the Front's Central Committee.

More importantly, as Pool (2001) suggests, the institutional arrangements created in the post-independence Eritrea made concentration of power in the hands of the president inescapable. With independence the president retained the post of secretary-general of the party (PFDJ) and assumed the post of commander-in-chief of the armed forces. He also chairs the National Assembly and ministerial meetings. The presidential office also has functions paralleling ministerial ones in the spheres of economy, security and foreign affairs (Pool, 2000:172). By the time the drafting of the constitution was completed the president had consolidated a power structure that did not require him to consult with anyone since there is no other institution that regulates or balances his power. The establishment of such a governance structure, of course, is a manifestation of the shift in the balance of power between the democratic and authoritarian tendencies within the leadership in favor of the latter. The removal of the G-15 from the political scene in September 2001 was merely a mopping-up operation of any feeble democratic tendency that remained within the leadership. In any case, the political system under such a power structure did not allow horizontal (constitutional) accountability between the different branches of government let alone vertical accountability of leaders to the population.

A related factor is the determination of the party's leadership to preserve the hegemony of the PFDJ, despite the past pronouncements of the EPLF that it was committed to a multiparty political system. The Front's participation in business activities to build its economic power basis is a strong indication. Additionally, in an April 12, 2001 interview with Voice of America, the president stated that, in his view, elections and the presence of multiple parties are not related. Yemane Gebreab also invokes the tired argument of some African leaders, such as Mugabe, that political pluralism has its negative aspects and that it could spark divisions among the Muslim and Christian populations of Eritrea (*Asmarino.com,* March 18, 2005). This view suggests that the president and other members of the PFDJ are determined to maintain a single party hegemony by disallowing the emergence of political parties. The suspension of the draft laws on the formation of political parties by the National Assembly, under the guise that the majority of Eritreans do not see the need for parties, was thus to preserve the Front's control of power at a time it appeared vulnerable.

Given its close relations with the masses cultivated during the long period of armed struggle, the EPLF was in a position to be a leader in the reconstitution of the African state. The EPLF could have opened the political system with little threat to its hold on power. It has squandered this historic opportunity. By opting against a democratic system of governance that enables the population to be engaged in decision-making, the EPLF also fractured beyond repair the organic links between the state and society that prevailed at the time of the country's independence. Moreover, by resorting to repression of opponents and denying a political space for legalized political opposition, where political struggle can take place peacefully, the Eritrean regime has joined the ranks of many African governments which turned politics into warfare, as Ake (1990) perceptively noted. The government's repressive measures have unleashed hostile forces and the conflict with such forces has the potential to divide Eritrean society, undermining the country's process of state building. Indeed, the country's future, which a decade ago appeared to be bright, has deemed significantly.

CHAPTER FIVE

POST-INDEPENDENCE
FOREIGN RELATIONS

Over a year and half before the formal installation of the Eritrean government, the intrinsic linkage that exists between the installation of democratic governance at home and the pursuit of a visionary foreign policy abroad can be put thus: "[The] sufficient development of political democracy is a prerequisite condition for the promotion" of cooperative framework in the African Horn. "This requires the formulation of prudent and coherent strategies and the implementation of those strategies in ways that preempt discord and disintegration. To be sure, the future political viability and economic prosperity of Eritrea will be as much a function of its internal making as the success of its external relations" (Yohannes, 1993). In light of what has transpired since that view was expressed, it seems that the observation is demonstrably correct, when considering the current difficulties the country is facing. Perhaps in the absence of received traditions and institutional memory necessary for the conduct of a coherent diplomacy to craft a regional identity and an international imagery for the young nation, it was unavoidable for the Eritrean leadership to go about doing its business by fits and starts. Given this reality, the leadership was more likely than not to fall into the pitfalls that leaders frequently run into in conducting international diplomacy. The first fundamental error the

Eritrean leadership committed was that it enunciated two contradictory policies from the start. On the one hand, the leadership declared the policy of internal self-reliance as the centerpiece of national economic and social development; on the other hand, it began to pursue an activist and even interventionist foreign policy. This was exemplified by the dispatch of an Eritrean fighting unit to Zaire to assist in the overthrow of Mobutu Sese Seko, only to replace him with an equally brutal dictator. This fundamental error was partially a result of a faulty assessment of the objective international conditions and correlation of forces and the erroneous subjective evaluation of Eritrea's ability to considerably influence continental events.

During the Cold War period, the EPLF taught its adherents that the Eritrean struggle was part of the third world anti-imperialist front in general and a continuation of the Middle Eastern struggle in particular. With the end of the Cold War, though, the provisional Eritrean government made a one-hundred-eighty-degrees turn about and chose to align itself with the United States, even with all its regional implications. Long before the Eritrean government was duly installed, the leadership readily internalized the U.S. self-proclamation as the *de facto* manager of the post-Cold War international order. In keeping with its understanding of the changed global environment coupled with the internalization of its pro-American orientation, the Eritrean government then chose an entirely new set of regional allies. Accordingly, Ethiopia and Israel became Eritrea's strategic partners under American stewardship. Symbolic of the radical shift in Eritrea's foreign policy orientation and the formation of a triangle of realpolitik was the fact that a U.S. air force plane whisked the Eritrean leader in January 1993 to Israel for immediate medical attention when cerebral malaria struck him, an event that deeply offended Arab sensibilities. In recognition of the shift of Eritrea's posture, western media and officialdom also hyped in short

162

order the particular importance of the Eritrean leader as one belonging to the "new breed of African leaders," destined to shepherd the African "renaissance" to a new height. This unavoidably made Eritrea party to a grand delusion. Indeed, the relations Eritrea cultivated and the contradictory policies it pursued with the United States, Israel, Ethiopia, the Sudan and Yemen have cumulatively defined its external imagery and have derailed the trajectory of its internal progress. In this chapter and in the next we will attempt to look into the character of Eritrea's foreign relations by analyzing its interactions with these countries. In studying Eritrea's external relations, however, one fundamental problem deserves mention before we delve into the analytical narrative. There is an objective problem of accumulation that must be acknowledged. For a nation that is only a dozen years old, with most of that marked by turbulence, the time frame is too short to establish discernible patterns of behavior. The bureaucratic infrastructure of its foreign policy is virtually nonexistent, making it exceedingly difficult to objectively study the processes of policy formulation and the mechanisms of policy implementation. The problem of accumulation is compounded by the *ad hoc* character of the country's foreign policy, which may have to do with the overbearing presence of the president himself at both the input and output ends of foreign policy. Thus far Eritrea's external relations appear to rest on a "make as you go" logic; making the effort to link the interpretation and explanation of Eritrea's foreign policy to existing paradigmatic perspectives a futile exercise. Given these difficulties, we have chosen to embed our analysis in an historical narrative.

Nevertheless, there are three important dimensions of Eritrea's foreign policy that make the Eritrean state ontologically and functionally analogous to the post-colonial African state. First, the absence of a differentiated institutional framework of foreign policy making is a discernable feature

163

of the Eritrean state. Policy analysis, policy making and policy implementation are all made in the office of the president. Thus the absence of a dialectical interaction of ideas and institutions and personalism rather than bureaucratic rationalism defines Eritrea's foreign policy. Second, like its African contemporaries, the Eritrean state does not recognize the role of domestic opposition groups in foreign policy making. Having denied them public space, the state uses its foreign policy to alienate the opposition groups from cultivating or establishing relationships domestically, regionally and internationally. Third, like in most other African states, Eritrea's foreign policy is harnessed more to insure the short term survival of the regime than to anchor the country's long term national interests in coherent strategic foundations.

Eritrea and The United States: Where The Future Meets the Past.

Immediately following World War II, the United States articulated a public posture that amounted to an open repudiation of Eritrea's right to self-determination. Washington saw the integration of Eritrea into the Ethiopian empire as consistent with its stated definition of Eritrea and Ethiopia forming a single strategic whole on which the realization of America's regional objectives presumably rested. Even after the unilateral Ethiopian abrogation of the federal arrangement in 1962, the United States readily endorsed Ethiopia's annexation of Eritrea by militarily and financially contributing towards the pacification of the territory. Between 1953 and 1969, U.S. military assistance to Ethiopia amounted to $147 million, which was half of the total U.S. military aid for all of sub-Saharan Africa, supplemented by another $195.1 million in economic aid (Machida, 1987; Halliday, 1971; Lobban, 1976; Pateman, 1998). The U.S. also provided Ethiopia a large contingent of military advisers and trainers in counter-insurgence maneuvers. This included a 55-member team from

164

Plan Delta which initiated a pacification program in Eritrea as part of the plan to weaken the mass support of the Eritrean struggle. By 1966, there were 266 American military trainers and advisers, who trained 2,523 Ethiopians in conventional and counterinsurgency warfare (Machida, 1987; Lobban, 1976; Pateman, 1998).

As the Cold War waned, however, Washington began calling for a peaceful resolution of the war of liberation in Eritrea, preferably by restoring Eritrea's federal autonomy. But this American idea was overtaken by events on the ground as the Eritrean liberators militarily evicted the Ethiopian army from Eritrea in 1991. In consequence, the U.S. was placed in a quandary that necessitated the grudging acceptance of Eritrean independence as a state of fact. The question confronting Washington now became how to reconcile America's regional objectives with the fragmentation of the African Horn. Although the first Bush administration mediated the provisional separation of Eritrea from Ethiopia, it fell on the Clinton administration to formulate a policy response to the no-contest divorce of Eritrea from Ethiopia, consummated by a referendum in 1993.

By fits and starts, the Clinton administration identified four broad American objectives in Eritrea that together defined what Eritrea's role in the reconfiguration of the African continent should be. These objectives were: the promotion of stability in Eritrea itself; the need to cement Ethio-Eritrean relations in ways that reinforced the promotion of Ethiopia's internal stability; the imperative to enhance Israel's regional security interest by distancing Eritrea from the Arab world as part of the effort to insure the de-Arabized status of the Red Sea basin; and the making of Eritrea into an active partner in forging a regional bloc under American leadership. Remarkably, these American foreign policy *desiderata* have remained constant under the Bush administration with minor tuning. The present Administration includes combating global terrorism and promoting democratization in Eritrea among its policy objectives (U.S. Department of State, March 2004). The Eritrean government readily accepted the above four American *desiderata* as compatible with its own vision and expectations. From the Eritrean government's point of view, the new partnership with the United States would provide the necessary inducements to the flow of American private and public capital into Eritrea, considered crucial to the economic rehabilitation of the economy. Secondly, the U.S.-Eritrean partnership would also provide the framework for the transfer of American arms to Eritrea, necessary not only to complete the internal pacification of the country but also to insure regime survival. Finally, the insertion of Eritrea in regional politics and increasing the role of the Eritrean leader in it required U.S. patronage. In this section we will assess the outcomes of U.S.-Eritrean "partnership" by juxtaposing the aims and efforts of each with those of the other.

In matters of both internal Eritrean security and economic rehabilitation, there was an apparent convergence of views in Asmara and Washington. Although the Clinton administration proved to be overly generous in preaching its moral and ideological views, it was extremely frugal in providing the necessary material assistance. The administration was nonetheless determined to address Eritrea's internal security and development needs by focusing its aid on five areas: food security, refugee resettlement, troop demobilization, humanitarian demining and promoting internal stability or pacification. To realize these goals, the U.S. provided Eritrea $6 million for fiscal year 1993, which was pitifully insignificant (*State Department,* March 1998). As the Eritreans began to complain about America's frugality, the Administration raised overall U.S. aid to Eritrea to about $20 million a year on average between 1994 and 1997. This included the aid channeled through private U.S. organizations, covering food, health, education, refugee resettlement and troop demobilization (*State Department*, March 1998).

The Clinton administration tried to lighten the burden of handling Eritrea's requests for assistance by encouraging the Asmara regime to involve other advanced countries as well as regional and international multilateral agencies in the country's development. In fact, the Clinton administration was an active participant in the December 1994 conference of the Paris Club, organized by The World Bank. Western governments and multilateral institutions collectively pledged about $285 million to cover an assortment of projects in agriculture, road construction, telecommunication and airport expansion, drinking water supply, refugee resettlement, troop demobilization, public health and primary education, micro-enterprise and fishery development. While Italy led the pack of donors with $50 million, the Clinton administration added a mere $9 million to the pot (*Indian Ocean Newsletter (ION,)* February 4, 1995).

From the Eritrean government's standpoint, considering the fact that Eritrea was designated by Washington as a frontline state in the fight against Sudanese fundamentalism, the overall U.S. economic assistance to Eritrea was disappointing. For example, between 1999 and 2002, Eritrea consistently ranked eighteenth among twenty-five African states that received U.S. aid. During those four years, Eritrea received $39.8 million in total aid while Uganda and Ethiopia, which ranked third and fourth in receiving U.S. aid and were also designated frontline states, received $194.1 million and $157.3 million respectively (*Congressional Research Service,* Jan. 2002). The area where American generosity was evident involved humanitarian assistance. Between 1998 and 2004, the United States provided Eritrea with 854,570 metric tons in emergency food aid, valued at $240 million (U.S. Department of State, July 23, 2003; *IRIN,* October 29, 2004). On the basis of per head of the Eritrean population, this is among the highest U.S. food donations anywhere in Africa.

In so far as Eritrea's internal security and size of armed forces were concerned, both governments were in agreement in that the country's 95,000-strong force was too big for the economy to support. Hence, the U.S. offered to help transform the Eritrean armed forces into a smaller yet highly mobile, efficient and professional national army, more suited for internal pacification and humanitarian crisis response than for offensive external engagement. To this end, the Clinton administration agreed to provide Eritrea with new light equipment, in-country military training teams, and to train Eritrean officers in the United States (*State Department*, March, 1998). However, U.S. military aid fell well short of the Eritrean regime's expectation. By 1995 the United States had already phased out military grants to or the financing of purchases of U.S. military equipment by African states. The only type of military grants left in place was limited to small allocations of between $100,000 and $200,000, administered under the International Military Education and Training program for which Eritrea was eligible (*Congressional Research Service*, January, 2002). However, receipt of such insubstantial amounts of military aid would not go far enough to transform the Eritrean armed forces into a modern and professional fighting force.

Perhaps the only relatively successful U.S. aid program in Eritrea was the de-mining scheme carried out between 1994 and 1997 under the "Training the Trainer" initiative. Even four years after independence, Eritrea's valleys, ravines, fields and roads were still littered with land-mines, antipersonnel and antitank devices and unexploded ordinance munitions. Apart from the fact that there were between 300,000 and one million land-mines spread throughout the country, hampering access to farmlands and grazing pastures, there were forty-four types of land-mines obtained from different countries that complicated the de-mining operations (Clemens, 2000). In addition to the wide dispersion of the landmines in uncharted patterns, some of the deadly landmines were fitted with anti-tampering features and plastics, making detection and detaining operations extremely hazardous. Eritrea lacked not only landmine clearance equipment but also trained personnel to carry out detaining operations.

America's recognition of the landmine problem in Eritrea first arose from a particular military interest, having to do with the planned joint exercise of U.S. Special Operations Forces and the Eritrean armed forces. The view was to expose U.S. forces to peculiar terrains and improve their endurance while at the same time contributing to the professionalization of the Eritrean troops. The plan was dubbed *Eager Initiative-94.* In light of this military necessity, in 1994 the Clinton administration found Eritrea eligible for humanitarian de-mining assistance. It was followed by the establishment of a U.S. military de-mining mission in Eritrea with the U.S. Special Operations Command of the U.S. Central Command tasked to train Eritreans in de-mining operations, information fusion and raising public awareness, and to help the country develop a self-sustaining national de-mining capacity (Clemens, 2000). With a modest investment of less than $3.3 million between 1994 and 1995, the U.S. team of thirty-four persons completed its mission in 1995, leaving behind a relatively effective Eritrean national de-mining organization, run by two hundred eighty-six de-mining personnel. Between 1996 and 1997, the Clinton administration allocated almost $1.2 million in additional aid to further strengthen Eritrea's national de-mining capacity (Clemens, 2000). To be sure, the "Train the Trainer" initiative in Eritrea was relatively successful in putting in place the necessary infrastructure for self-sustaining national de-mining capacity, although it was later overwhelmed by the magnitude and complexity of the mined fields left by the 1998-2000 war with Ethiopia. The U.N. Mine Action Coordination Center (MACC) estimates that Eritrea laid 240,000 landmines during the 1998-2000 Ethio-Eritrean war while Ethiopia laid between 150,000 and 200,000 landmines in Eritrea; as of April 2002, there were 592 areas, covering 660 square kilometers, which the MACC classified as hazardous (UNMEE-MACC, 2002). To deal with the latest minefields, the United States contributed a little over $1 million to the de-mining action in Eritrea for 2001, and pledged another $1.23 million in humanitarian de-mining operations for 2002. In addition, the Washington, DC-based Ronco Consulting Corporation provided training and equipment to over one hundred twenty Eritrean de-miners under contract from the U.S. Department of State (UNMEE-MACC, 2002). Given the enormity and extent of the problem of landmine hazards in the country, the U.S. contribution to the U.N. landmine action group in Eritrea is insubstantial, demonstrating America's waning interest in the country. In contrast to the small role of the U.S. in the landmine detaining operations, for example, Denmark made a contribution of $2.2 million to the U.N. landmine action group in Eritrea for 2002 while it gave another $3 million to the DanChurchAid for building de-mining capacity in Eritrea (UNMEE-MACC, 2002).

As far as external security interests and relations were concerned, there appeared to have been a congruence of views and interests between the Eritrean government and the Clinton administration. Early on, the Eritrean political elite staked out a position that the cultivation and promotion of regional stability was an integral part of Eritrea's economic development strategy. Hence, the Eritrean elite began to actively engage in forging a regional bloc, stretching from the Horn of Africa to the lake region of sub-Saharan Africa. The regular visits of the nation's president to Ethiopia, Uganda, Rwanda and the democratic Congo were meant to achieve this goal. Coincidentally, the Clinton administration had long identified the same region, which it called "greater" Horn of Africa, paralleling the Eritrean president's definition of a regional security and economic whole as the primary focus of its Africa policy. In keeping with this orientation, the U.S. Embassy in Addis Abeba launched a fresh program known as the Greater Horn of Africa Initiative or GHAI in 1994. The purpose seemed to create the requisite political conditions for the U.S. economic penetration of the region. Former U.S. Ambassador to Eritrea, Robert Houdek, was among the chief architects of the initiative, who was also placed in charge of the program, entrusted with the responsibility to monitor the effective implementation of the initiative (*Economist Intelligence Unit (hereafter EIU)* 1st quarter, 1997).

In the new definition, the "greater" Horn of Africa stretches from the Red Sea in the north to the shores of the Indian Ocean on eastern Africa, links to the southern African and the great lake regional systems that hug the connecting corridor of the Indian and Atlantic oceans. Forming the core of Africa's extractive resources, this regional system stretches over 5.7 million square kilometers, housing over a quarter billion people. The economic indispensability of the untapped markets and extractive resources of these regions to U.S. multinationals is all too clear. If during the Cold War America had defined the region in geopolitical terms, the Clinton administration defined it in geo-economic terms, signifying the growing competition between American and European, especially French, multinational corporations over the same markets and resources. Between 1985 and 1992 the United States spent over $4 billion in what it currently calls the "greater" Horn of Africa in emergency aid and political support of its local allies (EIU 1st quarter, 1997). In the post-Cold War era, however, when the U.S. had begun to feel the long-term effects of its imperial overstretch, the Clinton administration sought to achieve its foreign policy objectives in the "greater" Horn of Africa on the cheap, namely by relying on local surrogates and actively promoting the creation of a regional bloc of these surrogates. The talk in Washington became about the "new" breed of African leaders, like Isaias of Eritrea, Meles of Ethiopia, Kigame of Rwanda, Museveni of Uganda and Kabilla of the Democratic Congo, who were widely marketed as having been radically different both from their right-wing and left-wing predecessors. This was reminiscent of the Kennedy administration's strategy to recast U.S. foreign policy in support of the creation of a third force that was neither reactionary nor revolutionary and yet compliant.

The apparent convergence of Eritrean and American interests in the "greater" African Horn soon locked the two countries into unequal partnership, which the Clinton administration found perfectly in keeping with its design. U.S. Assistant Secretary of State, George Moose, publicly acknowledged the value of this partnership: "Thanks to its president, Eritrea had gained a reputation for being a viable partner for the U.S.A. in promoting regional peace and stability in key areas" (EIU 1st quarter, 1997: 26).

The U.S.-Eritrean partnership reached its crescendo in November 1996 when the United States formally conferred on Eritrea the dubious distinction of "frontline state" status in the struggle against Sudanese fundamentalism. The designation entitled Eritrea to receiving $3.85 million in U.S. surplus military supplies (EIU 1st quarter, 1997). By then, over 3,000 Sudanese opposition forces were receiving military training in Eritrea in preparation for an offensive against the Khartoum regime, something that provided an additional material basis to the growing confrontation between Asmara and Khartoum. Oddly, the escalation of tensions between them further served to cement U.S.-Eritrean relations. In December 1996, for example, President Isaias eagerly accepted the American plan to create a pan-African rapid intervention force to be deployed in crisis situations within the continent. Anticipating participation in such a multilateral force, Isaias was looking forward to the arrival of American green beret units to train Eritrean troops in counter-insurgency maneuvers.

The case was first taken up by Isaias and General Binford Peary, Commander of U.S. Central Command, on February 13th 1997 when the latter was visiting Eritrea (EIU 2nd quarter, 1997).

In addition to playing a continental role through the African rapid reaction force, the Eritrean elite hoped to use American military patronage to eradicate Islamist insurgency within Eritrea. Of course, the notion that the Eritrean opposition forces would be contained and eventually destroyed by military means alone was myopic. Successive Ethiopian rulers had tried the same means in vain against the Eritreans largely by relying on American and Soviet military patronage.

The Eritrean elite's response to the growing insurgency in the country was to ask for more American arms, reminiscent of old Ethiopian policy. After having accused the Sudan, Iraq and Iran of supplying arms and money to the anti-regime forces, Isaias traveled to Washington in September 1997 to seek U.S. military assistance. In Washington Isaias met with Sandy Burger, National Security Adviser, and Thomas Pickering, head of Political Affairs in the State Department. What came out of the meeting was for Robert Houdek, the trouble shooter within the framework of GHAI, to travel to Eritrea to assess the situation and Eritrea's need for U.S. training assistance (EIU 4th quarter, 1997). Meanwhile, General Binford Peary of the U.S. Central Command had visited Eritrea the previous July for the third time in two years, testifying to the seriousness of the war clouds hanging over Eritrea and the Sudan. Inasmuch as the U.S. and Eritrea collaborated on using the anti-regime forces to undermine the Islamist regime in Khartoum, the Sudanese government was equally determined to use the anti-regime Eritrean elements to destabilize America's "frontline state."

The increase in the frequency of Islamist penetration of Eritrea was further complicated in 1998 when a war broke out between Eritrea and Ethiopia, two "frontline" states that were expected to shepherd the *tabula rasa* of America's regional policy. To the profound dismay of Washington, Eritrea and Ethiopia escalated their ostensible boundary dispute into a full-scale war. Using Rwanda as a junior partner, the U.S. tried to mediate between its two "frontline" states without success. The peace plan, which was entirely an American undertaking, called on Eritrea to return to the ante-bellum state of affairs in exchange for the insertion of a token international observer force between the two countries to be followed by the establishment of an international commission to carry out boundary delimitation and demarcation tasks. Eritrea found this U.S.-Rwanda plan inadequate to guarantee a peaceful resolution of the conflict for fear that Ethiopia might refuse to abide by the provisions of the plan after Eritrea's withdrawal from the contested territory. The Eritrean government also found the U.S. embassy's apparent failure to share its prior knowledge with the Eritrean government about an impending Ethiopian bombing of Asmara airport grossly inconsiderate, leading the Eritrean leader to view the American mediation effort with suspicion. In fact, Isaias in a television interview later crudely accused the U.S. mediation team of complicity. As he told the interviewer:

> Unfortunately, the Americans were not free from the blame of complicating the issue right from the beginning. We know now that Ethiopian parliament was not alone in taking its bellicose decision. It was goaded by some quarters to take the move. Even before the Ouagadougou conference, the American team had been told by TPLF authorities about the bombing of Asmara. It was then that the team, instead of trying to prevent the bombing at a time when the peace process was going on, asked for a day or two in order to evacuate its citizens. Some American authorities were for a quick fix and bombing Asmara into submission was not overruled (Africa News, September 24, 1998).

174

The Ethio-Eritrean war thus served as a proxy to unravel U.S.-Eritrean relations. Overestimating Eritrea's value to the United States in the context of post-Cold War geopolitics, the Eritrean leader began to make imprudent diplomatic moves, which accorded American policy makers an opportune moment to size up the Eritrean leader and to question his reliability and predictability. One of the irritants, from Washington's standpoint, was that the Eritrean leader made at least five visits in a matter of six months in the second half of 1998 to Libya in an apparent defiance of U.N. longstanding sanctions on Libya. Not only did such visits unnerve Washington but they also heightened Israeli apprehensions about a possible radical shift in Eritrea's orientation. Susan Rice (1999), U.S. Assistant Secretary of State for Africa, noted this fact in a testimony before a congressional committee in these terms:

> Eritrea's President Isaias has made several trips to Libya—Africa's other state sponsor of terrorism—for frequent consultations with Colonel Qadhafi, and has joined Qadhafi's Community of Saharan and Sahelian states. We are very concerned by credible reports that Eritrea has delivered large quantities of weapons and munitions to self-proclaimed Somalia President Hussein Aideed for the use by a violent faction of the Oromo Liberation Front. The terrorist organization Al-Ittihad may also be an indirect recipient of these arms.

As is characteristic of all relationships between two unequal parties, the limits of Eritrea's ability to maneuver meaningfully in its relationship with Washington became evident, forcing the Eritrean leader to try mending fences with Washington after the third offensive of the war with Ethiopia in 2000. By then, however, Eritrea had not only exposed its external vulnerability but also exhausted its regional credibility and international respectability and the U.S. did not seem eager to embrace the Eritrean leader again. His imprudently heavy-handed moves on his political opponents, journalists and students under the cover of the "war" on terrorism did not help matters. More important, the regime further complicated its relationship with Washington when it arrested and imprisoned two Eritrean nationals who were working in the economic and political sections of the U.S. embassy in Asmara.

Following the terrorist attacks on the United States and the subsequent U.S. declaration of "war" on global terrorism, relations between the two countries appeared to be on the mend. The formulation of "preemption" as Bush's post-modern doctrine seemed to have elevated once again Eritrea's geopolitical relevance to Washington, and Eritrea's president seized upon the doctrine as an opportune vehicle to link Eritrea to the U.S. global mission. To elucidate Eritrea's perceived relevance to the Bush doctrine, a few words on that doctrine must be said.

Historically, America's realist cold warriors believed that the road to international security and stability was in promoting containment, deterrence and international balance of power as constitutive of a grand strategy needed to manage the bipolar international configuration. This grand strategy was credited with dragging the Soviet Union to the ground until ultimately it collapsed under its own weight (Ikenberry, 2002). However, in an open repudiation of the received grand strategy, President Bush enunciated in the spring of 2002 the unilateralist doctrine of "preemption," endowing the U.S. with the right to take a military action against any state considered either hostile to the U.S. or potentially dangerous to global stability. This revolutionary preemption doctrine has as its sub-text the concept of preventive strike in which a regime considered rogue will have its capacity to develop weapons of mass destruction utterly thwarted long before it puts its hands on the means to create them. This post-modern doctrine is formalized in "The National Security Strategy for the United

States of America," issued in September 2002. In addition to vowing to use America's "unparalleled military strength and great economic and political influence" to defeat global terrorism and the rogue states that harbor terrorists, the document states that, "[The] United States will use this moment of opportunity to extend the benefits of freedom across the globe. We will actively work to bring the hope of democracy, development, free markets, and free trade to every corner of the world" (National Security Council, 2002). Implicit in the preemption doctrine is a linear progression, which begins with taking out a rogue leadership in order to bring about a regime change in a country considered a potential threat to U.S. security interest and/or its global pre-eminence. A regime change in a particular country is but the first step toward effecting "regional change." The logical terminus of the doctrine is a unified global structure, made up of reconfigured and yet complimentary regional subsystems, managed by unregulated American hegemony, without peers or countervailing coalition of challengers. This has been the vision vigorously forwarded by a cabal of neo-conservatives, gathered under the canopy of the Project for the New American Century (PNAC). Seven of the original founders are in the current Bush administration, including the vice president and the secretary and deputy secretary of Defense. The touchstone of their strategy has been to transform the exceptionalism of America's position, prestige, technological prowess, and military power into undisputed global dominance for a long period of time. Against this backdrop Iraq emerged as the new paradigm test case for the application of this post-modern doctrine of open-ended warfare. "It is a doctrine without limit, without accountability to the U.N. or international law, without any dependence on collective judgment of responsible governments and, what is worse, without convincing demonstration of practical necessity" (Falk, 2002). In effect, as defense secretary Donald Rumsfeld refined it, the post-modern notion of preemptive strike rests on the projection and application of America's power "to combat unfamiliar enemies in unexpected circumstances" (Klare, 2002).

The exercise of the new Bush doctrine is not constrained by time and space. In the words of Michael Klare (2002), "[The] projection of U.S. power forward in time and horizontally across the earth's surface and the use of advanced surveillance and munitions to overpower less capable adversaries" are the core principles through which the Bush administration's military posture expresses itself. Furthermore, according to the overly rigorous definition of friends and enemies which recognizes no gray areas, states are either with or against the U.S. This post-modern grand strategy thus depends, for its operational viability, not on balance of power, containment and deterrence but on totalizing American hegemony, the elimination of global terrorism and the destruction of rogue states using surprise and/or pre-emptive strikes before they are in a position to harm Americans or challenge its dominion. "At the extreme, these notions form a neo-imperial vision in which the United States arrogates to itself the global role of setting standards, determining threats, using force, and meting out justice. It is a vision in which sovereignty becomes more absolute for America, even as it becomes more conditional for countries that challenge Washington" (Ikenberry, 2002: 44-60).

It is in the context of this newly enunciated doctrine that the invasion of Iraq must be understood, something that the Eritrean President sought to use as a proxy to mend his relationship with Washington. As a senior U.S. diplomat in Iraq during Desert Shield noted, the aim of the invasion was not about weapons of mass destruction, not about liberating the Iraqis from the dictator, and not about an attack on terrorism, but rather about "the imposition of a Pax Americana on the region and installation of vassal regimes that will control restive populations" (Wilson, 2003). It is this global reach nature of the U.S. post-modern preemption doctrine and Eritrea's strategic proximity to the Middle East that made Eritrea's geopolitical location loom large again as integral to the constellation of military bases and staging points.

A closer scrutiny of the new American architecture of the preemption doctrine would suggest that Eritrea has long been considered an important link of the ring needed to encircle the Middle East by a network of pro-American and non-Arab countries or vassal states. Robert Kaplan, who has been retained in the past as an adviser on Middle East affairs by U.S. Central Command, provides important clues for the long range American plan for the region. Because of his closeness to the military thinking, Kaplan's insight is invaluable. In his view, the invasion of Iraq and the consequent change of regime there would be crucial in terms of transferring U.S. military bases to Iraq from Saudi Arabia, where they have been a source of tension, inducing a change of regime in Iran, and insuring Israel's security interest. These byproducts of an attack on Iraq would supply the conditions for building "a coalition of the willing" or for creating permanent partnerships between the U.S. and other key states in the area. In Kaplan's words (2002: 88-90):

> This would undermine the Iranian-supported Hizbollah in Lebanon, on Israel's northern border, would remove a missile threat to Israel, and would prod Syria toward moderation and would allow for the creation of an informal non-Arab alliance of the near eastern periphery to include Iran, Israel, Turkey and Eritrea. The Turks already have a military alliance with Israel. The Eritreans, whose long war with the formerly Marxist Ethiopia has inculcated in them a spirit of monastic isolation from their immediate neighbors, have also been developing strong ties to Israel. Eritrea has a secularized

population and offers us a strategic location with
good port facilities in the Bab el Mandeb strait.

In Kaplan's conventional wisdom, only the secular character
and the pro-American orientation of regimes should guide U.S.
planners in forging a constellation of pro-preemption allies,
because to wish "a better alternative to dictators" only
represents "the fallacy of good outcomes."

With no other option, the Eritrean leader quickly jumped
on the U.S. anti-terrorist bandwagon to join the "coalition of
the willing" in the war on global terror under American
stewardship. He hoped that the U.S. would once again
designate Eritrea a "frontline" state in the war on global
terrorism. To attract the Bush administration's attention he
made an offer made to U.S. armed forces of unhampered access
to Eritrea's territory, airfields, waters and ports. In an interview
with a Japanese newspaper, Eritrea's ambassador to
Washington put the matter mellifluently: "It would benefit the
U.S. government to set up a military base in Eritrea. We are
perfect for America; we have deep water ports for its navy,
mountains very similar to those in Afghanistan that can be
used for training purposes and airfields that can accommodate
its aircraft" (Sipher, 2002). The Eritrean diplomat even
forwarded the proposition that the U.S. did not have to fly
sorties from Saudi Arabia, where U.S. troop presence was not
welcomed, since the same function could be performed from
Eritrea. Cloaking his reasoning in the need to fight terrorism
in the African Horn, Eritrea's Defense Minister also sent a
letter to U.S. Secretary Rumsfeld, urging him to give serious
consideration to the necessity to station American troops in
Eritrea (Sipher, 2002).

In the context of this enticing Eritrean offer and against
the backdrop of global terrorism looming large, the Bush
administration seemed prepared to overlook the authoritarian
character of the Eritrean government, reminiscent of the

bygone Cold War era. In May 2002, National Security Adviser, Condoleezza Rice, made it clear that, in the event that Eritrean extremists were to overthrow the regime, the U.S. would be placed under compulsion to opt for the "lesser evil" and would defend Isaias' presidency in order to preempt the possibility of Eritrea becoming a menace to Israel (ION, May 25, 2002). Defense Secretary Donald Rumsfeld's visit to Eritrea in December 2002, the first ever visit by a high-ranking U.S. official to that country since its independence, gave material substance to the above consideration. Unsurprisingly, Isaias utilized Rumsfeld's visit to highlight Eritrea's readiness to join the "coalition of the willing" in the war on terror by offering Eritrea's facilities to be used for purposes of military operations against Iraq and terrorists. To impress this upon the visiting guest, Isaias emphasized that the runway of the new Massawa airport "can handle anything the U.S. Air Force wants to land on it" (Kaplan, April, 2003). The Eritrean president added, "We have very limited resources, but we are willing and prepared to use these limited resources in anyway useful to fight the global war on terror" (Kellogg, 2002). The president's comment was, of course, very odd, considering that two-thirds of Eritrea's people were on the verge of starvation because of the unprecedented drought and famine and the regime's inability to secure enough international pledges of food to feed the hungry. On a crucial point, Isaias' offer to devote Eritrea's scarce resources to help America fight global terrorism, at a time when other countries in the region were working hard to use their geopolitical positions as a leverage to squeeze more American aid, simply exposed the president's utter desperation to insure regime preservation with U.S. military patronage.

In any event, the area which American military planners particularly covet is the port of Assab in southeastern Eritrea, staring at Yemen from just 60 miles distance on the other side of the Red Sea. U.S. planners are attracted to Assab because it has a large modern airport, modern cranes capable of loading and unloading large and heavy quantities of supplies, equipment and vehicles. U.S. military planners visited Assab several times since October 2001 to determine its value as a staging point for U.S. marines, navy and troops in the event of a war with Iraq or any other recalcitrant vassal states. Moreover, because Assab is situated in a somewhat desolate area, it is ideal for American forces to defend themselves easily (England, 2002). From the American point of view, the non-Arab character of Eritrea and its government's eagerness to provide the U.S. unhampered access to any and all facilities make Eritrea potentially valuable to the application of the preemption doctrine. In the words of Philip Mitchell of the International Institute for Strategic Studies, "A base within the area is something that they (U.S. officials) must be considering. They are not getting on too well and not getting well supported by the Yemenis, so anything bordering the Yemen area, which is where they want to go at some stage, would be absolutely ideal" (England, 2002). Moreover, unlike other leaders elsewhere, Isaias's offer of access to U.S. forces was unconditional and unqualified. In an interview with Terry Gross of National Public Radio (Fresh Air, March 11, 2003), Robert Kaplan recounted the value to Washington of the Eritrean offer:

> Here's the rub. Here's where it gets even trickier. The President of Eritrea, Isaias Afeworki, has offered the United States deep water port facilities, air bases to bomb anyone we want anytime we want anywhere we want. He's strategically placed at the mouth of the Red Sea, 50 miles from Arabia. And given the problems we've been having in Turkey, in other parts of Europe, if you're looking down the road five or ten years, it's almost inevitable that the Pentagon is going to want to have a deeper and deeper military relationship with this government.

The only problem that stands in the way of putting the American plan into place has been the fear of a potential danger of associating the U.S. with an authoritarian regime. The departments of Defense and State are apparently divided on this issue, with the former showing greater willingness to overlook Eritrea's human rights abuses while the State Department is hesitant about the potential cost of lending credibility to the Isaias regime. Pentagon officials seem to have staked out a position that, as demonstrated by Rumsfeld's visit to Eritrea, the U.S. could do business with the Eritrean regime by making a few winks and nudges along the way to prod the regime in Asmara toward moderate authoritarianism. When pressed by members of the media if the question of imprisoned government officials and journalists were raised in the discussion with Isaias, Rumsfeld gave an affirmative nod to the question while adding that sovereign nations had the right to "arrange themselves and deal with their problems in ways that they feel are appropriate to them" (Kellogg, 2002). Of course, Rumsfeld couldn't see the obvious contradiction between the Bush administration's enunciation as part of its neo-cold war mission of a verbal commitment to take democracy "to every corner of the world" and what the Defense Secretary himself said with regard to the question of democracy in Eritrea, which presumably could "arrange" itself in ways that it felt right in order to meet the requirements of its sovereignty.

The Department of State, however, seems poised to project a pro-democracy image of the United States by urging the Eritrean regime to address its gross democracy deficit and to undo the sweeping human rights violations it has perpetrated against U.S. embassy employees, senior government officials and journalists. In October 2002, the Department of State issued a stern warning against the Eritrean regime to that effect, followed by Secretary Colin Powell sending a letter in January 2003, admonishing the regime that failure to improve its human rights situation would result in Eritrea's deprivation of preferential market access to the U.S. under the "Africa Growth and Opportunity Act."

However, this division between the two bureaucracies within the Bush administration as to what approach to take toward the Eritrean regime seems inadequate to explain America's hesitancy to take advantage of Eritrea's facilities to the fullest extent. After all, the Bush administration has fully embraced the universally known authoritarian president of Uzbekistan in exchange for unhampered access to that country's military facilities. Therefore, there appears to be four additional reasons why the Bush administration is not eager, as of this writing, to go the full length to embrace Isaias. First, the administration seems to doubt the longevity of Isaias in power and has maintained low level contacts with some of the Eritrean forces opposed to the Isaias regime. Given the potential of the opposition forces coming to power, the Bush administration doesn't seem eager to put all its eggs in Isaias' basket. Moreover, American officials have increasingly come to question Isaias' dependability and diplomatic ability to manage Eritrea's external relations with some degree of coherence and predictability. Second, there is an unknown quantity, which the Bush administration fears, if the Isaias' regime is overthrown, because the Eritrean opposition is a mixed bag. In the aftermath of regime downfall, Eritrea may become a safe haven for Islamists, especially given its porous borders from the Red Sea and Sudan. After all, the Eritrean Islamic Jihad Movement was, as of this writing, still actively planting land-mines in Eritrea; in February 2003, Islamists took credit for a landmine that killed an Eritrean army colonel along with four soldiers (*IRIN,* March 21, 2003). On April 12, 2003, the Islamist rebels reportedly also murdered a British geologist, Timothy Nutt, as he was prospecting for gold in western Eritrea for Nevsun, a Canadian company (Johnson 2003). Hence, in light of the conspicuous presence of Eritrean Islamists among the opposition forces, the United States must carefully trade its options. Third, the Ethio-Eritrean border conflict and the lack of progress in normalizing relations between Asmara and Addis Ababa continue to interfere with the U.S. vision toward the African Horn. Some officials in the Eritrean government tend to blame the Bush administration's lukewarm attitude toward Asmara on Ethiopia's mischief. Indicative of this mood is the fact that Isaias was conspicuously excluded from the invitation extended to leaders of the African Horn to visit with President Bush in Washington in November 2002, intended to demonstrate the unity and solidarity of "the coalition of the willing" in the war on global terrorism. Fourth, the concern in regards to over-stretching U.S. military presence may have been another reason for the administration's waffling on the Eritrean matter.

Yet despite these liabilities, Washington did not want to slam the door shut; it still wanted to use Eritrea as a default option when the need arises. From a strategic standpoint, Eritrea can be an ideal frontline state in the war on terrorism in the area by virtue of its 600-mile long coast and its bordering Sudan, Ethiopia and Djibouti. This ideal geo-strategic position can potentially enable American forces to detect and disrupt the movement of terrorist groups from across the Gulf of Aden to the African Horn and vice versa: a fact acknowledged by Michael Westphal, a senior Pentagon official. "I can see a lot of benefits from us having a more formalized relationship with Eritrea, military-to-military" (*IRIN*, May 17, 2002).

The awkward relationship that has been evolving between Washington and Asmara, in spite of Eritrea's geo-strategic location, raises a fundamental question: why is Isaias so desperate as to literally beg the United States to base its troops in or use Eritrea as staging point for military operations against Iraq at a time when other countries in the region are openly skittish about U.S. moves, and view its requests for military facilities with serious reservations and apprehensions? The answer lies in Isaias' way of coping with the internal delegitimation and external isolation of his regime. The Eritrean leader seems to have pinned his hope on spending his antiterrorist currency to achieve three objectives—inducing the flow of American economic aid in the hope of resuscitating the national economy, bolstering his internal legitimacy to restore his international credibility and bringing America's influence to bear on the floundering prospect of boundary demarcation with Ethiopia. The Ethiopian regime has particularly been making every effort to block quick and smooth implementation of the decision of the International Boundary Commission on the matter while at the same time attempting to use external Eritrean opposition elements to overthrow Isaias. Therefore, from Isaias' standpoint, warming up to Washington would improve the prospects for Eritrea's territorial security and regime survival and help reduce the leader's political marginality.

In this context, Eritrea has retained the American law firm, Greenberg Traurig LLP, since April 2002 at $50,000 monthly fees to represent the Eritrean government before the Bush administration, Congress and other government agencies to entice the U.S. to base its troops in Eritrea (Bresnahan, 2002). The law firm's powerful lobbying team was headed by Jack Abramoff, known for having strong ties to Tom DeLay, the Republican majority leader in the U.S. House of Representatives. From the Eritrean regime's standpoint, the choice of Abramoff as the key lobbyist was no coincidence; it was a strategic move. Abramoff, who notably brings $10 million annually in revenue to his law firm and who single-handedly raises between $4 million and $6 million annually for Republican politicians, is among the highly paid elite influence-peddlers in Washington with multiple channels to high-powered Republicans (Bresnahan, 2002). There was something more which the Eritrean regime also saw in Abramoff: he is an orthodox Jew, a rabidly pro-Israel and a conservative Republican, crucial credentials that would presumably make him sympathetic to Eritrea. Isaias' rejection of numerous Arab invitations to join the Arab League and his disparagement of the Oslo process could not help but impress Abramoff. This appears to be an important consideration in Abramoff's decision to discount his monthly fee to $50,000 for Eritrea from $150,000 which he normally charges other clients. Abramoff cloaked his beneficence toward the Asmara regime in his admiration for Eritrea's acceptance of free market principles and open invitation to U.S. investors. In justifying the discounted rate he offered the Asmara regime, Abramoff referred to Eritrea as "a very exciting client. They want to be the Singapore of Africa—that is their goal. They want to set up policies that encourage investment, encourage free markets. They want to be a U.S. base" (Bresnahan, 2002).

As the first business of its relationship with the Eritrean regime, Greenberg Traurig developed an issue paper, entitled "Why Not Eritrea?" It tried to make a strong case for a formal alliance between Eritrea and the United States, based on Eritrea's strategic location in the Red Sea basin, its pro-American orientation, its willingness to serve as a staging point for military operations in the war against Iraq and the fact that the establishment of a U.S. military base would bring the much needed capital to that country, necessary to create a middle class and to provide "economic stability to U.S. companies" (Sarasohn, 2002). The issue paper emphatically added that, "Eritrea provides the United States with a strategic advantage and hospitable atmosphere that cannot be matched in the region. Based on the current sentiment of the Arab community and the geography of the region, it is increasingly clear that failure to form an alliance with Eritrea is unconscionable" (Kellogg, 2002).

The lobbying effort was taken to and picked up by some elements in the American media as they began to echo Eritrea's potential relevance to the "war" on global terror. The conservative columnist and a staunch defender of Israeli interests in America, Joel Mowbray, for example, made the Eritrean case in these terms, "One nation in the region that doesn't need its arms twisted is one that itself has been the victim of terrorism ... Eritrea has offered U.S. full option of using Massawa's new airport against Iraq. ... Eritrea's own experience with terrorism likely explains why it is the only country in the region that openly and defiantly supports Israel. That stand has inspired the wrath of the Arab League, which has badly wanted Eritrea to join as a member nation for years now" (Mowbray, 2002).

Eritrea's lobbying effort could not, however, rival that of its chief nemesis: Ethiopia. Between October 2001 and March 2002, for instance, Ethiopia paid out $5.6 million to an American law firm to finance its lobbying operations before the U.S. government and its agencies. The Ethiopian aim, among other things, was to bring the U.S. view on the boundary dispute with Eritrea in line with that of Ethiopia. The troops deployed to make a case for the Ethiopian cause included former Senators George Mitchell, Bob Dole and Lloyd Bentsen (*ION*, April 6, 2002). The first two senators were majority leaders in the senate for their respective parties and Bentsen was treasury secretary during the first term of the Clinton administration. Even in this small battle to win America's favor, Ethiopia was the relative victor as Washington unambiguously embraced Ethiopia as the geopolitical foundation of its policy in the African Horn and as a reliable partner in the "war" on terrorism. As America's new ambassador to Ethiopia told the senate, "Prime Minister Meles has been a strong partner of the United States on this global war on terrorism. Given its strategic location in the Horn of Africa, bordering the unstable countries of Somalia and Sudan, we have designated Ethiopia as a frontline state in the global war, and we are gratified to have its support" (Brazeal, 2002).

The sorry state of democracy in Eritrea and the roguish leadership style of its president are a crucial intervening variable in U.S.-Eritrean relations. The dilemma for America is how to reconcile its own rhetoric commitment to the promotion of democracy in the third world with the Eritrean government's subjection of its citizens to wanton violations of human rights and civil liberties. As noted earlier, the U.S. State Department has been attempting to walk a tight rope between an open confrontation with the Asmara regime, particularly over the arrest of its Eritrean employees, and quietly prodding the Eritrean regime toward making at least some minor political reform. On October 17, 2002, the State Department went public with a statement, asking the Eritrean government either to charge the two Eritrean employees of the U.S. embassy before a court of law or release them. The statement also lamented the continued detention of high government officials and journalists in undisclosed locations and the refusal to implement the constitution and hold the scheduled elections as clear manifestations of the "troubling crackdown on democracy and human rights violation in Eritrea" (Gollust, 2002).

In response to the U.S. statement, Eritrea's Foreign Ministry issued its own statement in which it characterized the American position as "unwarranted intervention" in Eritrea's internal affairs (*Foreign Ministry*, October 18, 2002). The statement openly accused three U.S. government officials in the Clinton administration of breaching the trust placed on them by siding with Ethiopia during the Ethio-Eritrean war. The statement added that, after having failed to make Eritrea knuckle under by giving unjustified concessions to Ethiopia, the said U.S. officials resorted to unlawful methods to overthrow the regime by using the CIA. According to the Foreign Ministry, the eleven high government officials still in detention at the time of writing were in the service of both the CIA and the Ethiopian regime through their advocacy for early surrender and fomentation of division within the country by religion and region in order to materialize their plot (*Foreign Ministry,* October 18, 2002). One of the accused American officials was Anthony Lake, who was the chief mediator between Eritrea and Ethiopia on behalf of the Clinton administration. In an op-ed piece, Lake (2002) characterized the Eritrean allegation of his involvement in a conspiracy to overthrow the government as utterly false and preposterous.

As of this writing, the diplomatic row between Washington and Asmara over the latter's poor record of human rights has continued. In mid-September, 2004, the American Department of State cited Eritrea for persistent violations of the religious rights of smaller Christian denominations, something that angered the Eritrean government. The Foreign Ministry of the Eritrean government issued a statement, condemning the American charges in these harsh terms:

> The statement by the State Department does not come as a surprise to the government of Eritrea as it has been no secret that the CIA and its operatives have long been engaged in fabricating defamatory statements in a bid to embark on other agendas and at the same time conceal its unwarranted intervention. It is only astonishing to see the United States, which lacks moral and legal high grounds on human rights and the respect for religions, make an attempt to become the self-appointed adjudicator (*BBC Monitoring Africa,* September 16, 2004).

The harsh tone in the Foreign Ministry's reaction is particularly astonishing in the context of the regime's apparent effort to improve its relations with the Bush administration. After all, the Eritrean regime had just hired the American lobbying firm, Alexander Strategy Group, at annual fees of $300,000 to assist in improving the regime's relations with the Bush administration (*ION,* September 4, 2004). The American lobbying firm is known to have a close relationship with the Republican Party and the firm's president, Ed Buckham, is former chief of staff to Tom Delay, a Republican representative from Texas in the U.S. Congress. Despite the Eritrean regime's angry reaction, the United States shipped to Eritrea in late October 2004 61,000 metric tons of emergency food to feed 600,000 drought-affected people, which is the largest single shipment of food to that country since its independence (*IRIN*, October 29, 2004). This American act of generosity was preceded by the USS Hopper having a port of call at the Eritrean port of Massawa between October 7th and 8th, the first navy ship to have done so since 1997 (*States News Service*, October 14, 2004). As a show of goodwill, 55 sailors lent their services to the Eritrean community by planting 500 mangrove trees along the Red Sea coast and by landscaping and painting the city's public library. Even though the navy ship's visit and the sailors' participation in community projects were symbolic, they nonetheless highlighted Washington's desire to relax tensions and improve relations between the two countries, perhaps a price to keep Eritrea in the "coalition of the willing."

All things considered, the Eritrean regime's expectation to thrive on America's back is rooted in grand illusion. America's imperial overstretch to combat global terrorism, to contain rogue states and maintain global pre-eminence, and the intensification of global economic competition are all likely to impose severe limits on what the United States can do in terms of foreign assistance and military patronage. What America could pledge in 2002 toward the long term rebuilding of Afghanistan, for example, was a mere $296 million. When some U.S. representatives attempted to raise the amount pledged, the Bush administration stubbornly resisted the effort. Moreover, when members of Congress proposed $150 million in aid to Afghanistan to modernize its agriculture and education, the administration said that it was not prepared to grant more than $40 million for that purpose (Hersch, 2002). In circumstances where American priorities are elsewhere with a variety of interest groups competing for its ever shrinking foreign aid budget are proliferating, Eritrea will be among the least priorities for Washington. Therefore, the Eritrean regime's permanent quest for an external patron as a substitute for an authentic and a genuinely democratic self-reliance is likely to remain as elusive as ever.

Eritrea and Israel: A Convoluted Relationship

Eritrea's relationship with Israel, which had the appearance of formal alliance, was melodramatically revolutionary in the diplomatic sense. Since the birth of the Eritrean liberation struggle, Israel was not only overtly hostile to the Eritrean cause but also vigorously supportive of Ethiopia in terms of providing training, weaponry, actionable intelligence and technical assistance to crush the Eritrean liberation movement. Well up until the independence of the country, Israeli leaders viewed the Eritrean movement as an organic extension of the Arab cause, having the potential of Arabizing the entire Red Sea region, thereby imposing a complete siege on Israeli commercial arteries and ominously endangering Israel's existential security. Upon the liberation of Eritrea, however, both countries made a one-hundred-eighty degree swing and agreed to bury the past and transcend normalization of relations to cultivate closer cooperation in all aspects of diplomacy, economy and military affairs. The Eritrean leader set the tone for revolutionary diplomatic relations between the two countries in June 1992, almost one year before the formal declaration of independence, when he told *The Jerusalem Report* that Eritrea was prepared to trade its Arab allies of liberation years for Israeli friendship if keeping both Israeli and Arab friendships was not attainable. As he unscrupulously put it:

> We said time and again, we're not limiting our relations. We consider Israel a partner in this area.

192

> If trade with Israel precludes trade with other
> nations, then Eritrea will nevertheless go with Israel.
> ... The Arab League has no function; it cannot
> deal with problems. But the political implications
> of joining it are very dangerous. It would limit
> African governments to following certain policies
> without regard for their national interests (Hamburg,
> 1992).

Why was the Eritrean leader prepared to trade his Arab allies
of liberation years for Israel in the post-liberation period? The
answer to this question consists in the president's austere
understanding of Middle East politics and his exaggerated
expectations of his alliance with the new Ethiopian regime
and by extension with the United States. Several veteran
interviewees noted that Isaias had long been obsessed with
Israeli military prowess and Singapore's economic progress,
two countries he considered worthy of emulation. By using
authoritarian manipulation of the levers of power, Isaias hoped
to meld Israeli militarism and the Singaporean economic model
into a distinctly Eritrean path to development and greatness.
This was seen early on in the symbolic imitations the Eritrean
president made. He made "The State of Eritrea" the official
name of the country in imitation of "The State of Israel," and
he named the national army "The Eritrean Defense Forces,"
just as Israel calls its army "The Israeli Defense Forces." The
Eritrean security forces were also made to imitate Mossad's
mode of operation. To demonstrate their invincibility and
omnipresence, Eritrea's security forces successfully kidnapped
ala Mossad some members of the opposition from Sudan. Three
Eritreans were also sent to Zimbabwe to supposedly
assassinate former Ethiopia's military dictator, Mengistu
Hailemariam, in his retirement ranch.

In the long run, Isaias has had two reasons for choosing
Israel over the Arab states. First, he apparently saw a potential

nexus between the Eritrean forces opposed to his regime and Arab support for the opposition. In this scenario, a close military relationship with Israel would serve as a counterbalance to Arab hostility. Second and more importantly, Isaias seems to have inherited the classic Ethiopian view that the road to Washington is through Jerusalem; a closer partnership with Israel would *ipso facto* translate itself into a closer relationship with the United States and all the benefits that accrue from that relationship.

Israeli motivations for cultivating warmer relations with Eritrea were certainly predictable. Preemption of the Arabization of the Red Sea was the primary aim of the Jewish state, and de-linking Eritrea from the Arab world would presumably achieve that *desideratum*. This would nullify the potential Arab effort to establish a military and economic stranglehold on Israel. Equally important was the Israeli vision to have access to Eritrean ports and islands by Israeli warships, submarines and surveillance vessels.

Continual Eritrean government denial notwithstanding, sources close to Israeli intelligence revealed that there was a sufficient Israeli military presence in Eritrea throughout the 1990s. According to the *Times* (June 27, 1998), in the spring of 1998, the British newsletter, *Foreign Report*, reputed for its reliability and proximity to Israeli sources, revealed that the Israelis did have crucial military networks, electronic listening posts and radar stations in Eritrea. The acquisition of three German-made advanced Dolphin Class Diesel-Electric submarines by the Israeli navy was connected to the importance Israel attached to the Red Sea region. According to some analysts, the primary aim of the nuclear submarines was to enable Israel to have the option of second strike capability in the event that the Arabs destroyed its land-based nuclear facilities by using air assets and ground to ground missiles. In circumstances of second strike option, Israeli submarines would be well positioned to launch retaliatory cruise missiles at Arab and Iranian targets from the Red Sea (*Times*, June 27, 1998).

Like other aspects of Israeli-Eritrean relations, the privileges Israeli military enjoyed in Eritrea experienced what proved to be a temporary setback during the 1998-2000 Ethio-Eritrean war. When an Israeli defense company offered to upgrade Ethiopia's fighter jets, the Eritrean government interpreted the action as Israel taking sides in the conflict. According to the London-based risk assessment journal, *Jane's Sentinel*, Israel's Red Sea-based second strike capability was put in jeopardy because of the war in the Horn. Without the use of facilities and supply networks in the Red Sea, it would be particularly difficult for Israeli nuclear forces to reach Iran if the need arose (Davis, 2000). It seems as though Israeli military presence in Eritrea's islands and territorial waters did continue, albeit at reduced levels. In fact, one of the issues that Prime Minister Sharon and President Bush discussed in their March 2001 meeting was how to persuade the financially strapped Eritrean government to allow the extension of the secret electronic listening post jointly operated by U.S. and Israeli intelligence forces in exchange for some financial aid to develop Eritrea's tourist sector (*Chicago Sun Times*, March 16, 2001).

Feeling isolated from the international community in the wake of the war with Ethiopia and the internal repression he enforced, the Eritrean leader saw ever closer relations with Israel as critical to regime survival. Indeed, he continued to ingratiate himself with Israeli politicians in the hope of keeping Israeli friendship or, at least, neutrality in matters pertaining to Ethio-Eritrean relations. The desire to have Israeli help in convincing Washington about the geopolitical importance of Eritrea could not be ruled out from Isaias' calculation either. In fact, Isaias made a habit of offending Arab sensibilities in order to ingratiate himself with Jewish leaders both in Israel and the United States. In one of his press conferences in May 2002, for example, he went out of his way to belittle the Madrid and Oslo accords that produced a framework for the Palestinian-Israeli dialogue. In his view, Madrid and Oslo were the problem not the solution. Then he gave the unsolicited verdict that the problem should be corrected "by returning to square one—the start of serious negotiations, the placing everything about Madrid and Oslo in the rubbish bin and the start of a new dialogue" (*BBC Monitoring Africa,* May 11, 2002).

Israel was not unappreciative of such gestures as it reciprocated by taking similar moves toward closer relations with Eritrea. In February 2002, Israeli Transport Minister, Ephraim Sneh, paid an official visit to Asmara, where he held a series of meetings with Isaias on a wide range of issues. Israel highlighted its desire to deepen its relations with Eritrea when officials from Israel's aeronautics sector, airlines and civil aviation accompanied Sneh to Eritrea. The inclusion of a representative from Elbit Systems, Israel's defense company, also demonstrated the desire on both sides to upgrade their military ties. Elbit Systems offered to undertake the modernization of the Eritrean air force and the renovation of its armored personnel by retrofitting them with advanced control systems (*ION* February 25, 2002). Following the visit of the Israeli delegation, the two countries signed a civil aviation agreement, which included flights by chartered planes from Israel to Eritrea transporting Israeli tourists. Also, Israel agreed to consider Eritrea's request to set up vocational training camps for demobilized soldiers, and an Israeli company was given the license to fish in Eritrea's waters (Ya'ari, 2002).

Sneh's visit was particularly important in the context of the scathing remarks the Israeli ambassador to Ethiopia made in early February about Ethiopia's behavior. The Israeli ambassador accurately castigated Ethiopia in no uncertain terms for dragging its feet to sign a permanent peace treaty with Eritrea (*ION,* February 25, 2002). The visit of the Israeli delegation to Asmara has had enormous symbolic significance because Sneh is regarded both in Eritrea and Israel as the chief advocate of deepening relations between the two countries. This is in contrast to bureaucrats in Israel's foreign office, who are inclined to nurture Israel's special relationship with Ethiopia and who also believe that warming up to Eritrea may have a negative impact on that special relationship (Ya'ari, 2002). Sneh and his supporters believe that closer ties with Eritrea and the latter's strategic asset outweigh Israel's special relationship with Ethiopia, which is merely mediated by the status of the Falashas and Ethiopia's economic and market potential for Israeli companies. The position of the pro-Eritrean officials in Israel seems to be strengthened by the importance of the landing rights Israeli planes have in Eritrea and port access enjoyed by its blue water navy. Writing in *The Jerusalem Report*, Ya'ari reflects the view of the pro-Eritrean group in Israel with regards to the relative advantage that Eritrea holds over Ethiopia. Moreover, a large number of influential Israeli politicians treat Isaias with high esteem because he "is the most consistent African head of state actively and openly seeking better ties with Israel and he is the only head of state outside the Arab world who publicly rejects the Oslo process, which he thinks was too hasty and half-baked.... More and more Israelis within the security establishment, the business sector and the political community, even at cabinet level, are waking to the potential of this northeast African republic" (Ya'ari, 2002).

The Eritrean President's declaration of unvarnished solidarity with Israel has also been warmly received by Jewish groups in the United States. The relationship that has been established between Eritrean officials and the Jewish Institute for National Security Affairs (JINSA) is particularly notable. JINSA, an advocacy group devoted to bringing American and Israeli foreign and defense policies into line, has been active in promoting closer ties among Israel, Eritrea and Ethiopia. The evolution of this relationship has been such that on December 13, 1996, the Eritrean President met a delegation from JINSA in Washington and briefed the members of the Jewish group on Eritrea's policy priorities. Isaias strongly defended Israel before the group against critics who blamed the Jewish state for slowing the peace process (*JINSA Reports,* December 18, 1996). On March 20, 2001, Eritrea's Defense Minister also briefed JINSA leaders on Eritrea's desire to deepen his country's relations with Israel and the United States and reiterated Eritrea's readiness to grant the U.S. military facilities on its Red Sea islands (*JINSA Reports,* March, 2001). As part of the effort to permanently tie Eritrea to Israel and the United States, JINSA continued to lobby Washington to accept Eritrea's offer of a military base. On June 20, 2002, for example, JINSA's Board of Directors passed a resolution, imploring the Bush administration and Congress to embrace Eritrea. Part of the resolution reads:

> Whereas the state of Eritrea ... has proven to be an island of stability in a volatile area, and is located in a particularly critical strategic location, along the Red Sea, and owns the historically important deep ports of Massawa and Assab;
>
> Whereas Eritrea, since its independence, has been friendly to, and cooperating with, the United States (including the U.S. military) and U.S. allies, including Israel;
>
> Whereas the Eritrean defense minister and other leaders have expressed strong willingness to cooperate with the United States and be of any assistance possible in the war on terrorism and other security imperatives;
>
> Whereas Anthony Zinni, the former Commander of CENTCOM, and General Tommy Franks, the current Commander of CENTCOM, have visited Eritrea and held talks with Eritrean military commanders;
>
> Be it therefore resolved that: the United States military should consider, and the Congress of the

United States should fund the establishment of U.S. military facilities in Eritrea (*JINSA Reports,* July 25, 2002).

JINSA's advocacy for closer links among the United States, Israel and Eritrea is particularly noteworthy if only because of JINSA's ideological partnership with the Project for the New American Century. Both advocacy groups have similar agendas and enjoy the dual membership of many defense intellectuals. The ideologically colorful Richard Perle, for example, holds dual membership in both groups. Moreover, in addition to having been the intellectual force behind the pre-emptive national security strategy together with Deputy Defense Secretary Wolfowitz, Perle chaired the Defense Policy Board, until he was forced to resign the post in late March 2003 in the midst of a business scandal that was euphemistically brushed aside as a conflict of interest. The Pentagon policy board is made up of unelected and unaccountable figures, ostensibly to lend their collective wisdom to the Defense Secretary on defense issues. Both Wolfowitz and Douglas Feith (Undersecretary of Defense) also migrated from JINSA to the Bush administration. This reality in part explains why the Defense Department, where JINSA and PNAC have firmer grips on the policy making process, has been more inclined than the State Department to deepen relations with Eritrea in the face of the political depravity of the Eritrean regime.

Predictably, Arab nations near and far viewed the Israeli-Eritrean cooperation with serious apprehension and at times hostility. From their point of view, the primary purpose of the Israeli military presence in Eritrean islands and territorial waters was to spy on Arab countries and to use Eritrean facilities to attack Arab interests. As recently as July 2002, Arab countries accused Eritrea of harboring Israeli military presence and requested that a special conference of Arab and African countries be held to discuss the Red Sea question, which Eritrea rejected forthrightly (*Deutsche Prez-Agentur,* July 9, 2002). Furthermore, Arab commentators and diplomats see something nefarious behind the solid relations that developed among Eritrea, Ethiopia and Israel under American stewardship before the Ethio-Eritrean conflict unraveled the tapestry of the partnership. As the *Mid-East Mirror* (June 9, 1998) put it, the United States linked Eritrea and Ethiopia to Israel in order "to fuel hostility between them and their Arab neighbors. Both Eritrea and Ethiopia were allocated tasks that involved meddling in inter-Arab disputes and sabotaging inter-Arab reconciliation efforts, and both provided scope for Israeli and American action aimed at undermining the security and stability of a large number of Arab states."

Irrespective of whether the above claim has a kernel of truth in it or not, the perception of a triangle of real-politik, composed of Eritrea, Israel and Ethiopia with U.S. hegemonic guidance, has posed a long term threat to the Arab cause that is widespread in the Arab world. And no doubt, such a perception will have serious ramifications for Eritrea's security. At both the elite and sub-elite levels, the transformation of the Red Sea into an Arab "lake" has long been a cherished Arab dream. But this dream is now seemingly frustrated by Eritrea's decision to align itself with countries considered hostile to that Arab vision. In consequence, this is likely to bring down the wrath of Arab states on Eritrea. Sudan and Yemen can potentially be used as frontline states to undermine Eritrea's security and development by forcing it to be in a permanent state of war. Even more dangerous is the possibility that Arab states and non-state Arab groups may sponsor Eritrean Islamist elements to undercut Eritrea's sense of security. Hence, Eritrea's partnership with Israel may not in the long run compensate for the potentially severe damage caused by strained Arab-Eritrean relations.

Certainly Eritrea has the right to develop and diversify its external relations. However, this can be done astutely and prudently. One should bear in mind that a number of Arab countries, like Egypt and Jordan, have maintained working relationships with Israel, without disparaging their relations with other Arab states. What is particularly disturbing about Eritrea's relations with Israel, from the Arab viewpoint, is the revolutionary character of that relationship and Isaias' continual belittling of the Arab League.

Eritrean-Sudanese Relations: A Partnership Betrayed

No other country had ever been more pivotal than Sudan to the unfolding and ultimate success of the Eritrean liberation struggle. Apart from having become the most hospitable host to hundreds of thousands of Eritrean refugees for almost four decades, successive Sudanese governments allowed the Eritrean fronts to take full advantage of the opportunity which its geography presented. For all practical purposes, Sudan was the rear base area of operation, sanctuary, the primary source of supplies and a strategic transit for the Eritrean liberation forces since the early 1960s. Moreover, Sudan was the first nation to enthusiastically welcome the liberation of Eritrea, as seen by President Umar al-Bashr's visit to Asmara in August 1991 to demonstrate the strategic partnership that existed between the two countries. Thus, in light of the enormous contribution Sudan made to the triumph of the Eritrean struggle, what has transpired since 1994 in terms of strained relations between them is very unfortunate.

The sources of the deteriorated relations between the two countries consist primarily in the radical shift in Eritrea's external orientation and secondarily in the Islamist character of the al-Bashr regime. During the Cold War, the Eritrean liberation fronts projected the Eritrean struggle as part of the anti-imperialist third world struggle, in general, and as an extension of the Arab cause, in particular. Against this background the two countries agreed to nurture the continuance of the strategic partnership when they signed a defense and security pact in August 1991. This was seen as crucial to the regulation and management of frontier relationships between the two countries. When Eritrea grew closer to the United States, Israel and Ethiopia, however, the Islamist regime in Khartoum began to distance itself from Eritrea. Subsequent Sudanese hostility toward the Asmara regime was thus, in part, a response to the global co-optation of Eritrea's elite and its melodramatically played pro-Israel position. Eritrea's decision to establish a seemingly strategic partnership with Israel, symbolically demonstrated in January 1993 when a U.S. air force plane whisked the Eritrean leader to Israel for medical treatment for deadly cerebral malaria, is what confirmed the deterioration of their relationship. The subsequent pact between Eritrea and Israel regarding economic and technical cooperation seemed to have decidedly placed Eritrea in the traditional pro-American camp. Eritrea, Israel and Ethiopia formed a partnership, which an astute observer characterized as "convoluted triangular relations" (Stein, 1993).

From the Sudanese and Arab perspective, the new triangular relationship that emerged between Eritrea, Israel and Ethiopia was not going to sit well with the political landscape of the regional system since it represented a new regional power configuration having the potential of offending the Arab sense of security and prestige. One Arab commentator, for example, raised a rhetorical question and answered it: "Why does Afwerki reject the Arabism of Eritrea? Eritreans could not and should not ignore the Arabic and Islamic dimensions of their history and culture" (Tash, 1993). According to this view, Eritrea failed to live up to its promise to align its interests and external relationships with those of the Arab Middle East. In the words of Iyad Abu Shakra (1998), a Saudi commentator, "There was a time in the 1960s and 1970s when many Arabs looked forward to an independent Eritrea with its close cultural, historical and human links to the Arab countries, joining the Arab League and becoming part of an expanded Arab world." The roots of the deteriorated Eritrean-Sudanese relationship, in particular, and Arab friendship, in general, lay in the frustration of those hopes and expectations. A critical lesson, which may have been lost on the Eritrean elite early on was the fact that Eritrea could not willy-nilly pursue an independent foreign policy without understanding the panoply of intricate relationships that underpin the entire complexity and particularity of Middle Eastern politics and the structure of international relations.

The role of the Eritrean leader in the conduct of the country's foreign policy has a lot to do with the negative Arab reaction to Eritrea's diplomatic moves. The Eritrean leader is characteristically known for his tendency to put arrogance in place of prudence, petulance in place of patience, contempt in place of deference and tactical calculations in place of strategic considerations. In his austere understanding of international politics and diplomacy, he could not anticipate the consequences of language. His inconsistent flirtation with the idea of joining the Arab League is a case in point. At times Isaias seemed to want to grow closer to the Arab world while staying far away from it. Such a position could, of course, be sustained through prudent diplomacy and great sensitivity to Arab interests. During a press conference in Qatar in May 2002, for example, the Eritrean President once again openly belittled the Arab League when he said, "We are not thinking of joining the Arab League. There is not one appropriate condition for doing so and there is not a regional organization that deserves to have Eritrea join. The Arab League does not represent anything in the world and is ineffectual. There is no need to join it, whatever emotions the issue raises. Ask any Arab about this organization and its role. The Arab League does not have a role or a presence" (*BBC Monitoring Africa,* May 31, 2002). Apart from the fact that the above passage reflected a blend of arrogance and imprudence, it needlessly offended Arab sensibilities and its negative impact on Eritrea's external relations was immeasurable. Paradoxically, just four months after his Qatar press conference, the Eritrean President sent a special envoy to Cairo carrying a letter to the Secretary General of the Arab League, seeking the organization's intercession with Sudan to avert a war. Instead of mediating between Eritrea and Sudan, however, the twenty-two members of the Arab League held an emergency meeting on November 9th 2002 and issued a stern warning to Eritrea to cease and desist from meddling in Sudan's internal affairs (*Xinhua,* November 15, 2002).

Another crucial conventional lesson lost on the Eritrean leader has been the necessity to appreciate the linkages that undergird the continual transactions between internal and external forces. The absence of national cohesion, the fragility of democracy, the unevenness of societal value orientations and rampant economic dislocations can definitely influence foreign relations. Consider Eritrea, for example, where societal orientations reflect the existence of two competing religions, Islam and Christianity, whose quantitative relationship is marked by a rough equilibrium. Perhaps partly in recognition of this reality and partly out of ideological necessity, the Eritrean leadership appears committed to the secularization option. But the leadership doesn't seem to have a full grasp of the qualitative aspect of politics—perception. There is a large section of the Eritrean population which actually feels that the Eritrean government is not democratically bi-religious or not religious enough at all. The sectors that hold these views tend to look to the Arab east for historical connection and spiritual inspiration. In this context Islamic fundamentalism has been spreading among Eritreans in the refugee camps of the Sudan. Predictably, this is bound not only to threaten the national cohesion of Eritrea but also to affect the nature and texture of Eritrean-Sudanese relations. The rise of Eritrean Jihadists, who began to use Sudan as a launching pad for attacks inside Eritrea, has been pivotal in despoiling the strategic friendship between the two countries.

Beginning in 1992, the Eritrean government implored Sudan not to allow its territory to be used by the Islamist elements. Although the Khartoum regime initially responded favorably to the Eritrean request by closing the offices and schools run by the Islamic Jihad of Eritrea, Sudan later changed course when relations between the two countries turned sour (*Parmelee*, January 5, 1994). In response to the changing political environment, the Eritrean government quietly expelled the Sudanese Consul from Asmara after identifying him as the key handler of the Eritrean fundamentalists. The incident was initially downplayed by both governments in order to prevent further damage to the already delicate balance in their relationship (*Arab News,* January 13, 1993). In December 1993, a contingent of jihadists infiltrated Eritrea and actually engaged the Eritrean security forces, and the president of the young republic could no longer keep quiet. Twenty jihadists were killed, most of whom were reportedly non-Eritrean Afghanis from Morocco, Tunisia, Algeria and Pakistan. Sensing the seriousness of the matter, the Eritrean president publicly identified the Sudan as the main source of the trouble for the first time. (Parmelee January 5, 1994)

In 1994, several attempts were made on both sides to mend fences. In August 1994 the two countries agreed to solemnly adhere to the principle of nonintervention in each other's territory. They would also expedite the repatriation of the 450,000 Eritrean refugees from Sudan, who were considered the main source of recruits for the anti-regime cause. The following November Isaias and Bashr joined Ethiopia's Prime Minister to discuss possibilities of repairing Eritrean-Sudanese relations without any palpable result to show for it. In 1995 the Organization of African Unity was also engaged in shuttle diplomacy to find ways to smooth over the worsening relations between Eritrea and Sudan; it, too, failed to produce any meaningful agreement. Consequently, in June 1995 Eritrea invited all Sudanese opposition groups to Asmara where they held a unity conference. Subsequently, the National Democratic Alliance (NDA), the umbrella organization for the Sudanese anti-regime forces, was allowed to occupy the Sudanese embassy in the Eritrean capital (Cliffe, 1999).

The explanation for the failure of the diplomatic efforts was to be found in three crucial dimensions of the problem. In the first instance, Eritrea's pro-American posture, its relations with Israel and its secular orientation were problematic for the Sudanese regime to accommodate. Sudan saw Eritrea as having turned into a staging ground for anti-Sudanese and anti-Arab forces. Moreover, Eritrea's regional activism and international visibility was seen in Khartoum as impeding the Islamist vision to transform the African Horn into an Islamist hub. The Islamist conquest of Eritrea was considered the necessary prelude to the Islamist transformation of Ethiopia and the rest. Once the Eritrean crucible was effectively handled, the other pieces of the Islamist puzzle would presumably fall into place. In Hassan al-Turabi's words, "Ethiopia will self-destruct in the future, thus paving the way for the establishment of an Islamic Oromo state and resulting in a chain of Islamic polities, extending from Sudan to the Indian Ocean" (Cliffe, 1999).

Second, the conduct of Eritrean diplomacy, bordering on adventurism and haphazard arrogance, was a major contributing factor to the collapse of the diplomatic efforts. Again, the Eritrean leader seemed to lack the capacity for appreciating the delicacy and sensitivity of the issues that were of concern to both countries. Equally important was that he exaggerated the utilitarian value of Eritrea's partnership with the U.S., Ethiopia and Israel in the event of a military confrontation with Sudan, as the manner in which the Eritrean leader expressed himself on the matter attested to the foregoing observation. In an interview with *The Economist*, for example, he boastfully warned: "We are out to see that this (Sudanese) government is not there anymore. We are not trying to pressure them to talk to us, or behave in a more constructive way. We will give weapons to anyone committed to overthrowing them" (*The Economist,* October 14, 1995).

Third, determinants to the strained relations between Eritrea and Sudan were internal. The authoritarian character of both regimes was not amenable to discursive communication and constructive dialogue. The anti-regime forces in both countries were internally produced in response to the repressive political systems. Therefore, if Sudan used the Eritrean anti-regime elements to further its policy of de-stabilization strategy that was simply a function of mutual convenience between the Khartoum regime and the Eritrean opposition forces.

Having established an intimate relationship with the National Islamic Front (NIF) in the Sudan, Eritrean jihadists naturally looked to the Sorbonne-educated leader of the NIF and architect of Sudanese fundamentalism, Hassan Al-Turabi, for theological inspiration and guidance, as much as to the Al-Bashr regime for military and material support. The NIF presented itself and the Islamist government in Khartoum as the salutary alternative to the failed institutions of Africa and hence as the premier model to be emulated by other organizations and governments. The state minister for political affairs and top adviser to Al-Bashr, Ghazi Atabani, unabashedly declared that it was imperative for other organizations to follow the example of his government because it "embodies the values of Islam and the tools of modernity" (Parmelee, January 5, 1994). Noting his theocratic prominence in the Islamist movement, Turabi also congratulated himself on his centrality to that movement by proclaiming: "I am the symbol of a new movement that will change the history of humanity" (Dewal, 1994). Indeed, the spread of Islam to the African Horn and beyond to sub-Saharan Africa had long been an integral part of Turabi's vision. In the eighties, he created the Islamic Africa Relief Association, ostensibly to establish humanitarian networks in sub-Saharan Africa in order to reach those in destitution with the distribution of relief supplies. The association was later renamed the Islamic Relief Association, which better reflected Turabi's globalist vision; the charity received a continual stream of funding from the oil-rich gulf states, including Saudi Arabia and Iran (Dewal, 1994; Gunaratna, 2002). He also created the Popular Arab and Islamic Congress (PAIC) which brought together forty Islamist parties and terrorist groups, among which was the Eritrean Islamic Jihad Movement, all committed to spreading the Islamist vision. When the PAIC held its conference in Khartoum in early December 1993, Turabi reassured the five hundred delegates in attendance—representing sixty nations including Eritrea—that his Islamist regime was prepared to face up to the challenges of western conspiracy and to realize the universalism of the Islamist vision (Lusk, 1993). Osama Bin Laden's occasional presence at PAIC meetings certainly enhanced Turabi's stature in the eyes of the Islamist parties and groups in the region. Thus, given this universalist orientation of the Islamist vision, not to support the Eritrean Jihad would have been incompatible with the stated objectives of Turabi and the Al-Bashr regime. After all, in addition to being part of the regional network of the Islamist movement, the Eritrean Jihad openly aspired to the creation of an Arabized and Islamized Eritrean State. The transformation of Sudan into an al-Qaida hub also placed the Eritrean Jihad Movement in a favorable position.

In 1991, Hassan al-Turabi invited Osama Bin Laden to relocate al-Qaida headquarters from Pakistan to Sudan. Osama took up on the offer in the hope of making a deeper strategic penetration of the African Horn and north Africa while at the same time buttressing the long term security of the Islamist movement under the patronage of the Sudanese state. In Sudan al-Qaida transformed itself overnight into a multinational terrorist organization, comprising over one hundred loosely connected associate groups and affiliates (Gunaratna, 2002). In Khartoum Osama and Sheikh Arafa, leader of the political wing of the Eritrean Islamists, developed a deferential and intimate working relationship. Based on an analysis by Abul Bara' Hassan Salman, deputy commander of the Eritrean Islamists, Osama noted the strategic importance of the African Horn to the furtherance of the Islamist cause in the Red Sea basin and east Africa. Consequently, the Eritrean Islamic Jihad Movement was designated the Islamist vanguard to spearhead the deep penetration of the region. To insure the close coordination of the operations by the Eritrean Islamists with those of al-Qaida, the Eritrean Islamic Jihad Movement appointed a certain Muhammad al-Kheir as a liaison officer between itself and al-Qaida (Gunaratna, 2002). The Eritrean Jihad Movement was now counted among the most dependable salafist affiliates, committed to the puritanical restoration of the Islamic golden age under al-Qaida's ideological direction, theological guidance, political indoctrination, military training and material support. Several hundred Eritrean Jihadists were said to have received military training in al-Qaida's camps in Afghanistan and Sudan (Gunaratna, 2002). In his August 1996 *Fatwa*, Osama lamented the claim that Eritrea was stained with the blood of thousands of pious Moslems under the infidel and secular Eritrean regime, which aligned itself with the Zionist-crusader bloc (Gunaratrna, 2002).

Like other States in the region, the Eritrean leadership was justifiably concerned over the growing salience of religious fundamentalism in the area, as it threatened to interfere with the religious equilibrium of Eritrean society and the imperatives of moving forward with the secularization of the Eritrean State. In this context the Eritrean leader lashed out at the Saudis in early 1994 for encouraging and sponsoring Eritrean fundamentalists (*Horn of Africa Bulletin*, 1994). Although the exchange of accusations subsequently subsided, the nature and extent of the Saudi connection to the anti-Eritrean Islamists was going to depend largely on the degree to which the Saudi leaders felt threatened by the progressive secularization process in Eritrea and on the final structure of the triangular relationship between Eritrea, Ethiopia and Israel.

Fortunately for Eritrea, however, the Asmara regime escaped the wrath of Riyadh as the Saudis chose rapprochement in place of confrontation with the Eritrean regime, purely out of their own tactical calculations. The Saudis did, in fact, later make some attempt to mediate between Eritrea and Sudan. Some analysts explain the Saudi change of heart in this area through fear of Israel establishing a foothold in the Red Sea region by exploiting the Eritrean-Sudanese conflict. In this view, the Saudis found co-optation of the Eritrean regime a better alternative than distancing it (*ION*, March 15, 1997). In addition, the Saudis saw a large window of opportunity to spread their socio-religious, cultural and political influence in Eritrea by other means, namely using the mosque. In 1994, for example, the Saudi government made a grant of $5 million for mosque construction in Eritrea, in addition to the $55 million it pledged in concessional loans to the Eritrean government for various projects (*ION*, February 4, 1995). The total amounts of Saudi aid extended to Eritrea between 1994 and July 2002 reached over 230 million Saudi *rial*, making the kingdom the single largest contributor to Eritrea (*Arab News*, July 18, 2002).

The religionization of normal inter-state relations could make the Eritrean Islamists the convenient instruments of internal subversion, serving the interests of outside forces. If a convergence of particular Sudanese policy and general Arab attitudes toward the Eritrean fundamentalists were to crystallize, the territorial reach of the Sudan was bound to loom even larger. The Eritrean Islamists could capitalize on this to carry out subversive activity in Eritrea. The presence of an Iranian element in the equation was also relevant to the political evolution of the Eritrean Jihad. Under-resourced

Sudan needed Iranian arms and money in order to realize its Islamist vision. Although the two countries espouse divergent versions of militant Islam, they had much in common, including international isolation, deep-rooted suspicion toward the west and strong devotion to the spread of their respective brands of Islam. These factors appeared to have provided a sufficient basis for such a marriage of convenience between the two governments as to have required President Ali Rafsanjani to pay an official visit to the Sudan in December, 1991. Among his two hundred-member entourage were the heads of the Iranian intelligence units and the Revolutionary Guards (Makinda, 1993). Subsequently, Iran supplied the Sudan with $300 million worth of arms, together with eight hundred Revolutionary Guards, sent there to assist in the training of the Sudanese Defense Forces and other Islamists, including those from Eritrea (Makinda, 1993). By early 1995, with generous Iranian funding, Turabi and Osama were able to securely establish twenty-three training camps in Sudan. The Eritrean jihadists were the chief beneficiary because of their geographic proximity to both the training camps and the source of their recruits in the Eritrean refugee camps (Gunaratna, 2002). Thus, in this remarkable collaboration in the division of labor, Shi'ite Iran stood to marshall financial resources and arms while the Sudan was geopolitically well positioned to furnish training camps, shelter and passports to members of various Islamist organizations. To be sure, by the mid-1990s a new arc of crisis, punctuated by the rise of fundamentalism, was shaping up in the area stretching from Iran and Afghanistan to Yemen, passing through the African Horn to north Africa. This exportation of radical Islam to these areas by Sudan and its allies began to haunt Eritrea and its neighbors.

For example, despite dusk to dawn curfew throughout western Eritrea and heavy troop concentrations along the Sudan-Eritrea border, anti-regime elements managed to infiltrate the country, planting deadly land-mines. In July 1997, fifteen passengers were killed when the bus carrying them hit a landmine. The audacity of the anti-regime elements was taking on xenophobic dimensions as they also began to target foreigners. On December 27, 1996, for example they killed five Belgians and their drivers.

Subsequently, the military and propaganda activities of the anti-regime forces continued to deepen in direct proportion to the growing confrontation between Asmara and Khartoum. In November 1997, three radio stations began to broadcast—presumably from inside the Sudan—anti-Eritrean government propaganda. The first identified itself to its listeners as the "Voice of Free Eritrea," a mouth-piece of the Eritrean Liberation Alliance, reportedly made up of three fronts, beaming virulent propaganda to Eritrea in both Tigrinya and Arabic. "The Voice of Truth" was the second station, which broadcast in Arabic only as the mouthpiece of the Eritrean Islamic Jihad Movement. "The Voice of Democratic Eritrea" was the third station, which broadcast in the name of the Eritrean Liberation Front Revolutionary Council; its messages were broadcast bilingually. The inescapable conclusion was that, so long as Eritrea remained committed to the secularization and non-Arabization option, cushioned by its cozy relations with Israel and the United States, Eritrea was bound to receive the wrath of Sudanese Islamism via the Eritrean Jihadists and other political dissidents. If a coincidence of geographic opportunity and religion emerged to threaten the security of the Eritrean State, then the leadership was bound under pressure to respond to that threat. This led to continual strained relations between the two countries, especially after fundamentalism achieved greater transnational connectedness when Osama Bin Laden moved his al-Qaida headquarters to Sudan in December 1991.

One must qualify the above observation by stating that geographic opportunity and religion were by no means causal variables; they simply contextualized the evolving relations between Eritrea and the Sudan. The divergent internal political dynamics and the contradictory external orientations prevailing in both countries were the intrinsic factors that accounted for the strained relations between the two countries. The existing strained relations between Eritrea and the Sudan were derivative reflections of the authoritarian character of the two states. The opposition forces being used by both against each other were mere instruments to promote de-stabilization in each other's territory. Normal equilibrium in Eritrean-Sudanese relations could have been established only when and if the leaders in both countries were prepared to begin the de-authoritarianization of their respective political systems and allow their peoples sufficient latitude of political freedom. As *The Economist* intelligence unit correctly noted in reference to Eritrea's problems, "These ongoing external difficulties, which can be seen in the context of Eritrea's evolution as a sovereign State, are a focus for the strong nationalism built up during the years of war, allowing the government to divert attention from the pressing issue of domestic political reform" (EIU 4th quarter, 1997: 16).

Paradoxically in the end, Sudan not Eritrea, emerged triumphant from the neo-containment strategy that was designed to encircle and then suffocate to death Sudanese fundamentalism under sustained assault from internal Sudanese insurgents with active support from the front-line states and American military patronage. When Eritrea's triangular relations with Ethiopia and Israel unraveled in the aftermath of the 1998-2000 Ethio-Eritrean war, both Eritrea and Ethiopia began to woo the al-Bashr regime, each vying to alienate the other. Ethiopia succeeded in achieving that objective when Ethiopian, Sudanese and Yemeni leaders met in October 2002 in the Yemeni capital to plan ways of isolating Eritrea and overthrowing its leader.

Quietly admitting the failure of the neo-containment strategy, the Bush administration, too, decided to change course, now preferring direct negotiation over confrontation with Sudan. The Bush administration signaled its desire to normalize relations with the al-Bashr regime by simultaneously appointing former Missouri Senator, John Danforth, as a special envoy to the Sudan to broker a peace deal between the central government and the insurgents, on the one hand, and maneuvering the U.N. Security Council into lifting the economic sanctions which it imposed on Sudan eight years before at the behest of the United States, on the other. Lubricating the new U.S.-Sudanese rapprochement was, of course, oil.

Upon assumption of office, the Bush administration quickly discovered that American oil multinationals were disadvantaged by the economic sanctions regime as other oil companies from such countries as China, Malaysia and Canada rushed to grab a lion's share of Sudan's oil riches. The three billion barrels of oil sitting in the bowel of the Muglad Basin, already flowing through a 1,000-mile long pipe into tankers in the Red Sea, and the $900 million that Sudan garnished from oil export in 2001 were too enticing for the Bush administration to leave the country to others (Hartman, 2002). Furthermore, in the wake of September 11, 2001, Sudan effectively demonstrated its readiness to discard its Islamist label and to join "the coalition of the willing" in the war on global terrorism. To improve its antiterrorist credentials, the regime promptly allowed CIA and FBI operatives to operate freely in Sudan. Apart from the fact that the Sudanese regime apprehended and deported thirty suspected Al-Qaida followers, the regime handed over to the U.S. Department of State some two hundred files on Osama Bin Laden and his operations while he was in the country (Hartman, 2002).

Openly pleased by the expected dividend from its mediation initiative, the Bush administration was quick to claim credit for the prospect of peace in Sudan when the contending parties announced on November 18, 2002 a breakthrough in the mediation and negotiation process. On November 22, Walter Kansteiner, assistant secretary of state for Africa, briefed diplomats, think-tank intellectuals and journalists on developments in Sudan. The assistant secretary credited President Bush for making the Sudanese problem a top priority of his administration, demonstrably validated by his selection of John Danforth as the chief trouble shooter and broker. The positive outcome was a function of the fact that the Bush administration was "involved, committed and forceful in peace negotiations…. The war had gone too long and we were going to put our time, talent and resources to getting this resolved and stopped" (Kansteiner, 2002).

Paradoxically, the "frontline" states which the United States lined up to encircle and then kill Sudanese fundamentalism weren't mentioned by name in Kansteiner's presentation. Seemingly anxious to know whether the omission was inadvertent or intentional, the Ugandan ambassador commented that the "frontline" states, especially Eritrea and Uganda, played a critical role in the multilateral effort to contain the Sudanese problem. Kansteiner then thanked the ambassador for raising it while acknowledging that neighboring states, like Uganda, did play a constructive part. He once again dreaded mentioning Eritrea by name, even though the Eritrean ambassador was sitting in front of him. Since Eritrea was the leading player among the "frontline" states and disproportionately bore the effects of the neo-containment strategy, it would only make sense that Eritrea's contribution to the effort would be acknowledged. The news which Kansteiner reported as extremely positive was that the central Sudanese government and the opposition forces agreed to extend the cease-fire for a considerable period of time to create a favorable negotiating environment and to put in place confidence building measures and a veritable companion to the six years transition period expressed by power sharing arrangement. In short, although the long term prospect of the U.S.-brokered peace remains to be seen, the Sudanese peace deal meant that Eritrea had run out of cards to play in order to prove its importance to the United States.

Eritrean-Yemeni Relations: A Sudden Descent

Eritrea's ill-managed relations with Yemen also contributed to the pejorative external image of the country as a warlike nation. The crude and confrontational diplomatic style of the nation's leader did not help to project Eritrea as a positive and peaceful actor. Indeed, the poor diplomatic managerial skills of Eritrea's elite provided ammunition to some misguided intellectuals and political adversaries that were bent on undermining Eritrea's international imagery. Their proof was the Tribunal's disposition of the matter, seen as favorable to Yemen when in truth though, the Yemeni-Eritrean dispute over a group of islands was a result of legitimate interactions between neighboring states, interactions mediated by ambiguities surrounding their maritime possessions and delimitation.

Contrary to what critics purport to portray, the Tribunal's decision was not lopsidedly favorable to Yemen. Even though both countries have had complaints about certain aspects of the final outcome, both did express equal satisfaction at the process as having been fair and balanced (Antunes, 2001). To its credit, Eritrea did give unqualified commitment to abide by the final decision of the Tribunal. Although Eritrea was not a signatory to the Law of the Sea Convention, it nonetheless authorized the Tribunal to apply the provisions of the law if pertinent to the case in question and that Eritrea agreed to respect the resulting decision. The Yemeni-Eritrean maritime dispute was not limited to the two of them alone. There were similar maritime disputes between Yemen and Saudi Arabia, Egypt and Sudan, Saudi Arabia and Qatar, Iran and the United Arab Emirates, and Qatar and Bahrain. These disputes and other maritime conflicts elsewhere are manifestations of global capitalism's reaching for its outer limits, and the evolutionary incompleteness of the international maritime regime.

The Yemeni-Eritrean conflict was part of a global scramble for more resources. In this case, the prospect of oil, the exploitation of marine resources and the desire to develop tourism in the Red Sea basin underlay the Yemeni-Eritrean competition (Tal, 1996). Although the islands in dispute are barren and without water and historically no one has wanted them, in the context of the contemporary struggle to control ever greater portions of the maritime regions of the world, the geo-economic significance of these islands loom large. For resource poor Eritrea, the Red Sea holds great promise for resource extraction, considered critical to kick-start its national economy. When the conflict with Yemen flared up in 1995, the annual fish catch by Eritrea's fishermen was a mere four hundred tons while the annual potential fish catch was 70,000 tons (Sutton, 1994). This was enough of a motivating factor for Eritrea to look eastward to the Red Sea for extractive resources. The Hanish and Zuqar islands were seen as integral to the development of the fishing industry since they had been used by Eritrean Afars in particular for centuries as way stations to dry their catch, repair their fishing gear and market their fish catch. Furthermore, because of the war with Ethiopia, eighty percent of Eritrea's fishermen had abandoned artisan fishing, making the fishing industry the most un-skilled sector (Sutton, 1994). In the wake of Eritrea's independence, rehabilitating and expanding the fishing industry held great promise for creating jobs and means of livelihood for thousands, not to mention the potential to make the export of marine products an important hard currency earner.

The numerous islands located along the entire length of the Red Sea also offered potential attraction to tourists. Eritrea had already signed with an American developer to transform the Dahlak islands off Massawa into a tourist haven with the injection of over $200 million into building casinos, luxury hotels, golf courses and related amenities (Tal, 1996). As an extension of this development, Eritrea had also granted permission to an Italian investor to develop tourist complexes. This included a luxury hotel and scuba diving on the Hanish islands and work had begun in mid-1995 (Plaut, 1996).

Likewise, Yemen had similar ambitions and plans for the Hanish islands. It had issued a permit to a German company to develop tourist villages on the same islands where the Eritrean tourist projects were in progress. Eritrea's warnings notwithstanding, Yemen deployed its troops on December 16, 1995 to the islands to create a state of fact on the ground. Eritrea responded to Yemen's military undertaking by dispatching its units and by the next day the skirmishes ended in Eritrea's favor (Plaut, 1998).

The way in which Yemen resorted to the use of force to claim possession of the Hanish islands was mysterious since the two countries had agreed to establish a negotiating framework to settle their differences cooperatively. In fact, by November 1995 the two countries were already engaged in a flurry of diplomatic activity to bring about a peaceful end to their differences. The major issue separating the two parties was one of methodology. Eritrea sought a comprehensive settlement of some two hundred islands while the Yemeni delegation insisted on restricting the negotiation to Greater Hanish only. Having failed to reach agreement on the procedural question, the parties then agreed to defer the matter until February 1996. For some unexplained reasons, however, Yemen provoked the military exchange in mid-December (Plaut, 1996). One plausible explanation is that Yemen was trying to capitalize on the general Arab irritation with Eritrea over its "convoluted" relations with Israel. This was a time when Sudanese-Eritrean relations were at their lowest ebb and the Arab media throughout the Middle East was arousing anti-Eritrean sentiments. The fact that the Arab League wasted no time to give unqualified support to Yemen, which the Organization of African Unity censured, was illustrative not only of the general Arab mood but also of the Arab versus African dimension of the conflict (Kwiatowska, 2001; Tal, 1996). Despite a stunning victory, Eritrea agreed to create an international tribunal to settle the matter by arbitration. In May 1996, the two countries agreed on the arbitration principles in Paris, crafted with the help of France, Ethiopia and Egypt. Subsequently, a five-man tribunal was impaneled to receive the respective complaints of the two parties.

Yemen invoked historical titles to the islands, dating to the medieval period. In addition, Yemen contended that it was Yemen, not Ethiopia, which Egypt approached during the 1967 war with Israel with a request to use the islands for military purposes, affirming the continuity of Yemeni juridical rights over the islands in dispute. To bolster its case, Yemen produced twenty volumes of materials, accompanied by one hundred twenty maps (Kwiatowska, 2001; Plaut, 1998). For its part, Eritrea used state succession and the principle of effective occupation to make its case. In other words, Eritrea claimed to have inherited the islands from Italy. Furthermore, since the 1960s the Eritrean liberation fronts had used the islands as a base of operation against Ethiopian troops without asking for or receiving Yemeni permission. When independent Eritrea asserted sovereignty over the islands in 1993, Yemen did not raise any objection. Eritrea, too, generated twenty volumes of materials and sixty maps to support its presentation (Kwiatowska, 2001; Plaut, 1998).

Even though both Yemen and Eritrea tried to embellish their respective cases with voluminous historical documents and maps and legal arguments, the Tribunal did not find the presentation of either country persuasive, which meant that it was primarily guided by other principles, rules and practices of international law. The Tribunal found the ambiguities surrounding the status of the islands intractable, having to do with the manner in which Turkey relinquished its Red Sea possessions. One incontrovertible fact was that the Hanish islands were under the Ottoman empire, which built and operated lighthouses in order to protect ships against navigational hazards. The 1923 Treaty of Lausanne between Turkey and the Allied Powers failed to determine the future status of the islands. In the meantime, Great Britain, Italy, Germany and the Netherlands shared the costs of maintaining the lighthouses on the islands. From the Eritrean perspective, one point of importance is the 1938 agreement between Great Britain and Italy, which allowed Italy to establish its presence on the islands in order to provide protection to the fishing community. By implication, the agreement administratively linked the islands to Assab, without prejudice as to their legal status. This was the basis for Eritrea's claims to the islands (Plaut, 1996).

After having deliberated meticulously, the Tribunal gave its decision in stages, the first in October 1998 determining the scope of the dispute and the legal status of the islands, and the second in December 1999 establishing maritime delimitation. Even though the Tribunal tried to fall back on its "Solomonic wisdom" rather than on the arguments of the contenders, Yemen received the majority of the benefits from their ruling. The Zuqar-Hanish islands were made subject to the territorial sovereignty of Yemen while Eritrea got a group of smaller islands, namely the Mohabbakkah islands, Haycocks and southwest islands (Kwiatowska, 2001; Reisman, 2000, Antunes, 2001). Since the Mohabbakahs lay within the 12 nautical mile coastal belt of Eritrea, the Tribunal found it reasonable to award the islands to Eritrea. Likewise, the Haycocks and Southwest islands were awarded to Eritrea on account that these islands had historically been connected to the African coast. The controversial part of the Tribunal's decision involved the disposition of the Zuqar-Hanish Islands. Even though Yemen's case with regard to Zuqar appeared to be stronger, its claim on the Hanish islands was far from certain. In fact, the coastal median line put a larger portion of Greater Hanish on the Eritrean side of the delimitation line; but because the islands that were on the Eritrean side of the line formed part of the group, the Tribunal used the "unity theory" to justify their award to Yemen (Evans, 2001). With regard to the islands in the Jebal al-Tayr and Zubayr group in the northern section of the Red Sea, the Tribunal decided to give them to Yemen, not on the basis of evidence but because the islands are more easterly toward Yemen than to the Eritrean line. Moreover, the Tribunal's decision to adopt a single all-purpose international boundary line, on the basis of equidistance principle, tilted the disposition of some of the islands in Yemen's favor (Evans, 2001).

Contrary to the claims of some analysts, especially Ethiopia's ideologues that the Tribunal's verdict would serve as a precedent for the Ethio-Eritrean dispute, the Tribunal was guided by the principle of equity, which underpins the normative structure of the international maritime regime. Methodological equidistance or the geographical proximity of the islands to the coast lines of the respective parties and the principle of proportionality influenced the Tribunal's decision (Kwiatowska, 2001; Reisman, 2000, Antunes, 2001). After all, the two countries are set apart by one hundred sixty nautical miles in the Red Sea at its widest point in the north, which is far short of the two hundred nautical miles of exclusive economic zone each country is permitted to control under the law of the sea Convention. In fact, as the maritime boundary moves southward, the maritime delimitation zone narrows down significantly until the two countries are set apart by just twenty-four nautical miles. Thus, the coastal and geographical configurations of the territorial sea under the jurisdiction of Yemen and Eritrea and the locations of the islands were determining considerations in the disposition of the islands.

As Brilmayer and Klein (2001) cogently posited, the international maritime regime is both structurally and jurisprudentially distinct from the regime that governs interstate conflicts mediated by physical occupation of land. The distinction is one of prior establishment of sovereign rights over land through appropriation sanctioned by force and the acquisition of maritime rights by allocation justified in terms of equity or geographic proximity. In other words, interstate conflicts over land boundaries are settled by reference to historical facts and juridical considerations, whereas maritime spaces are allocated on the basis of equity. The latter are justified by the method of equidistance or geographic proximity and the proportionality principle where evidence is scarce with regard to prior presence.

The international jurisprudence of the maritime regime has historically been grounded in Hugo Grotius's formulation of oceans and seas as "Res Communis," or things held in common, because bodies of water are not amenable to occupation. Therefore, what could not be physically possessed or enclosed could not be declared private property (Brilmayer and Klein, 2000). Thus the Yemen-Eritrea Tribunal disposed of the case on the basis of normative considerations while de-emphasizing the contending claims of the two parties. Thus the tribunal's decision may have very little transferrable value to settling disputes involving physical territorial dispute, like the Ethio-Eritrean dispute.

Apart from the determination of the scope of the dispute and the allocation of the islands, the Tribunal's decision to establish a common fishing regime is significant in terms of both jurisprudential and practical implications. In doing so, the tribunal emphatically asserted that the allocation of the disputed islands to Yemen could not and should not disturb the pre-existence of the traditional fishing regime. In practice, the fishing community that was historically constituted by Eritrean and Yemeni fishermen should continue undivided in the exploitation of marine resources, including using the islands as way stations to dry their fish, repair their fishing gears and to market and sell their catch without discrimination by Yemeni authorities. Eritrean fishermen can also use the islands as fishing grounds or for diving to acquire pearls, shells and the like. Thus, in so far as the artisan fishing regime is concerned, the allocation of the disputed islands to Yemen "entails the perpetuation of the traditional fishing regime in the region, including free access and enjoyment for the fishermen of both Eritrea and Yemen." (Reisman, 2000; Antunes, 2001; Kwiatowska, 2001). Substantively, the tribunal's decision endows the Red Sea fishing community with intrinsic rights, making it subject to international law by virtue of its distinct existence prior to the formation of Eritrea and Yemen as modern states; although the two states can jointly make regulations to strengthen the traditional fishing regime and/or deepen their cooperation, neither country can tamper with the integrity of the fishing regime (Kwiatkowska, 2001; Antunes, 2001). Here again, the tribunal's recognition of the artisan fishing regime as distinct and separate from the Eurocentric notion of sovereignty is grounded in the normative structure of the international maritime regime. This time it is articulated by reference to Islamic jurisprudence which places the premium on the unitary conception of a community, whose members are fully and equally entitled to the exploitation and use of nature as God's providence (Reisman, 2000, Antunes, 2001).

Even though the tribunal's decision to leave the communitarian artisan fishing regime intact is laudable, it may have, however, created conditions for conflicts between Eritrea and Yemen. First, the decision recognizes Eritrea's right to act on behalf of its nationals in the event that the fishing regime is violated by Yemen or its nationals. In this case, Eritrea may use diplomacy to smooth over a particular violation of the regime in consultation with Yemeni authorities or seek an international remedy by submission of complaints to the

Tribunal itself. In a country where the rule of law is a scarce commodity, Yemen may find it to be against its national interest to insure equal access and enjoyment of the fishing regime by Eritrean fishermen. Or, local Yemeni authorities and nationals may resort to practices that amount to *de facto* exclusion of Eritrean fishermen from making full use of the traditional fishing regime. Such a scenario can potentially invite armed clashes between the two countries.

Second, there is a practical implication unforeseen by the Tribunal's decision. According to the specific rules governing the fishing regime, Eritrean fishermen are entitled only to artisan fishing; Yemen has the juridical right to exclude Eritrean fishermen from engaging in industrial fishing. In practice, this could mean that Yemen and its nationals can embark on the modernization of their fishing industry by virtue of which they may be able to drive out Eritrea's fishermen from the area, in effect making artisan fishing dysfunctional.

Third, the Tribunal makes the promotion of ecological welfare in the Red Sea a joint responsibility of Eritrea and Yemen; both countries must consult and mutually agree on the health of the maritime environment because the "protection and preservation of marine environment" is integral to the continued sustenance and viability of the traditional fishing regime (Reisman, 2000, Antunes, 2001). Here Yemen's competence is theoretically limited because it cannot undertake environmental measures without prior agreement from Eritrea. However, the two countries may have divergent understandings of the maritime ecology, which can potentially become a source of conflict. In sum, the Tribunal's decision accords Eritrea and Yemen the opportunity either to use the decision to fashion a new framework for regional cooperation or to use the ambiguities implied by the decision to perpetuate friction. Indeed, several extrinsic circumstances, such as the intensification of competition over fishing grounds in response to the depletion of fish stock, may be elevated to a state of high politics. Despite settlement of the juridical question under international law, the dispute over fishing has yet to subside. In late September 2002, for example, Yemen openly complained about "repeated provocations by Eritrean authorities against Yemeni fishermen as well as seizure of their boats" (*Zawya.com,* September 23, 2002). Early in the same month, Yemen had put its armed forces on heightened status after having accused Eritrea of conducting military exercises near the Yemeni coasts (*Zawya.com,* September 23, 2002). The Yemeni government has, of course, been incredulous in its treatment of the international decision on the maritime delimitation and demarcation. In December 1999, the government issued a press release informing its fishing population that the tribunal had allowed them to fish in Eritrea's territorial waters. This prompted the Eritrean government to seek clarification from the international tribunal on the issue in January and again in March 2000. However, Yemen contended that there were no differences between the two countries over the characterization and interpretation of the tribunal's decision. Because "Yemen chose not to contest the declared Eritrean stand," the Tribunal then informed both governments that Yemen's decline to do so amounted to fully accepting the Eritrean interpretation of the matter (*Eritrea Profile,* September 21, 2002). Despite such clarification, Yemeni fishermen continue to violate Eritrea's fishing waters, which attests to the delicacy of Yemeni-Eritrean relations. Without the genuine will and commitment to observe them, the mere international articulation of norms and principles of law may be insufficient to promote interstate solidarity and regional cooperation.

Conclusion

The discussion in this chapter has brought two essential lessons about foreign relations into a sharper focus. The first involves the fact that foreign policy is always an intrinsic continuation or a reflection of domestic politics. The second lesson pertains to the decisive role leadership plays in articulating a coherent diplomatic vision and in conducting a credible and consistent foreign policy. In order to appreciate the fluidity, particularity and complexity of regional politics and the chaotic state of international politics, a leadership equipped with vision and prudence is required. The cases we reviewed in this chapter clearly demonstrate that Eritrea has hitherto been endowed with a leadership incapable of understanding the dialectics of the relationship between means and ends, on the one hand, and the capabilities and limits of its society, on the other. Fixated on liberation empiricism, the Eritrean elite failed to comprehend the dialectical interplay of domestic and external factors as having the capacity to produce certain unforeseen implications for the domestic economy and society, on the one hand, and for inter-state relationships, on the other.

In the context of the rapidly shifting balance of forces after the demise of the bipolar international system, the lesson should have been obvious to a visionary leadership that Eritrea is destined to gain nothing and lose much from open confrontations with its neighbors, especially the Sudan. Eritrea's fragile state institutions, the chemistry of her ethnic and religious makeup, her geographic location and poor resource endowment are such that the country is as equally vulnerable to external manipulation and destabilization efforts as her neighbors are. The search for and reliance on external patronage and a dubious alliance network—as the Eritrean elite have practiced—are dangerously myopic undertakings. So if one is at liberty to give a retrospective prescription based on the arguments we developed in this chapter, then that advisory prescription must go to Eritrea. The reason is simple enough; external relationships are inherently perishable quantities. Ethiopia, for example, on which the Eritrean leader had pinned his grandiose ambition to construct a regional whole, was continually reassessing during the second half of the 1990s its regional orientation in general and its policy with Eritrea in particular. The dialectical escalation of the row with Eritrea over strained bilateral trade relations—arising from Eritrea's introduction of a new currency and Ethiopia's subsequent decision requiring that all commercial transactions between the two countries be handled by the use of hard currency—to full-scale bloody warfare illustrates our point. Moreover, Ethiopia was appreciably moderating its hostile posturing toward the Sudan while Eritrea continually raised the ante against its most important neighbor. This suggests that Eritrean and Ethiopian regional interests have not necessarily been identical. Thus by way of recapitulation, two cardinal points relevant to Eritrea must be emphasized.

First, it is essential to understand the dynamic interplay of external and internal factors. Given this reality, the surest way to insulate the Eritrean political order from negative external pressure and influences is to construct a viable political and economic order—although admittedly this is easier said than done. If the state of the Eritrean economy is such that the various segments of society are relatively satisfied with the system and if they feel that they are well represented in the political order, then the factors of geographic opportunity, religion, ethnicity and region are likely to have only a passing relevance for Eritrean foreign policy toward her neighbors. Hostile external forces could also be neutralized by the absence of such readily available factors that, if present, would have the potential to facilitate the manipulation of the internal affairs of the country. Thus, the restoration of Eritrea's dynamism may ultimately depend on whether the government is able to solve the "bread and butter" questions, and whether it is prepared to construct representative political institutions while insuring the promotion of human rights governance.

Second, it is essential to understand that the regional and international environments do produce particular factors over which Eritrea is unlikely to have any control. It is important to note that Eritrea's potential power is so limited as to be unable to shape the direction of future regional power configurations. It should have been obvious that even at the height of its military standing after liberation, Eritrea's revolutionary vigor and relative military standing were likely to dissipate quickly unless Eritrea embarked on a costly rearmament program for which it had no resources. The Eritrean elite's moves to rely on patronage to forge special relationships with the United States and the new regimes in the "greater" Horn of Africa seem to have been intended to address this reality, but they proved to be illusory.

The relative advantage which Eritrea enjoys is that it occupies a strategic geopolitical position in the African Horn, which may permit it to play the role of a regional balancer in relations between its two giant neighbors, the Sudan and Ethiopia. Indeed, given Ethiopia's perennial quest for regional dominance, future Eritrean-Sudanese relations may enormously benefit from a configuration that will place both countries on the same side of most regional and international issues. Such innovative diplomacy does certainly demand of the elite mastery of the imponderables of politics and diplomacy.

CHAPTER SIX

THE 1998-2000 ETHIO-ERITREAN WAR: ORIGINS AND EFFECTS

After jointly overthrowing the military dictatorship of Mengistu Hailemariam in 1991, the Eritrean People's Liberation Front (EPLF) and the Ethiopian People's Revolutionary Democratic Front (EPRDF), of which the Tigray People's Liberation Front (TPLF) was the dominant partner, brought to a peaceful conclusion the thirty-year-old war between Eritrea and Ethiopia. When the Eritrean population voted for independence in a referendum conducted in 1993, Eritrea obtained Ethiopia's as well as the rest of the world's recognition as Africa's newest state. Ethiopia's Prime Minister, Meles Zenawi, visited Eritrea during the independence festivities and, in his public address marking the occasion, asked the Eritrean people not to scratch their wounds sustained during the years of war.

The two regimes agreed to cooperate in broad security matters and to maintain many aspects of the economic ties that prevailed before Eritrea became independent. The key components of the "Friendship and Cooperation Agreement" they signed in July 1993 included:

1. Preservation of the free flow of goods and services, capital and people,
2. Ethiopia's continued free access to Eritrea's sea ports paying for port services in its own currency, the *bir*;

3. Cooperation in monetary policy and continued use of the *bir* by both countries until Eritrea issued its own currency;
4. Harmonization of customs policies and
5. Cooperation and consultation in foreign policy.

Ethio-Eritrean relations appeared to have been transformed at the time of Eritrea's formal independence. However, the cooperation agreement did not address some important issues and did not provide details on others. For example, it neither addressed the border issue nor provided sufficient mechanisms for dealing with differences that might arise on a number of issues, including matters of trade and currency. The agreement also did not address the system of payments to be adopted or how the two countries were to dispose of the *bir* notes in circulation in Eritrea after Eritrea had issued its own currency. The issue of citizenship of Eritreans in Ethiopia, Ethiopians in Eritrea and pensions of Eritrean workers were also never adequately clarified. Nevertheless, peace and cooperation enabled the two countries to register notable progress in rehabilitating their respective economies. Their cooperation also had a stabilizing influence on a part of the world long characterized by turmoil, as evident by Somalia's total disintegration and Sudan's perpetual civil war. Revitalization of the Intergovernmental Authority on Development (IGAD), an organization of the countries of the Horn of Africa, was one of their important but short-lived achievements. Eritrea's open border policy with both the Sudan and Ethiopia was another. Unfortunately, this too was short-lived.

By November 1997 the two regimes had largely squandered their close ties and, to the shock of the populations of the two countries and most observers, an unexpected war broke out between Ethiopia and Eritrea merely five years after the signing of their "Friendship and Cooperation Agreement." Between May 6th 1998 and June 2000 Ethiopia and Eritrea fought over an alleged border dispute. The number of casualties in the two years of intermittent fighting is estimated to be over 100,000 and, despite the Algiers peace treaty of December 12, 2000, which brought the war to an end and the delineation of the border by the Eritrea- Ethiopia Boundary Commission, in line with the Algiers peace treaty, the border dispute remains unsettled. This chapter has two principal objectives. The first, is to explore the factors that led to the conflict and the reasons why Ethiopia has not yet fully accepted the border delimitation ruling by the Hague-based independent Eritrea-Ethiopia Boundary Commission. The second is to examine how the war has affected Eritrea's socioeconomic landscape.

Factors that Contributed to the Conflict

Many observers described the war as "absurd," "nonsensical" and even "the stupidest war in Africa." At the time it was fought, the foreign ministers of the two countries themselves referred to the war as "insane." Nevertheless, the war had manifested a complex set of latent causes. The primary manifest cause was the border dispute between Eritrea and the Tigray region of Ethiopia, which goes back to at least the 1960s, when Eritrea was incorporated into Ethiopia, if not to the creation of Eritrea as an Italian colony during the last decade of the 19th century and the first decade of the 20th century.

The borders between the two countries were delimited during the early period of Eritrea's colonization by three treaties between the government of Italy and Ethiopia's government under Emperor Menelik II. The first one is the Treaty of 10 July 1900 signed in Addis Ababa. This rather brief treaty sets the western boundary between Ethiopia and Eritrea to be the line Tomat- Toduluc-Mareb-Belassa-Muna (Hertslet, 1967:460; Brownlie, 1979:863).

The second treaty, which was signed in Addis Ababa on 15th May, 1902, is a modification of the first treaty. Article I of the second treaty states that the frontier treaty between

Ethiopia and Eritrea, previously determined by the Tomat-Toduluc line, is mutually modified in the following manner:

> Commencing from the junction of the Khor Um Hager with the Setit, the new frontier follows this river to its junction with the Maieteb, following the latter's course so as to leave Mount Ala Tacura to Eritrea, and joins the Mareb at its junction with the Mai Ambessa.
>
> The line from the junction of the Setit and Maieteb to the junction of the Mareb and Mai Ambessa shall be delimited by Italian and Ethiopian delegates, so that the Canama [Kunama] tribe belongs to Eritrea (Hertslet, 1967:433; Brownlie, 1979:868).

The third treaty is the "Convention" between Italy and Ethiopia of 16th May, 1908 which was signed in Addis Ababa. Article I of this Convention, which establishes the eastern boundary, states:

> From the most easterly point of the frontier established between the colony of Eritrea and Tigre by the convention of the 10th July, 1900 the boundary proceeds in a south-easterly direction, parallel to and at a distance of 60 kilometers from the coast, until it joins the frontier of the French possessions of Somalia (Hertslet, 1967:1225).

These treaties define Eritrea's territorial identity and its boundaries with Ethiopia. However, the boundaries were not demarcated on the ground. Another source of complication was that with Ethiopia's annexation of Eritrea in 1962, many people from Tigray as well as from Eritrea settled in the Badme planes with little regard for the border. Often Tigrayan regional authorities also infringed on the area with efforts to establish *de facto* control over some territories claimed by Eritrea. In 1966, for example, Emperor Haile Selassie dismissed a protest by the administrator of the Barentu locality in Eritrea against incursions and interferences by the administration of Shire in Tigray in the now disputed area of Badme by saying "it is all Ethiopia" (Peninou, 1998). In the late 1970s, the TPLF contested ownership of Badme, which was liberated in 1975 by the Eritrean Liberation Front (ELF), the oldest of the Eritrean liberation movements.

The border dispute, however, subsided following an understanding between the EPLF and the TPLF and the disintegration of the ELF in 1981. In a meeting held between April 4 and April 8, 1978, the EPLF and the TPLF discussed the border issue. According to the EPLF, the TPLF accepted that the colonial boundaries constitute the boundaries between the two countries but requested time to study the relevant maps and treaties (Hiwyet, no. 14, July, 1998:28-29). TPLF documents corroborate the EPLF claim as the following statement shows.

> In TPLF's view, Eritrea was organized as a state during the Italian colonial era. If they exist and can be found, there were official treaties between Menelik and the Italians and the borders were delineated. If the question of border demarcation comes up, it should be based on the Menelik-Italian treaties (TPLF, Miyazya 1978 Ethiopian calender; April 1985 in Gregorian calender).

Relations between the two fronts were not always smooth (Young, 1996). However, given their April 1978 understanding and the realization that their cooperation was essential in defeating the Mengistu regime, they were able to put the border dispute on the back burner. According to an eyewitness observer who visited the area in 1985, Badme was under the control of the EPLF at the time but the TPLF did not rescind its claim over it either (Connell, 1999:197). By the time the two movements successfully overthrew the Ethiopian military government in 1991, resolution of the border issue was still pending.

The two regimes, however, failed to address the border dispute seriously before tensions escalated, although they created a bilateral commission to deal with the issue as early as 1994. According to the Eritrean government, before such discussions rendered an outcome the Tigray administration carried out several creeping encroachments to control the contested areas. Among the infractions was uprooting Eritrean farmers from their farms in the Badme plains in order to resettle Tigrayan farmers and demobilized TPLF fighters. According to the Eritrean government, such border provocations intensified in July 1997 with fresh expulsions of Eritrean peasants from the Badme area.

Worsening matters, in October 1997 the Tigray administration released a new "official" map of Tigray that incorporated several areas that Eritrea considered its own, including the small town of Badme and parts of the Badme plains (for a good description of the disputed areas see Ghidewon Abay Asmerom and Ogbazgy Abay Asmerom, 1999). The conflict exploded when on May 6, 1998 Tigrayan militiamen fired on an Eritrean patrol near Badme, killing four and wounding three. On May 12 Eritrea's Defense Forces reacted by driving the Ethiopian militia out of the area and on May 13, 1998 Ethiopia's Council of Ministers issued Eritrea with an ultimatum to withdraw its forces from Badme. The conflict escalated from a border skirmish to a full blown all-out-war on June 5th when Ethiopia bombed Eritrea's capital city, Asmara, and Eritrea retaliated by bombing Meqelle, the capital city of the Tigray region of Ethiopia.

Eritrea claims that the small town of Badme (Baduma), where the conflict started, is within the Eritrean boundary as specified by the first two treaties between Italy and Ethiopia.

[handwritten: LEVELLAS ON POLICY ON BORDERS]

Moreover, in Eritrea's view, given the identified treaties and the Organization of African Unity's (OAU) resolution AHG/RES 16(2), which sanctifies colonial boundaries, what is needed to settle the border dispute between the two countries was to demarcate the boundaries on the ground. Accordingly, the Eritrean Government proposed the redeployment of the troops of both countries out of the disputed areas and demarcation of the boundaries on the basis of colonial treaties with the help of neutral third parties.

Needless to say, Ethiopia also claims that Badme falls on the Ethiopian side of the border. Moreover, in Ethiopia's view the May 12 retaliation by Eritrean Defense Forces amounted to an invasion. It thus insisted that Eritrean troops withdraw from the contested areas they captured after May 6 and Ethiopian administration be reinstated before negotiations on demarcation of the border can take place.

At the time of its independence in 1991, the Eritrean government underestimated the potential seriousness of the border dispute, viewing it as an issue that could be settled by demarcation on the basis of existing colonial treaties, and with arbitration if the need arose. It also sought open borders with both Ethiopia and the Sudan. The Ethiopian government was more equivocal but it too seems to accept the OAU principle that colonial boundaries are sacrosanct and that the colonial treaties are the basis for demarcating the boundary, as the following statement by Prime Minister Meles indicates.

> The Eritreans have to accept that they have to withdraw from the territories that they occupied after May 6. We have all agreed that, the border issue would be delimited and demarcated on the basis of the colonial treaties (Meles' interview with *Voice of America*, Associated Press, April 14, 1999)

The TPLF communique of Myazya 1978 (on page 240) as well as Ethiopia's acceptance of the Algiers Treaty of December 12, 2000, which specified that the border would be demarcated on the basis of the colonial treaties and relevant international law, are other indications that suggest that the Ethiopian regime recognizes the colonial treaties as the basis for demarcating the border.

Given this apparent acceptance by both sides that the colonial treaties constitute the basis for demarcating the border, it is rather difficult to understand how the two fronts and their leaders, who had cultivated close ties for over two decades as liberation fighters, allowed a border dispute to explode into a fratricidal war. As noted, the war produced close to 100, 000 casualties, led to the deportations of thousands of each other's citizens and the displacement of hundreds of thousand of people, and cost hundreds of millions of dollars in destroyed property and arms imports that the two countries, which are among the poorest countries in the world, could ill afford. There are no estimates of Eritrea's financial costs of the war but Ethiopia's total costs are estimated to be about $2.9 billion by the Ethiopian Economic Policy Research Institute (Styan, 2005: 184).

The border dispute could have been resolved amicably before it escalated into a full- fledged war through arbitration, as is often done by African countries. Several African countries have referred their border disputes to the International Court of Justice for peaceful resolution. Botswana and Namibia, Nigeria and Cameroon, Benin and Niger, Equatorial Guinea, Cameroon and Nigeria are among the countries that have taken this peaceful route. The U.S.-Rwanda sponsored peace plan, which proposed redeployment of troops to pre-May 6, 1998 positions, and demarcation of the boundaries on the basis of colonial treaties also provided a good opportunity for Eritrea and Ethiopia to stop the war after it started and to seek peaceful means. The OAU-mediated "Framework, Modalities, and

Technical Arrangements" was another opportunity for peaceful settlement of the conflict. The "Technical Arrangements" specified four critical steps to deal with the border problem. These steps included: cease-fire, redeployment of the troops of both countries to pre-May 6, 1998 positions, deployment of peace-keeping forces and demarcation of the boundaries on the basis of colonial treaties by U.N. technical experts.

Eritrea was close to accepting the U.S.-Rwanda plan, despite some reservations. When the mediators publicized the proposal as accepted by both countries before they obtained Eritrea's official response, however, it rejected the proposal and insisted that the troops of both countries be redeployed out of the contested areas until demarcation takes place. The second peace plan, the "Technical Arrangements," generated different interpretations by the two countries. Eritrea accepted the plan after obtaining clarification from the OAU. Ethiopia, however, rejected the plan, even though the country's prime minister had publicly accepted it initially and he had called on Eritrea to accept it "without ifs and buts." After the failure of these two peace initiatives and a third round of fighting, mutual exhaustion induced both countries to sign the Algiers peace plan on December 12, 2000. The mediators of the Algiers Peace Treaty arranged for the establishment of a neutral commission with the mandate to delineate and demarcate the border on the basis of pertinent colonial treaties and applicable international law.

The Hague-based commission was made up of five commissioners with each country selecting two commissioners and the fifth commissioner, the president of the commission, selected by the four commissioners. The Algiers treaty specified that the delimitation and demarcation determination of the commission was final and binding and that the United States, the European Union, the UN, and the OAU would guarantee the implementation of the commission's ruling. The commission rendered its determination on April 13, 2002.

However, this seemingly air-tight arrangement has not yet rendered resolution of the border dispute. Ethiopia, initially celebrated the commission's ruling as a victory for its cause, and Eritrea officially accepted it too. Following the commission's clarification that the town of Badme, the flashpoint of the war, rested on the Eritrean side of the border, on September 19, 2003 Ethiopia officially rejected the ruling, declaring it "totally illegal, unjust and irresponsible." Perhaps as a result of external pressure, and the removal of the leading figures of the hard line "Greater Tigray" faction of the TPLF from key positions through purges, Ethiopia recently modified its position and announced on November 25, 2004 that it has accepted "in principle" the boundary commission's ruling and called on Eritrea to enter into dialogue for adjustments on the ruling. However, Eritrea insisted that it would not engage in any dialogue that would undermine the commission's ruling. Instead it called on the guarantors of the Algiers treaty to put pressure on Ethiopia to accept the ruling in full.

Latent Causes of the War

Many African countries have border disputes. Benin has disputes with Togo, Nigeria, and Burkina Faso; the Republic of the Congo has disputes with the Democratic Republic of the Congo; Sudan has disputes with Egypt, Ethiopia, Chad and the Central African Republic; Libya has disputes with Niger and Chad; Equatorial Guinea has disputes with Gabon, Nigeria and Cameroon; Nigeria has disputes with Cameroon and Chad; Botswana has disputes with Namibia; Swaziland has disputes with South Africa; and Tanzania and Malawi have squabbles over the border of Lake Nyassa. In some cases, the disputes are over territories that are known to be rich in resources, as the Bakassi Peninsula between Nigeria and Cameroon, the Corisco Bay between Equatorial Guinea and Gabon and the Aozou region between Chad and Libya. However, none of Africa's border disputes erupted into wars of the magnitude that Ethiopia and Eritrea fought. Escalation of the Ethio-Eritrean border dispute is unusual on the African political scene, matched only by the Ethio-Somali conflicts over the Ogaden, which was much more than a border dispute. This uniqueness along with the overall deteriorating relations between the two countries before the outbreak of the war and some of the developments that transpired since the outbreak of the war, including the large scale deportations of innocent people under conditions of gross violations of human rights and the expansion of the goals of the war to include regime change, suggest that the border dispute was one among many factors although not a mere pretext, as often suggested (Leenco Lata, 2005). With the outbreak of the war many political actors in Ethiopia, including opposition parties, advocated for the expansion of Ethiopia's objectives to include the undoing of Eritrea's independence or, at least, the carving out of one of Eritrea's sea ports, Assab, for Ethiopia. Some Ethiopian scholars have also argued that there will never be peace between Ethiopia and Eritrea unless Eritrea cedes Assab to Ethiopia. Many such arguments can be found on several Ethiopia-related web sites, including, www.mediaethiopia.com; www.dekialula.com; and www.waltainfo.com. The Ethiopian government did not officially endorse these calls, but its repeated attempts during the war to capture Assab were in line with the popular sentiments. In any case, there is little doubt that the war had broad latent factors. Some observers suggest that economic factors, elite insecurity, interpersonal antagonisms and rivalry between the leaders of the two countries were among the main factors (Khadiagala, 1999). Even this list omits some critical factors related to the history of the relations of the two countries and the mindset of the two peoples.

Our own thesis is that, in addition to the identified list, a confluence of three broad factors contributed to the war. One is the nature of the relations between the EPLF and TPLF at the conclusion of the war of Eritrea's independence. A second factor is the nature of Ethiopia's political landscape and the country's ethnic rivalries in the aftermath of Eritrea's independence. A third factor relates to Eritrea's autocratic rule which personalized relations with the Ethiopian regime precluding a careful process of developing policies appropriate for the competing dynamics in Ethiopian policies.

The Nature of the EPLF-TPLF Relations

At the conclusion of the war when the EPLF and the TPLF jointly overthrew the military regime in Ethiopia, Eritrea agreed to conduct a referendum for independence in two years while remaining *de facto* independent. A regional organization from Tigray which represented less than 10% of Ethiopia's total population of roughly 60 million, the TPLF had its immediate goals set at pacifying the rest of Ethiopia and consolidating its power. The TPLF was in no position to prevent Eritrea's independence and, in fact, relied on Eritrean support in its process of pacification of Ethiopia. The EPLF also relied on the TPLF's economic cooperation in easing the economic hardship of transition.

The cooperation between the two fronts, however, created problems for the TPLF, especially among its detractors in Ethiopia, who accused it of betraying the territorial indivisibility of Ethiopia by allowing Eritrean independence to take place without at least obtaining Assab for Ethiopia. One problem was that the TPLF was perceived as a junior partner of the EPLF and that Ethiopia was under indirect control of Eritrea (Asefa Negash, 1996). A second misperception was that the two fronts had conspired to dominate and exploit Ethiopia (Negussay Ayele, October 2001). The fact that the Tigrayans and highland Eritreans share a common ethnic identity and common language, Tigrigna, made such allegations relatively easy to sell. Under these conditions, the TPLF's alliance with the EPLF, which

240

was important in pacifying Ethiopia, became a liability for the TPLF in consolidating its power in the country. The alliance was thus of a tactical nature from the perspective of the TPLF. In order to change the perception that it was a junior partner of the EPLF and to stem the accusation that it sacrificed Ethiopia's interests in its dealings with Eritrea, distancing itself from the EPLF became a strategic option. The border dispute and the differences that arose in other areas, such as in trade and monetary policies, became opportunities to be exploited instead of differences to be resolved, especially within the TPLF's hardline faction.

TPLF's Conflicting Ambitions
A second major factor that contributed to the conflict is the nature of the TPLF as a ruling party. Since its creation in 1975 the TPLF has been characterized by two conflicting objectives. Its initial objective was to free Tigray from Ethiopia's repressive rule and to form an independent Tigray state (TPLF, 1976; Clapham, 1988:213; Markakis, 1987; Gebru Tareke, 1991:209). An alternate objective was to free Ethiopia from a repressive and exploitative military regime and to build a democratic state with equality among all its ethnic groups. This duality of objectives created serious and lasting problems for the TPLF and led to the emergence of factions within the movement. Its ethno-nationalist image along with the duality of its objectives also made it difficult for the TPLF to win acceptance in the rest of Ethiopia. During the late 1970s when the TPLF was a liberation movement, it had forcefully driven some Ethiopian movements, such as the Ethiopian People's Revolutionary Party (EPRP), out of Tigray instead of working with them in overthrowing the regime of Mengistu Hailemariam.

With military success against the regime of Mengistu Hailemariam, the TPLF's alternative objective became dominant, although the Front never completely shed its initial objective. In line with its alternative objective, the TPLF created two small organizations from Ethiopia's other two major Ethnic groups; the Amhara and the Oromo. The Oromo People's Democratic Organization (OPDO) and the Amhara-dominated Ethiopian Popular Democratic Movement (EPDM), which in 1994 changed its name to Amhara National Democratic Movement (ANDM), were the two movements the TPLF brought into a coalition to form the EPRDF.

Following its assumption of power in July 1991, the EPRDF undertook some encouraging steps towards democratizing the country's political system. It organized a national conference in which twenty assorted political groups with some four hundred delegates participated (Henze, 1998). The conference adopted a provisional charter and formed an EPRDF-led transitional coalition government, with a number of other movements and political groups. A new constitution was ratified on December 8, 1994, and the highly centralized political system that existed before 1991 was replaced by a federal arrangement among the newly demarcated and largely ethnic-based eleven states, including two cities; Addis Ababa, the capital city, and Dire Dawa, which constitute separate administrative units. The other nine *kilil* (zones) were; Tigray, Afar, Amhara, Oromia, Somali, Benishangul/Gumaz, Southern nations, Gambela, and the Harari people. The constitution recognized the unconditional right of every nation in the country to self-determination, including the right of self-governance, cultural autonomy, as well as secession.

In addition to the introduction of a new administrative structure, the EPRDF allowed some freedom of political organization and more freedom of press compared to the two regimes preceding it. A private paper which is often highly critical of the government, for example, admits the progress in this regard by saying, "we have never been so free to speak our minds in Ethiopia" (*Addis Tribune*, December 4, 1998). The democratization process, however, faced a number of obstacles.

The TPLF's ethno-nationalist tendency and its unwillingness to devolve power are among the major factors impeding the country's democratization process. The Front's notion of what constitutes Tigray is particularly relevant. Claiming to "restore" historical boundaries, in the late 1970s TPLF redrew the provincial map, vastly enlarging Tigray's size (Gebru Tareke, 1991:209). While creating the ethnic-based federal arrangement *(kilil)*, the TPLF acted upon its "Greater Tigray" objective by incorporating two districts that Tigray had lost after Emperor Haile Selassie ruthlessly suppressed Tigray's Woyane rebellion in 1943 (Markakis, 1987:250). In order to "restore" historical boundaries, the TPLF reclaimed the Hummera area from the former province of Begemdir and the Raya district from Wollo, another former province. Understandably, such redrawing of regional boundaries did not go very well with other ethnic groups in the rest of Ethiopia, especially the Amhara, who were affected the most by the identified changes. Such redrawing of the inter-ethnic boundaries, along with the loss of power has played a role in instigating Amhara nationalism, as evident from the creation of an all-Amhara party.

The TPLF is also often accused of favoring Tigray in its allocation of resources (Kiflu Tadesse, 1998; Leenco Latta, 1998; *Addis Tribune*, September 4-9, 1998), although Tigray was one of the most deprived and destitute provinces during the previous two regimes. As Markakis (1987:251) notes, not a single industrial establishment existed in the province during the *ancien regime*. The federal government's budget allocations to the states do not reflect any glaring pro- Tigray bias (Mengisteab, 1997). However, as Young (1997) notes, the close affiliation of the Endowment Fund for the Rehabilitation of Tigray to the TPLF leadership and the business activities of the Relief Society of Tigray and the Tigray Development Association while securing tax benefits are mechanisms through which Tigray might obtain preferential treatment. Regardless, the TPLF has maintained a firm monopoly of power. While giving the appearance of devolution on power through the ethnic-based federal arrangement, it has retained real power in its hands and has often used it repressively leading to continued ethnic conflicts. As a result, the objective of creating a democratic Ethiopia with ethnic equality and an ethnically-neutral state has not materialized. For all practical purposes, the previously Amhara-dominated state has been replaced by a Tigray-dominated state although the Tigray-dominated regime, unlike its predecessor has neither established dominance over the bureaucracy nor established cultural hegemony (Young, 1997).

The "Greater Tigray" objective of a faction of the TPLF, which contributed to reigniting ethnic rivalries within Ethiopia, also contributed to the war with Eritrea. The pursuit of this objective at the expense of Eritrea was evident from a number of measures. The creeping confiscation of Eritrean owned farms and the expulsion of their owners from the Badme plains, occupation of some areas administered by Eritrea, including Adi Murug in July 1997, and the release of a new map of Tigray that incorporated territories disputed with Eritrea in October 1997 are the most obvious. The militant TPLF faction that supports this position became influential within the organization and especially within the administration of Tigray as elements of this militant group, who rivaled Prime Minister Meles Zenawi in Addis Ababa, were sent by Meles to Tigray, where they regrouped (Calhoun, 1999). Moreover, there are strong indications that the ambitions of this group were not simply to gain chunks of land but to establish Tigray's hegemony in the Horn of Africa by weakening any challenges from Eritrea as well as from other ethnic groups within Ethiopia. According to Reid (2005) the "Greater Tigray" faction also had aspirations of obtaining a sea outlet for Tigray through Dankalia. Speeches in various Radio Tigray broadcasts by some TPLF politburo members after the outbreak of the war suggested that the war was not simply a border dispute. Rather, the objectives were to "crush Eritrean supremacy" and to break "Eritrea's back." After the termination of the war the hardline nationalists, who had pushed for regional boundary changes to enlarge Tigray, were unhappy that the war had failed to secure access to the coast (*UN-IRIN News*, March 28, 2001). Some of the now purged hardliners of the TPLF, including the former governor of Tigray, have also accused the prime minister of failing to obtain the Eritrean port of Assab for Ethiopia. Despite their internal differences, the two factions within the TPLF, namely the group that supported "Greater Tigray" objective and the group that supported consolidation of TPLF power in Ethiopia shared a common vision with respect to Eritrea. Advancing the goals of both groups required weakening Eritrea and possibly reducing it to a subservient state. This perhaps explains why regime change in Asmara was adopted as one of Ethiopia's goals during the war.

Ethiopia's Ethnic Politics
Another critical aspect of Ethiopia's political landscape that contributed to fostering conditions for the conflict is Ethiopia's ethnic politics. Eritrea's independence and its post-independence relations with Ethiopia became issues of contention in Ethiopia's ethnic rivalries. Modern Ethiopia is a multi-ethnic country largely created through conquest around the middle of the 19th century. From its creation in the mid-19th century up until 1991, when the EPRDF took power, modern Ethiopia's political system was highly centralized and ethnic relations were essentially hierarchical and antagonistic. As a result, various ethnic-based organized insurgency movements have operated in the country since the early 1960s while sporadic uprisings took place in different parts of the country since the creation of the state (Gebru Tareke, 1991). Ethnic rivalries and power struggle among the three largest

ethnic groups have largely continued despite the institution of an ethnic-based federal arrangement by the current regime.

The three ethnic groups that are dominant in the country's political landscape are the Oromo, the Amhara and the Tigray. The Oromo are the largest single ethnic group in the country but, since they were incorporated through conquest into the modern Ethiopian state during the last part of the 19th century, they were largely subjected to political, economic and cultural subservience. With much of their land taken by northern landlords, the Oromo masses were reduced to tenants and second class citizens. The land reform of 1975 largely eliminated the landlord-tenant relations by restoring land to the former tenants. However, in the view of Oromo nationalists, the new federal arrangement has not given Oromia a genuine self-rule since the TPLF, through the satellite parties it has created, controls all the regions (Mohammed Hassen, 1999). After forging a coalition with the EPRDF for a brief period of time, the Oromo Liberation Front (OLF), which had conducted armed struggle to liberate Oromia before 1991, withdrew form the governing coalition to continue an armed struggle. The OLF claims that the federal arrangement has not led to genuine devolution of power and the Oromo remain dominated by the northern ethnic groups (Leenco Lata, 1998).

The Amhara, who occupy the central and north western parts of the country, constitute the second largest group. The ruling elite of pre-1991 modern Ethiopia came mostly from this ethnic group. In the 1960s, for instance, about three-quarters of the senior officials in the country were from the Amhara of Shoa (Clapham, 1968:85). Even in the post 1991 era, the Amhara continued to dominate the bureaucracy. Figures released by the Federal Civil Service Commission in 1996, for example, revealed that about 57% of federal government employees were Amhara, 14% were Oromo and 12% were Tigrayan (Young 1996). With the 1991 change of government, however, the TPLF largely dislodged the top echelons of the Amhara elite from power. As Paul Henze (1998) notes, bitter at losing the dominant position they enjoyed since the creation of the modern Ethiopian state, Amhara centrists have fiercely opposed the TPLF. They have also responded by creating the All Amhara People's Organization, a party that aims to mobilize the Amhara.

The Tigray nation, at less than 10% of the country's total population, is the smallest of the three major ethnic groups. Tigray was the center of the ancient Axumite Empire but, with the exception of a brief period of Emperor Yohannes IV's rule between 1872 and 1889, it was largely marginalized during the era of the modern Ethiopian state. Since 1991, however, the TPLF has dominated Ethiopian politics. By forging a coalition with the OPDO and ANDM to create the EPRDF, it has forged the appearance of a multi-ethnic national party. It has also expanded its national reach by sponsoring the emergence of several other affiliated ethnic-based parties. However, observers note that the satellite parties, including those within the governing coalition, are essentially mechanisms by which the TPLF controls power rather than instruments of advancing ethnic equality and genuine decentralization (Harbeson, 1998; Tegegne Teka, 1998; Ottaway, 1999; Keller 2001).

The satellite parties are challenged by a plethora of ethnic-based independent parties. However, charging that they are manipulated and rigged by the EPRDF, most of the independent parties boycotted the 1992 regional elections, the 1994 Constituent Assembly elections and the 1995 national elections. In conjunction with the withdrawal of the OLF from the coalition government, the boycott of the independent parties allowed the EPRDF to monopolize power in the country. Participation of the opposition parties in the 2000 national elections did little to change the dominance of the EPRDF, as it won close to 90% of the seats in the parliament.

Many of the opposition parties blame election irregularities for their poor showing.

The opposition parties that aspire to restore a centralized "Greater Ethiopia," such as the All-Amhara People's Organization, oppose Eritrea's independence as well as the ethnic-based federal arrangement and the nominal right of nations to secede. As noted, there is very little that the TPLF could have done to prevent Eritrea's independence, in 1991. Yet, opposition groups question the TPLF's patriotism and accuse it of allowing the country to be landlocked by recognizing Eritrea's independence. Eritrean support of the TPLF to consolidate its power in Ethiopia during the period of friendship and cooperation between the EPLF and the TPLF (1991-97) also served as a cause for galvanizing the opposition parties. The stronger the ties between the EPRDF government and Eritrea became, the more unpopular the EPRDF became among the opposition parties and the private press in Ethiopia. As noted, given the common language and culture shared by highland Eritreans and the people of Tigray, some even viewed the TPLF-EPLF alliance as a prelude to the formation of a Tigray-Tigrigni (Tigrigna-speaking) state, as Mengistu Hailemariam charged during his last days in power (Alemseged Abbay, 1998:200).

Even after the war these parties have continued to question the patriotism of TPLF and particularly that of the prime minister, who is of Eritrean origin on his mother's side. According to its chairman, the Ethiopian Democratic Party, for example, holds Prime Minister Meles Zenawi responsible for the loss of a seaport and the secession of Eritrea (*UN-IRIN*, December 18, 2000).

Much of the private press that is affiliated with the opposition parties also strongly opposes Eritrea's independence, as the following statement by one private newspaper indicates. "Prime Minister Meles Zenawi has played a key role in the secession of Eritrea. The prime minister's mother voted in public in the referendum for secession. As things stand, we are facing war with Eritrea. Ato Meles can apologize to the Ethiopian people and /or restore our natural sea port. Then only can he expect forgiveness" (*Fiyameta*, February 3, 1999).

An editorial in the *Tobia* newspaper also charged that the government and ruling party of Ethiopia had "willfully renounced Ethiopia's legitimate claim to sea outlet," and that Meles was "unwilling to champion the national cause" (*UN-IRIN*, December 18, 2000). When the border conflict started some of these presses argued that there is no border problem since all of Eritrea is an integral part of Ethiopia.

Perceptions about the Economic Integration

Misconceptions among opposition parties about the distribution of the gains of the economic integration scheme that existed between the two countries during the 1991-97 period also show the impact of Ethiopia's ethnic rivalries on the Ethio-Eritrean war. As noted at the outset of this chapter, at the time of Eritrea's independence the two regimes agreed to retain the free flow of goods, capital, and people that existed before Eritrea gained its independence. They also retained the Ethiopian *bir* as a common currency. However, the integration scheme in general and the *bir* arrangement in particular created concerns and misconceptions on both sides but primarily among opposition parties in Ethiopia.

Given its small size and limited resources, Eritrea's choice of development strategy, at least in the early years of its independence, was based on an open economy with export and service orientation. Eritrea also aspired to develop itself into a regional center of financial services. Accordingly, Eritrea formulated investment, taxation, customs and foreign exchange policies largely compatible with an open economy. By contrast, Ethiopia's policy involved relatively more regulations on customs, foreign exchange and trade. Thus, the two countries had different exchange rates while using the same currency. According to the governor of Eritrea's National Bank, Tekie Beyene, lack of control over its monetary policy was hampering Eritrea from achieving some of its key policy objectives (*Reporter*, November, 1997). The governor added that the absence of a national currency made it difficult to gauge the growth of the economy or to check the amount of money in circulation as Eritrea was not represented in the making of monetary policy (*Eritrea Profile*, November 21, 1998). Thus, Eritrean authorities viewed the *bir* regime as a temporary arrangement and issued Eritrea's own currency, the *nakfa*, in 1997 (*Reporter*, November, 1997).

Whether Eritrea had to issue its own currency in 1997 or should have waited longer is debatable. Similarly unclear is if the disadvantages of the *bir* regime had exceeded its benefits by 1997. Also unclear is why, in the prevailing era of globalization, in which most African countries, have little control over their monetary policies, Ethiopia and Eritrea paid so much attention to the differences in their monetary policies. At the time of the outbreak of the war, both countries had progressively liberalized their economic and financial policies and the differences between them had been narrowed. Ethiopia, for instance, liberalized its foreign exchange policy on August 31, 1998 by authorizing commercial banks to conduct foreign exchange transactions that previously were carried out only by the National Bank of Ethiopia. The country's weekly wholesale foreign exchange auction had also been gradually replaced by an inter-bank foreign exchange market.

There was a widespread perception among Ethiopia's opposition parties, the private press and even some high ranking government officials that the common currency arrangement benefited Eritrea disproportionately by allowing it to purchase Ethiopia's export commodities, such as coffee, with *bir* and re-exporting them for hard currency (Kiflu Tadesse, 1998; *Addis Tribune*, September 4-9, 1998). It was also widely believed in Ethiopia that the common currency enabled Eritrea to buy with *bir,* goods that Ethiopia imported with hard currency.

These allegations have little empirical support. The integration agreement between the two countries, which was signed on September 27, 1993, had arrangements to prevent the two countries from re-exporting each other's exports. Exportable commodities were excluded from the agreement for free movement of goods and services between the two countries. For example, Eritrea was not allowed to buy with *bir* exportable coffee of all grades that were under strict control by the Ethiopian government. Only coffee that was designated for the domestic market could be purchased with *bir.* There were also quantitative restrictions on how much of the lower grade coffee Eritrea could import. According to official figures, Eritrea's annual coffee imports, 78% of which were from Ethiopia, were estimated at about $2,250,000 (*Eritrea Profile*, October 10, 1998). Eritrea's total annual exports for the period 1993-1996 were also valued at about $70,000,000 and over 60% of Eritrea's exports went to Ethiopia (Eritrea, Customs Office 1998; World Bank, 1994). Thus, even if the allegation that Eritrea re-exported Ethiopia's coffee were true, it is highly unlikely that the amount would have been significant.

The allegation that Eritrea was raiding Ethiopia's imports also has little merit for at least two reasons. One is that over 60% of Eritrea's exports went to Ethiopia and Eritrea was paid for them in *bir.* In addition, Ethiopia paid for Eritrea's port services in *bir.* Under these conditions, Eritreans who hold *bir* would be free to buy from Ethiopia whatever they want, within the law, with their *bir.* Ethiopians were able to do the same with their *bir* in Eritrea. This is a normal aspect of the integration agreement. A sensible solution to Ethiopia's concerns would have been to adopt a realistic exchange rate policy.

A second reason why the allegation lacks merit is that Eritrea's official imports from Ethiopia for the period between 1993 and 1996 averaged about 6.15% of its total imports. Eritrea's import-reliance on Ethiopia would unlikely be so modest if Eritrea was re-importing Ethiopia's imports. There is, of course, the unrecorded trade that went on between the two countries, but the volume of such trade could hardly be large enough to justify the concerns of the opposition parties.

The opposition parties' suspicions may have emanated from the view that Eritrea does not have notable sources of foreign exchange to meet its import needs. This view, in turn, was reinforced by the widely held belief, cultivated by Ethiopian authorities during Eritrea's struggle for independence, that Eritrea was not economically viable as an independent state. Undoubtedly, Eritrea's resources are limited. However, IMF (2003) figures show that Eritrea's current account balance, including official transfers as a percentage of GDP for the 1993-97 period was positive and rather healthy with the exception of 1996. This is explained by the amount of hard currency Eritrea received from its diaspora population in the form of remittances, which averaged roughly 35% of its GDP over the first ten years of its independence. It is thus not very likely that Eritrea would raid Ethiopia's imports. Contrary to the allegations, Eritrea's trade statistics indicate that Eritrea's re-exports to Ethiopia for the years 1995, 1996, and 1997 were 94.57 million, 60.0 million, and 19.8 million *bir* respectively.

Absence of supporting evidence not withstanding, opposition groups in Ethiopia, especially those that were hostile to Eritrea's independence opposed the economic integration essentially for three reasons. For them an economic integration that benefited Eritrea was unacceptable even if it also benefited Ethiopia. Secondly, due to their lack of trust of the EPRDF government, any deal that it made with Eritrea was viewed as sacrificing Ethiopia's interests to benefit Eritrea. Thirdly, as Latta (2005) notes, the goal of these groups was to create a wedge between the EPLF and the TPLF and to weaken both movements. As a result, some described the integration scheme as "Eritrea's exploitative and hegemonic economic relations with Ethiopia" (*Addis Tribune*, September, 4-9, 1998).

The simmering crisis of the integration scheme between the two countries finally unraveled when the monetary union was terminated. In November 1997, Ethiopia issued a new *bir* note as Eritrea was preparing to issue the *nakfa*. Surprisingly, although both governments had agreed for Eritrea to issue its own currency, the measure was undertaken without any agreement on how to conduct their bilateral trade or manage their economic integration under a two currency system.

A two currency system, of course, does not preclude a lower level of economic integration. However, economic relations between the two countries plunged into a crisis when the new *bir* and the *nakfa* were issued. One problem which is of a short term nature was what to do with the old *bir* that was in circulation in Eritrea. Eritrea viewed the *bir* as Ethiopia's liability since Ethiopia paid in *bir* for port services as well as its imports from Eritrea. The Ethiopian Government reluctantly agreed that these notes constituted its liability.

The second and more fundamental problem was how to conduct trade between the two countries. The Eritrean Government proposed that the two currencies become legal tender in both countries and that they be pegged at parity. When Ethiopia rejected this proposition Eritrea proposed that the two currencies float freely against each other and that any imbalances be settled periodically through dollar transfers. A third option that Eritrea proposed as a second-best option was using the dollar to conduct trade between the two countries. Ethiopia rejected all of Eritrea's proposals. Instead, it declared that all major trade between the two countries be conducted on the basis of U.S. dollar-denominated letters of credit (L/C).

Ethiopia's rejection of Eritrea's proposal that the two currencies become legal tender in both countries may have been due to concerns that the *nakfa* would not be able to maintain its value *vis-a-vis* the *bir* given Eritrea's weak export base. A weak *nakfa*, of course, would make Ethiopian products too expensive for Eritrean consumers and lead to the decline of Ethiopia's exports to Eritrea. Eritrea's exports to Ethiopia, in contrast, would become inexpensive in Ethiopia disadvantaging Ethiopian competitors. These concerns are, however, not supported by the available data. As shown in Table 1, Eritrea had a modest positive balance of trade with Ethiopia, if the 1997 figures, which do not cover the whole year, are excluded. Moreover, considering that Ethiopia under the new agreement would pay Eritrea in hard currency for port services, it was not apparent that the *nakfa* would depreciate relative to the *bir*. The *nakfa* depreciated more rapidly than the *bir* in the aftermath of the war but what transpired after the war is not a good indication of what would have happened under conditions of peace.

Table 1
Eritrea's Trade with Ethiopia (in *bir*)

Year	Imports	Exports	Balance
1993	63,968,197	123,579,747	59,611,550
1994	90,796,808	181,491,011	90,694,203
1995	146.820,200	259,700,000	112,880,000
1996	261,781,354	273,400,000	11,618,646
1997	274,600.000	218,200,000	-56,400,000

Source: Government of Eritrea, Customs Office, 1998.

Eritrea's proposal to float the two currencies freely or conduct trade using the dollar would have alleviated most of Ethiopia's concerns over the *nakfa*. Ethiopia, however, insisted on a dollar-based L/C system of trade, which was set up between the two countries in November 1997. There is little doubt that hard currency constraints would limit the trade between the two countries. Intra-African trade, including among members of integration schemes has remained limited partly due to this problem. Under this system, citizens of the two countries would have to obtain hard currency first in order to be able to carry out trade between them. This is not very different from the old colonial days when telephone calls from Accra to Lagos had to be connected through London. In the 21st century one would have expected from African leaders a little different than this sorry situation that prevails among African countries.

Ethiopia's insistence on the L/C system further complicated matters. It implied that all major trade between the two countries would have to go through government channels. Bureaucratic inefficiency could make it become an indirect and inadvertent mechanism for protectionism. Moreover, many of Ethiopia's bureaucrats, who were hostile to Eritrea's independence, could use it to sabotage the flow of trade between the two countries.

The economic integration that the two countries had built collapsed mainly due to misconceptions and considerable pressure from opposition groups in Ethiopia. The Ethiopian government, which in the past defended the integration arrangement as beneficial to both countries, decided to side with the opposition forces that always opposed the integration scheme (*Addis Tribune*, August 14, 1998). Possibly the Ethiopian government adopted such a policy in order to weaken the Eritrean economy by limiting its access to Ethiopia's markets. Also possibly the government simply succumbed to pressure exerted by the opposition parties. In any case, the collapse of the economic integration arrangement, together with the border problems that had already deteriorated brought the two countries into a collision.

Severing relations with Eritrea appeared to bring a tactical rapprochement between the TPLF, especially its militant wing, and the opposition parties, which continued to oppose Eritrea's independence passionately. This apparent reconciliation, however, was unlikely to be sustained for long for two reasons. One was that Tigray's militant ethno-nationalists, who wanted to establish a Tigrayan regional hegemony, and the centrist elements, who aspired to restore Amhara power, had little in common other than their common view towards Eritrea. Centrist parties continued to demand changes in the federal arrangement as well as in the constitution that allowed nations to secede. Even with the purges of many of the militant elements of the TPLF, following the end of the war, it is unlikely that the TPLF will agree to such changes which are likely to undermine Tigray's autonomy. As the smallest entity among Ethiopia's three main ethnic groups, Tigray is likely to view decentralization as a safeguard from possible domination by the larger ethnic groups, although while in power the TPLF has not promoted genuine decentralization other than Tigray's. In the unlikely event that the TPLF agrees to change the federal arrangement, such a reversal of policy is likely to alienate most of the Oromo political organizations which prefer a more decentralized federal arrangement as an alternative to secession.

A second reason is that for many of the centrist elements, annexing the Eritrean port-city of Assab to give Ethiopia a sea outlet was a goal of the war and a minimum condition for peace. Many of these groups even supported the ethnic cleansing deportations, which represented an arrogant disregard of human rights. One newspaper, in fact, suggested that all Eritreans must be expelled from Ethiopia or assembled in special camps (*Ethop*, September 30, 1998). Another newspaper (*Morsh*, August 25, 1998) argued that all Eritreans in Ethiopia belong to the EPLF. None of these publications drew any distinction between Eritreans and Ethiopians of Eritrean origin.

Ethiopia's ethnic rivalries along with the parallel aspirations of restoring "Greater Ethiopia" by the centrist parties, which exerted relentless pressure on the TPLF, and building a hegemonic 'Greater Tigray' by the hardline nationalists within the TPLF played a major role in bringing the conflict between Ethiopia and Eritrea. The same factors explain why Ethiopia has failed to accept and implement the demarcation ruling by the independent Eritrea-Ethiopia Boundary Commission. For the centrist parties in particular, the war accomplished very little. Eritrea's independence is still intact. Ethiopia remains landlocked and the TPLF still controls power in Ethiopia. For the remnants of the hard-line nationalists in Tigray too, the war did not achieve its goals since neither the territorial claims nor the goal of bringing Eritrea to its knees materialized. Both groups thus continue to pressure the government not to accept the Eritrea-Ethiopia Boundary Commission's ruling. As noted, on November 25, 2004 the government of Prime Minister Meles Zenawi officially accepted "in principle" the commission's ruling and proposed a five-point peace proposal. Uncertain, however, is if the proposal would lead to peace since it entails dialogue to readjust the boundary commissions ruling. From Eritrea's point of view, the border dispute, which now has a legal settlement, cannot be taken back to the negotiating table.

As noted, the African continent faces numerous border disputes that can erupt into wars if mishandled. Settling border disputes peacefully through independent commissions or through the International Court of Justice is a very promising mechanism of conflict resolution. If the Eritrea-Ethiopia Boundary Commission's ruling succeeds in bringing about peace, it is likely to boost such mechanisms of settling border disputes, which are likely to increase in Africa over the coming decades. If the commission's ruling fails, however, it may have a dampening effect on conflict resolution through a similar mechanism.

Eritrea's Deficient Policy-Making Process

Unlike Ethiopia, post-independence Eritrea did not have political parties or interest groups that opposed close relations with Ethiopia. The importance of close economic and political cooperation with both Ethiopia and the Sudan was widely recognized among the Eritrean population. The Eritrean government, however, contributed to the conflict through a series of poorly conceived policy decisions. At least five such cases can be identified as examples. One is failure to establish clear mechanisms by which its borders would be demarcated if not demand immediate demarcation at the time it gained its *de facto* independence. As noted already, the roots of the border dispute between the EPLF and the TPLF predate Eritrea's independence and, although the two fronts had some understanding, there was no clear and official agreement at the level of governments on what basis the demarcation of the border would be executed. Understandably, both governments had many other pressing issues to deal with at the time and, since both had open border policy, the demarcation issue did not seem to be pressing. However, for Eritrea as a new country not to seek at least an unambiguous and official agreement that the colonial treaties would constitute the basis for demarcating the border reflects a failure to understand the dynamics of Ethiopian politics and the multiple identities of the TPLF. A serious policy-making process would have accounted for possible future policy shifts in Ethiopia and formulate policies that would protect the country's interests and allow it to engage more carefully in diffusing hostile tendencies among Ethiopia's political actors. In short, the Eritrean government did not have any planned course of action to guard against possible policy shifts on the part of the TPLF towards Eritrea or the possibility of a delayed hostile reaction to Eritrea's independence within the Ethiopian polity.

A second policy failure relates to the nature of the 1993 Ethio-Eritrean Economic Cooperation agreement, which had a number of deficiencies. First, the agreement failed to protect the right of Eritrean civil servants to retirement pensions. With independence, pension benefits of all the retired civil servants or those verging retirement were completely disregarded, throwing many people into economic hardship as neither Eritrea nor Ethiopia assumed responsibility. Secondly, the agreement was of a short term nature, having little to say about how trade between the two countries would be conducted if and when Eritrea issued its currency. Lack of basic agreement in this regard led to abrupt disruption of their trade relations when Eritrea issued the *nakfa*. This, in turn, spoiled their overall relations.

Another major problem leading to tensions in the economic relations between the two countries was participation in business activities by both the PFDJ and the TPLF. As noted in chapter three, engagement in business activities by the PFDJ through direct ownership of several firms had many adverse political and economic implications within Eritrea. The party's engagement in business also had averse implications on Ethio-Eritrean relations. Like the PFDJ, the TPLF also actively engages in business activities in Ethiopia through direct and indirect ownership and control of various private and quasi private firms. Even before their political relations soured, the two fronts increasingly became economic rivals adding to the strain in the economic relations between the two countries.

A fourth policy failure on the part of the Eritrean leadership relates to its failure to publicize the growing border tension between the two countries, choosing to deal with it through quiet diplomacy. This strategy was understandable initially but not after things began to get out of hand. When a Tigrayan militia group attacked an Eritrean patrol, killing four and wounding three on May 6, 1998 in the contested surroundings of Badme, the Eritrean government's reaction changed swiftly from quiet diplomacy to what appeared to be disproportionate application of force, driving the Tigrayan militia out of the area on May 12, 1998. Given the open border policy of the two countries and that the border was yet to be demarcated, the Tigrayan administration was wrong to engage in expulsion of farmers from their farms or in dismantling Eritrean administration in the Adi Murug area of Bada. Yet Eritrea failed to bring the dispute to the attention of the OAU and the UN. Given the tendencies of the hardline nationalists within the TPLF and the Ethiopian opposition parties, Ethiopia reacted by hastily declaring war on Eritrea. Eritrea's failure to publicize the border encroachment and displacement of Eritrean farmers by the Tigrayan administration and to seek diplomatic involvement by the OAU and the UN allowed Ethiopia to present itself as a victim of an Eritrean invasion. Thus very quickly at the start of the war, Eritrea largely lost the diplomatic war, although its claim over Badme was legitimate, as affirmed by the Eritrea-Ethiopia Boundary Commission's ruling, which declared Badme a sovereign Eritrean territory. We don't know if war would have been averted if Eritrea had taken only a measured action against the Tigrayan militia and quickly brought the dispute to the attention of the UN and the OAU for mediation. However, it would have sheltered Eritrea from being viewed as the aggressor state.

Failure to accept the U.S. - Rwanda peace plan was another policy failure on the part of Eritrea. The US-Rwanda plan called on Eritrea to redeploy its troops to reestablish the pre-May 6th status quo. The plan then called for demarcation of the border to take place on the basis of colonial treaties with the involvement of third parties. If the plan would have been accepted by Ethiopia had Eritrea accepted it is unclear. The problem of defining the pre-May 6th status quo, which undermined subsequent peace plans, would have been used by the hardline elements within the TPLF, who opposed the plan, as a pretext for rejecting it. But Eritrea's fundamental interest was to obtain the demarcation of its border and it had little to lose by accepting the peace plan. Unfortunately, Eritrea rejected the plan on a technicality angered by the mediators' announcement of an agreement before they obtained Eritrea's formal acceptance of the plan.

If the identified examples reflect poor policy making in Eritrea, as we believe they do, then a brief explanation needs to be provided why the country's policy making was so deficient. We suggest two explanations. One is that, as a new country, Eritrea did not have the experience or the infrastructure necessary for careful policy making. A second and more fundamental explanation is the nature of the political system that emerged in post-independence Eritrea. As described in chapter four, excessive concentration of power in the office of the president with little mechanism for accountability simply did not allow for the establishment of a process of policy making conducive for careful exploration of various scenarios and options. The president's response to a letter from one of the country's high ranking officials and a member of the national assembly, who wrote to him urging that Eritrea accept the U.S.-Rwanda peace plan as Eritrea could win its case peacefully without sacrificing any human and material resources, is a telling example. The president wrote back to the official one brief sentence stating that Eritrea does not have a reason to raise its hands to surrender. The exchange suggests that even the national assembly was not involved in the decision-making process.

Eritrea's realistic gain from the war, even if it had emerged victorious, would have been minimal other than the demarcation of its borders on the basis of colonial treaties and perhaps a false enhancement of the stature of its president. There was little doubt, however, that the costs of the war and, especially the costs of losing it could be enormous. One likelihood is that Ethiopia would have attempted to reverse Eritrea's independence or to dismember Eritrea by wresting Assab from it. Of course, such outcomes would have led to another cycle of protracted war similar to that of the war of independence. Given these possibilities, one would expect Eritrea's policy making to be a lot more careful and more determined to avoid the war than it was.

Impacts of the War

The war produced serious social, economic, and political dislocations in Eritrea. By the time it came to a conclusion in June 2000, thousands of Eritreans had lost their lives. The government puts the number of casualties at 19,000, but the actual figure could be higher. One-third of Eritrea's population was displaced, with many refugees pouring into Sudan. While thousands of Eritreans from the western parts of the country sought refuge in Sudan, thousands from the southern parts of the country were internally displaced. Four years after the guns were silenced, thousands remain internally displaced as the border has not yet been demarcated and their fields remain un-mined. Over 80,000 Eritrean and Ethiopians of Eritrean origin were expelled from Ethiopia under conditions that grossly violated their human rights. Many families remain split, most of the expelled had their properties confiscated, and they were forced to walk several miles under harsh climatic conditions and through mine-infested areas to cross the border (*Human Rights Watch*, 2003).

The economic impacts of the war on Eritrea were also severe. The war entailed the mobilization of large segments of the Eritrean workforce into military service, resulting in severe shortage of labor throughout the economy but especially in the agricultural sector. Four years after the end of the war demobilization has yet to take place as the border dispute remains unresolved. Eritrea also lost the bulk of its export market due to the war and continued tensions with the Sudan. Tight supply of goods, partly due to the shortages of labor and foreign exchange, has resulted in sharp increase in inflation.

Many of the macroeconomic dislocations the Eritrean economy has faced as a result of the war are captured in Table 2.

Table 2.

Selected Indicators of the Economic Impacts of the War

Indicators	1996	1997	1998	1999	2000	2001	2002
Annual Change in Real GDP %	9.3	7.9	1.8	0.0	-13.1	10.2	1.8
Annual Change in GDP/Capita %	15.0	-3.7	5.6	-4.9	-14.2	7.7	-10.1
Consumer Price Index	-	3.7	9.5	8.4	19.9	14.6	16.9
Exports in millions $US	200.2	203.3	110.4	65.7	97.5	147.3	184.4
International Reserves in months of imports of goods	3.8	5.0	1.4	1.1	0.9	1.1	0.7
Official Exchange Rate (*Nakfa* vs. US $)	6.4	7.2	7.4	8.2	9.6	10.9	14.0
Current Acct. Balance % of GDP	-7.0	2.1	-23.0	-27.9	-16.2	-18.5	-15.7
Domestic Debt % of GDP	6.7	11.0	18.8	37.5	51.4	60.8	78.6
External Debt % GDP	31.7	30.5	58.2	96.7	125.9	119.9	123.2
Ext. Debt Service in % of GDP	0.2	0.3	0.5	3.0	4.1	7.6	19.5
Earnings from port fees % of GDP	6.4	8.9	1.8	1.8	1.0	1.3	1.6

Source: IMF. *Eritrea: Selected Issues and Statistical Appendix.* IMF Country Report No. 03/166, Washington D.C., June 2003.

The political impacts are perhaps the most lasting impacts of the war. The war exposed the deficiencies of the Eritrean leadership and more importantly the structural problems of the country's political system. The war did not go very well for Eritrea. No doubt, Ethiopia's hardliners were unable to reverse Eritrea's independence or to wrest the seaport of Assab from Eritrea. The Ethiopian government was also unable to achieve its stated goal of regime change in Eritrea. However, in ending the war, Eritrea was forced to accept terms that were worse than those that were offered to it by the U.S.-Rwanda peace plan at the beginning of the war. After the war many of the government's senior officials, including members of the parliament demanded more accountability from the president's office, a review of the country's political system, and implementation of the country's constitution. The president, however, rejected the proposals, as noted in chapter four, and locked up the dissidents, who have remained incarcerated since September 2001 without trial. As resistance to the regime grew, human rights violations also intensified. In contrast to the promise of a democratic rule following its independence, Eritrea is now ruled without the freedom for political pluralism and political parties, without a free press and without a constitution.

CHAPTER SEVEN

CONCLUSION

As stated in the opening pages of this book, we wanted to examine whether Eritrea lived up to its hopeful promise or followed in the footsteps of the post-colonial African states. With this fundamental task in mind, we began our analytic review of post-independence Eritrean politics, economics and foreign policy. To our dismay, Eritrea's record of performance, as the chapters in this book amply show, is disappointing. Rather than becoming an exception to the African rule, the Eritrean state actually completed its evolution in a short span of time to typify the post-colonial African state both ontologically and functionally. The symmetry between the Eritrean state and the typical post-colonial African state in patterns of political evolution, economic policy, foreign policy orientation and ideology of justification is indeed striking. In a way, our study of the post-liberation Eritrean state serves as a template to assess the political decay and economic and social crisis that characterize post-colonial Africa. In view of our analytic purview and the findings of our inquiry into post-liberation Eritrea, the comparative significance of our research program is unmistakable. Indeed, the sorry outcome of our research effort invites three tantalizing questions that beg closer attention. Why has the Eritrean state repeated the fatal mistakes that its sisterly African states made after decolonization? What is the pedagogical relevance of this study to understanding the phenomenon of political decay in post-colonial Africa? What are the prospects of Eritrea overcoming the challenges of democratic transition and restoring its historic trajectory?

Formation of a Single Party System

With the drive toward decolonization having become unstoppable, most African states began the second half of the 20th century progressively looking forward. Once political independence was achieved, the ruling assumption was that the African states would be poised to mobilize their untapped raw materials and human resources to realize rapid progress and prosperity. This forward-looking optimism was captured in Kwame Nkrumah's famous biblical recitation: "Seek ye first the political kingdom, and all the rest shall be added unto you." This view was widely shared by both the new African elite and the departing colonizers. African countries inherited from colonialism fragmented societies and fragmented economies. The global economic system was also stacked against them given their place in the global division of labor. To have a fighting chance in overcoming these obstacles and bringing about socioeconomic development, they needed to unify their societies through effective strategies and programs of state-building and to establish mechanisms of regional and continental cooperation. Liberal multi-party political systems with the French presidential system or the British parliamentary order that were erected during the process of decolonization were quickly deemed inappropriate for African realities by one state after another. The new African elite literally tore up the liberal constitutions and repudiated the multiparty system as alien to Africa sooner than the colonizers had completed their departure from the continent, even though in some cases phony opposition parties were allowed to exist to provide the appearance of pluralism.

The notion of a single party was somehow presented as compatible with the purpose and mission of the post-colonial state. This necessitated the construction of an ideology of justification in which the multiethnic and multi-religious character of the African polity in combination with the primacy of economic development were seen as incompatible with western-style political pluralism and competitive multiparty politics. In other words, the benefits deriving from the negation of democratic pluralism outweighed the advantages that could be had from tolerating the salience of religious and ethnic diversity. Soon the single party became the trademark of the post-colonial African polity, in theory charged with the historic mission to weld together the disparate ethnic and religious forces under the rubric of a single national identity. Far from promoting internal cohesion, the single-party system became a mechanism for monopolizing political power by the elite in power with detrimental effects on state building. The system facilitated the suppression of political forces with views that differ from those of the ruling elite. Absence of legal mechanisms for the expression of alternative views, in turn, led to internal strife and civil wars that have plagued many African countries. With many African civil wars inviting covert or overt intervention by other African countries, regional and continental cooperation among African countries has remained largely ineffective. Many African countries have, in fact, become major players in the de-stabilization of other African countries.

The foregoing description of the realities in post-colonial Africa applies to Eritrea with equal force. When the nationalists proudly turned a page in the seminal chapter in the country's history and happily proclaimed the passing of an era and the dawn of another, after the 30-year armed struggle successfully ran its course with the liberation of Eritrea in 1991, the country's international supporters and distant observers alike charitably shared this view. Many were quietly sanguine about Eritrea's bright future, full of potential to become an exception to Africa's tragic post-colonial history. Even western media, not known for having a benign attitude to the Eritrean struggle before, saw in Eritrea an alternative development trajectory, one that would serve as a premier model for the rest of Africa to emulate. Underpinning this euphoric optimism were two factors. First, there were numerous declaratory statements made by the Eritrean elite seemingly militating in favor of political pluralism, competitive multiparty system, human rights governance and economic freedom under a modern constitution. Second, there was an objective factor that seemed to nurture the hope of a bright future in Eritrea, and that had to do with the onset of the second wave of African "liberation." Following the collapse of the Soviet Union, which opportunely coincided with Eritrea's liberation, the wind of political change was sweeping through all the continents, including Africa. "Democratization" or "democratic transition" had become a buzz phrase in the political lexicon of African elite everywhere. This was a period when the second phase of Afro-optimism had reached its apotheosis, which soon found full expression in the fleeting notion of "African renaissance", shepherded by a "new breed" of African leaders. In light of this exuberant mood, the ruling assumption was that Eritrea was not going to escape the reality of political change and democratization.

Contrary to the sanguine expectations of many, however, Eritrea took a sharp u-turn from its historic trajectory. Shortly, the post-liberation Eritrean elite emulated the single party model. Numerous public pronouncements in favor of a multiparty system and competitive electoral politics within the framework of a liberal constitution, notwithstanding, the Eritrean elite proceeded to construct the PFDJ as the sole party in the country. The rationale was so familiar to students of African politics: the multiplicity of ethnic and religious forces in combination with the primitive state of the economy and politics rendered the notion of pluralism inoperative in the Eritrean context. The rationale was that adoption of a

European style mode of political governance would invite ethnic fragmentation and religious polarization, making Eritrea vulnerable to potential threats from de-stabilization and even disintegration. The Eritrean president himself affirmed the reification of this orientation when he publicly pronounced that the call for pluralist institutions "would amount to moving the institutions of formerly colonialist states to different societies" (*EIU* first quarter, 1994). The president was never shy to restate the view that political democracy was an article of luxury, which Eritrea could dispense with until the economic reconstruction of the country was completed. But nothing was new in this orientation, since the old shepherds in the first wave of African politics had said the same thing, when they invoked the ethnic and religious heterogeneity of their societies as a justifying reason for the postponement of the democratization project. In this context the PFDJ was given total monopoly over what comparativists call the input functions of politics. Interest articulation, elite preference aggregation, political socialization and political communication have all been carried out under the direction and guidance of the PFDJ in the name of promoting political stability, cultural brotherhood, national unity and economic development. The formation of rival political organizations or civic associations outside the space officially delineated by the single party has been seen as inimical to the post-liberation order.

Authoritarian Institutionalization of Leadership
Accompanying the formation of the single party as the permanent fixture on the African polity, the notion of a single central figure became widespread throughout the African continent during the first wave of African liberation. The justification for the centrality of what analysts call "the strong man" to political stability and national unity acquired a new currency. Phony elections were simulated every now and then to ostensibly confer legitimacy on the post-colonial order while

the "strong man" would run unopposed. The result was the emergence and proliferation of what David Apter called "presidential monarchs." Likewise, the simulation of elections for parliamentary seats became the standard operating procedure; the screening and certification of candidates by the single party under the direction of the "presidential monarchs" became commonplace. Jam-packed with quiescent political clients, parliaments could only legislate the will of the "strong man." This made the African "strong man" quintessentially an ex-officio legislator, with absolute control over the output functions of national politics in terms of rule making, rule application and rule adjudication. For its longevity, "presidential monarchism" required the widespread use of containment politics. Dissidents and critics were either co-opted into the patronage system or coerced into exile or eliminated.

Here again, as shown in chapters two and four, the parallel between the political role of the typical African leader and the role of the Eritrean president in the polity is unmistakable. Apart from the fact that the Eritrean leader has remained the undisputed head of state and government for thirteen years since independence, he has been chairman of the so-called national legislature with total control over the operations of the legislature, which rarely meets and, when it does, meets only at his pleasure. A criticism by anyone of the suffocatingly totalizing political process in the country more often than not invites the wrath of Eritrea's "strong man." Those who dare to question any aspect of Eritrea's economic policy, the conduct of its foreign relations, and the day to day operation of the government are today languishing behind bars, and the lucky ones have managed to flee the country.

Economic Statism

Upon the departure of the colonial powers, Africa's political elite quickly learned the importance of control over public resources as a crucial means to the perpetuation of political power and the expansion of the patronage system. In consequence, the state was steadily pushed to the center of the economy in the name of accelerating economic development, together with the promotion of social equity. African socialism *a la* Nyerere, African comunitarianism *a la* Ture and Afro-communism *a la* dos Santos were but a few of the development ideologies put forth to purportedly justify the insertion of the state at the center of the national economy. Other elite, like Jomo Kenyatta and Kenneth Kaunda, who shied away from associating themselves with such seemingly radical ideologies chose to quietly champion the construction of parastatals and the role of the state in the economy within the framework of capitalism. These parastatals are public economic bodies, theoretically autonomous, but in practice tightly controlled by the state. Like the political institutions of the post-colonial state, the public economic institutions had been typically staffed by men who were like mere clients, connected and therefore loyal to the African "strong man."

The structural and functional similarities between the typical post-colonial African economic order and the one that prevails in Eritrea today are quiet striking. In the name of promoting national self-reliance, the post-liberation Eritrean elite have anchored the economy within the framework of a statist ideology. Not only has the PFDJ government followed in the footsteps of the post-colonial African regimes in constructing public economic bodies but also expanded further the role of the state and party in the economy. As shown in chapter three, there are three economic sectors in Eritrea today: the public sector, the party sector and the private sector. Of these three sectors, the party sector is the hegemonic player in the economy. The net effect of the regime's economic centralism has been that a large number of national entrepreneurs with substantial capital have been discouraged from investing in the country. In fact, because the regime's investment policy was so stifling in the 1990s, a few Eritrean entrepreneurs chose to invest their capital in neighboring Ethiopia. Unfortunately the Ethiopian regime confiscated much of these investments when the Ethio-Eritrean war erupted in 1998.

Militarization of Civil Society

In a short decade after decolonization, most African states began to grapple with the classic crisis of legitimation. The "presidential monarchs" were unable to deliver on their inflated promises of economic development and social equity. The economy everywhere, rather than growing, faltered and sank into grim circular stagnation. Predictably, the conditions of political repression and economic stagnation set the stage for the military to step into politics. Coups and counter-coups became commonplace throughout the continent. Before the onset of the second wave of African "liberation" in the early 1990s, there had been over seventy successful coups in Africa. In countries where coups weren't successful, the civilian "presidential monarchs" increasingly relied on special security forces to maintain law and order. The end result had been the militarization of civil society almost throughout the continent. Only by transforming the post-colonial state into a police state could the African elite manage to deflect mass frustration and anger away from their squalid record of performance, which has manifested itself on a continental scale in unchecked population growth and environmental degradation, mass unemployment and growing poverty, rampant corruption and wanton political repression, inter-ethnic violence and interstate conflict, internal displacement and refugee formation.

As in the other areas of governance, the one-party Eritrean state has failed to become an exception to the African rule. Both civil society and state in Eritrea are structured on the military model. Even the so-called "national service" program is structured along military lines. Early military indoctrination of the youth is regarded by the party and president as crucial to the transformation of discipline and obedience into national duty. Moreover, unable to govern by democratic means, the Eritrean state has fully deployed coercion as an instrument of control. At the time of writing, the country is divided into four military zones, each under a military general, who is above civil authorities. Freedom of the press is indefinitely banned and journalists are imprisoned, together with political dissidents and critics under trumped up charges of compromising national security without evidentiary foundation. The government doesn't respond to international pressure from human rights organizations, non-governmental organizations and/or foreign governments. Under stress from grinding poverty and horrific human rights violations, Eritrea's able bodied citizens are today voting on their feet. In the hope of making it to Ethiopia or Sudan and beyond and at huge risk to their lives, Eritreans are again on the road in ever larger numbers.

The Inheritability of History.

The Eritrean state is similar in structure and function to the typical post-colonial African state. But this begs the question: why has the Eritrean state followed in the footsteps of other African states? Perhaps the answer is the burden of history. As the late Ernest Gellner (1983) notes, the state, like every other social formation, is a historical contingency. It cannot be understood apart from its specific historical, social, economic and political contexts. To begin with, the African state was constructed by the colonizers as an authoritarian entity in order to insure the unconditional submission of the colonized peoples to the will of the colonizers. Corresponding to this coercive political apparatus the African economies were structured in such ways as to maximize the exploitation of African labor and the extraction of natural resources. By the same token, the political culture that held together the repressive political order and the exploitative economic system

273

was inherently authoritarian. Thus, in all dimensions of politics, economics and culture, the African society was historically frozen. In such an all-encompassing repressive environment, almost all African nationalist movements were conceived. The leaders and the movements they created could not help but be influenced and shaped by the contextual contours of their immediate material and historical environment. Despite decolonization, there was no clean break between the colonial state and the post-colonial state. To think otherwise would be utterly undialectical.

Even on the surface it may appear that Eritrea's experience was different from the experience of a typical African state because of its protracted armed struggle, but closer examination of the two experiences reveals remarkable similarities between them. The Eritrean armed struggle was beset from the start with profound internal contradictions and their resolution eventually resulted in the formation of an authoritarian political order. The unconditional unity of purpose, mission and organization was seen as central not only to the survival of the national movement but also to the final liberation of the country. Secrecy and centralism, embedded in a "Spartanized" culture, was regarded as crucial means to secure national unity, organizational coherence and individual discipline in order to ensure survival of the movement and achieve the liberation of the country. Upon independence, Eritrea inherited what the fighters had historically developed during the 30-year armed struggle. There has never been a clean break between the EPLF of yesteryear and the PFDJ of today in terms of political culture and methods of governance.

In more crucial respects, the pre-colonial history and colonial experience of Eritrea is analogous to those of other African countries. By virtue of the fact that the capitalist mode of production and the corresponding political institutions were uniformly superimposed on the entire continent by external forces, the conditions for the organic development of indigenous forces were not favorable. In addition, because African colonies were assigned to specialize in the production and supply of primary commodities for metropolitan economies, the conditions conducive to growth and expansion of the capitalist mode of production were either severely controlled or virtually nonexistent. This reality not only severely circumscribed the spatial contours of politics but also undermined the prospects for the rise and growth of autonomous civil societies. These nascent civil societies had neither the economic strength nor the political means to influence the state of affairs. Consequently, unchallenged by competing counter-narratives from differentiated civic forces, a narrow band of nationalist elite proceeded to establish their hegemony in the post-colonial state without a legacy of accountability to the governed. Given the absence of structural conditions and a tradition of accountability to the governed conducive to the democratization of the post-colonial state, the best scenario that could have occurred—and which has occurred in selected African states—was what Guillermo O'Donnell (1996) termed "delegative democracy," one in which national legislatures and the courts are impotent and the executive is not answerable to voters, even though phony elections are held regularly to bestow some sort of legitimacy on the political system.

The state of affairs peculiar to democratic governance is the unambiguous presence of "horizontal accountability" in which the executive, the legislature and the judiciary operate on the basis of a system of checks and balances under the watchful eye of a robust press and vigilant citizenship. But this requires mass structural transformation, corresponded to by a comprehensive reorganization of state institutions along democratic lines as a requisite condition for putting a genuine political progress on a steady trajectory. Post-colonial Africa in general and post-liberation Eritrea in particular lacked such a requisite condition. One of the glaring tragedies of history is that structural impediments to progress and the poverty in intellectual and political leadership dialectically feed on each other. Even though researchers seem to have almost limitless ability to come up with multiple strategy designs for policy makers, the ability to supply readily usable operational prescriptions or practicable visions for how to overcome the leadership deficiency and create the necessary structural conditions for building democratic institutions may suffer from the same inadequacies that hobble the forces that we frequently criticize.

What Are Eritrea's Prospects for the Future?

In the post-Cold War era, most African countries have implemented some reforms to liberalize their economic and political systems due to internal pressure and the requisites of globalization largely imposed from outside. Most have restructured their economies by reducing state involvement in economic activity, opening up their markets and liberalizing their monetary systems and capital mobility. In the political sphere, they have allowed modest freedoms to the press and allowed the establishment of multiparty political systems. Although often marred by irregularities, elections are now regularly conducted in many African countries. More than forty countries have carried out multiparty presidential or parliamentary elections. In most cases, however, these political reforms have not been accompanied by independence of the judiciary, without which the rule of law cannot be firmly established. The executive has also not conceded the power of policy making over taxation and spending, allowing it to operate with little accountability.

The impacts of liberalization on African societies, in general, and on their state-society relations, in particular, have so far been paradoxical. While liberalization has resulted in the spread of some of the formal institutions of democracy, contrary to the expected outcomes of democracy, liberalization

276

has failed to narrow the discrepancy between policy and social interests, which is rampant in the continent. As Sklar (1996:39) notes, democracy implies the public management and nurture of markets so that they flourish with affordable fairness in the distribution of opportunities, services, and wealth. Democracy is expected to bring about such management of markets because it entails representation through which society at large can exert influence on policy regarding access to social services and productive assets.

Brought about by broad representation, societal influence on policy would be expected to be reflected in the advancement of the most basic societal interests, but to determine what constitutes societal interests, which vary from place to place and over time, is difficult. In Africa's present socioeconomic context, however, they are very likely to include expansion of societal access to public services, such as education and health, reduction of levels of poverty, increasing food availability and diversification of the economy to facilitate growth and job creation. On the basis of such criteria, African countries have made little progress in coordinating policy with broad social interests despite the spread of formal institutions of democracy since the early 1990s.

Many sub-Saharan African countries have retrenched their expenditures on public services since adopting liberalization policies. At a time when malaria and the HIV/AIDS epidemic are eroding the economic and social fabric of many African societies, *per capita* public expenditure on health has declined in many countries since the early 1990s (The World Health Organization, 2003; The World Bank, 1999). In many cases budgetary stringency has severely limited the capacity of governments to train health workers and to attract, retain and maintain the morale of professional health workers (*USAID*, 2003). Public expenditure on education has also declined steeply in many countries, although modest increases are reported in a few cases. For sub-Saharan Africa, expenditures on education as a ratio of GDP declined from 4.5% in 1992 to 3.3% in 1999 (World Commission on the Social Dimension of Globalization, 2004). Access to education, as measured by the percentage of relevant age groups enrolled in elementary schools, has largely stagnated. Out of twenty-eight countries with consistent data, enrolment in elementary school in 1997 declined in ten countries compared to enrolments in 1980 (*UNCTAD*, 2002). In two countries the changes were positive but minimal and in sixteen countries there were modest positive changes.

Levels of poverty, measured by the ratio of the population living on less than US$1 a day, which is the a widely accepted conventional measure of poverty, has also increased between 1989 and 1999 in thirteen of twenty-four countries for which data is available (*UNCTAD*, 2002). The absolute number of the destitute has increased from 241 million in 1990 to 323 million in 2000 (World Commission on the Social Dimension of Globalization, February 2004).

Food production and availability as measured by the annual changes in total and *per capita* food production and by *per capita* calories intake have also remained stagnant in much of the continent. Between 1990 and 1999 *per capita* food production declined in seventeen out of thirty-five sub-Saharan African countries (*UNCTAD*, 2002). Of course, food production is affected by various factors besides policy. Weather conditions have, for example, a strong influence on the variation of food production in the continent. However, sound policy that is devoted to advancing social interest would be expected to stabilize and improve food production and availability overtime. Economic and political liberalization has not yet reversed the worsening food conditions in much of Africa.

Liberalization has also not led to diversification of production in sub-Saharan Africa. The overall picture of Africa's industry since the implementation of liberalization policies has been rather grim. Average annual growth rates of value added in industry have declined from 2.2% for the 1975-84 period to 1.7% for the 1985-1989 period and to 1.3% for the 1990-2000 period (The World Bank, 2001). According to an UNCTAD study (2001), the elasticity of industrial value added with respect to GDP, which was 1.10 and 1.03 during the 1960s and 1970s respectively declined to 0.75 for the 1980s and 0.65 for the 1990s. A comparison of average annual growth rates of output in the manufacturing sector between the 1980-1990 and 1990-2000 periods also shows that the rates declined in fifteen countries while modestly higher rates were registered in eleven countries (*UNCTAD*, 2002).

The identified basic economic indicators hardly suggest that economic and political liberalization has been accompanied by better coordination of policy with broad social interests in Africa. Yet the political changes that have occurred in several African countries are not inconsequential. Political freedom, as an end in itself, is invaluable, even when not accompanied by rapid economic improvement. Moreover, the multiparty political system, provided that it leads to real competition among political parties in conjunction with a freer press can expand the political and economic space for civil society, which, in turn, would allow civil society to struggle through legal means, towards narrowing the gap between policy and social interests. Eritrea has largely remained an exception to the liberalization process taking place in Africa. Its economy is highly regulated. As already noted, it is one of the few African countries that have not allowed political parties and the private press. Eritrea also remains a country devoid of a constitutional rule, where the executive is unencumbered by any checks from a functioning legislature or judiciary. The government's ability to formulate and change policies at whim has created an acute "sovereignty paradox" problem. The government's ability to change its policy at any time has, for example, made the risk of uncertainty for investors, both domestic and foreign, very high. In the long run, the country is not likely to remain an exception, since neither its economic nor its political conditions are sustainable. In the short to the intermediate runs, however, the obstacles for change are considerable.

The Warsai-Yikeallo Campaign of Free Labor

Among the country's many unsustainable economic policies is the Warsai-Yekeallo campaign. Since the outbreak of the Ethio-Eritrean border war in 1998, a large number of Eritrea's work force has been tied up in military service followed by the Warsai-Yekeallo campaign, which forces much of the country's workforce to provide free labor in the public and party sectors of the economy. Disregarding the opportunity costs, the government claims that the campaign has expedited rehabilitation of the economy from the effects of the war. There is little mechanism for assessing the productivity of those serving in the campaign, but forced labor cannot be expected to produce high productivity, as it lacks basic incentive mechanisms. In any case, the program has led to widespread discontent among those serving and their families, who are forced to put on hold the pursuit of their own private interests for such a long time. Most Eritreans have a high sense of nationalism and many served and fought selflessly to win their country's independence and to preserve its independence and territorial integrity. But many don't see the Warsai-Yekeallo campaign in the same light. As a result, an increasing number of the most productive segment of the country's workforce is leaving the country and joining the ranks of refugees.

The acute labor shortage produced by the campaign has also hurt the private sector, especially the agricultural sector. Eritrea is unlikely to be able to feed itself under the current conditions of labor shortage even if weather conditions turn favorable. The campaign, which has a major role in bringing the Eritrean economy to the brink of collapse, is fundamentally unsustainable.

The Land Policy

The country's land policy, which firmly places ownership, control, and distribution of land in the hands of the government is also economically and politically unsustainable. The government's appropriation of land from peasants in semi-urban areas without paying any compensation has generated discontent in the affected areas. As evident from the acute shortage of housing in the urban areas, the government has also not been efficient in the distribution of urban land. Sky rocketing rental prices, triggered by the policy, have also depressed the standard of living of large numbers of urban dwellers, especially the poor.

The government has not yet implemented fully many aspects of its 1994 rural land reform program, which places ownership of all land in the hands of the government. It has, however, given land concessions to commercial farmers and mining corporations. So far, the government has developed little mechanism for compensating peasants and nomads who are affected by government acquisition of the land they hold or use customarily. As the number of the concessions given to commercial farmers and mining corporations increases, the rate of evictions of peasants and nomads and land disputes are likely to rise with serious political, economic, social and environmental implications. Resource rich areas in many African countries, such as the Nigerian Delta or Ethiopia's Awash valley in the Afar region, have long faced evictions, local poverty and environmental disaster. Eritrea's land policy is likely to duplicate such problems.

Unconstitutional Rule

The government's unwillingness to implement the 1997 ratified constitution and to allow the formation of political parties, its banning of the private press, and violations of human rights, including imprisoning of journalists and political opponents for long periods of time without formal charges and trial, have created political crisis and instability. Such political conditions have also hurt the country's external relations, its image and its ability to attract foreign investments. Even the Eritrean diaspora, which helped sustain the Eritrean economy during the country's first decade of independence, has shown signs of serious concern over the lack of civil liberties in the country. Given all these economic and political costs, the Eritrean government is not likely to withstand the pressure for change in the longer run. There are, however, some serious obstacles in the short term.

Obstacles to Change

One of the main obstacles is related to the weakness of the country's civil society. Governments rarely are agents of change. They maintain the *status quo* unless pressured to bring about change. In Eritrea civil society organizations are essentially integral parts of the government as they are run by cadres of the party. The absence of independent civil society organizations has allowed the government to operate unencumbered by serious public pressure from within the country.

Eritrean opposition organizations operating from outside of the country have also not been effective in exerting pressure on the government for a variety of reasons. They are highly fractured and lack a coherent political platform on the basis of which to mobilize support and, as a result, they face a credibility-deficit among the population.

The Border Conflict

Continued tension with Ethiopia due to lack of resolution of the border conflict is another obstacle to change in the short term. Following the war the government has consistently argued that the country remains under grave threat of war and that implementing the constitution, forming political parties, conducting elections and having a free press are secondary issues that can wait until the border dispute is resolved and the country's territorial integrity is preserved. Given Ethiopia's failure to abide by the "final and binding" ruling of the independent boundary commission and failure to allow the demarcation of the border, another round of war is not improbable. Lack of resolution of the border conflict has, thus, become an important factor in obstructing change, by giving the government a pretext for denying constitutional governance.

Lack of respect for the muted civil society and the fractured opposition groups along with the risks the government faces in the event of change have made the government recalcitrant. Given the loss of popularity it has faced over the last several years, the PFDJ runs a high risk of losing power in implementing the constitution and conducting multiparty elections. Loss of political power is also likely to bring about loss of the party's economic power, as the party's extensive ownership and control of economic assets would be incompatible with the constitution's spirit, even if the constitution fails to make an unequivocal provision on the issue.

Under these conditions, the prospects for change in the country in the short to intermediate runs remain uncertain. Furthermore, given the weakness of civil society organizations and the opposition groups, it is difficult to predict what kind of change, if any, might take place. Absence of institutions and civil society organizations, which is one of the critical legacies dictatorial regimes leave behind, often tend to reduce changes to a mere recycling of the elite.

BIBLIOGRAPHY

Abbay, Alemseged. *Identity Jilted or Re-Imagined Identity? The Divergent Paths of the Eritrean and Tigrayan Nationalist Struggles.* Lawrenceville, NJ: The Red Sea Press Inc, 1998.

Acemoglu, Daron, Simon Johnson, and James Robinson. "The Colonial Origins of Comparative Development: An Emirical Investigation." *American Economic Review* 91 (December 2001):1369-1401.

Addis Tribune, weekly English-language newspaper, Addis Ababa.

Ake, Claude. *Revolutionary Pressures in Africa.* London: Zed Press, ltd., 1978.

Ake, Claude. "The Case for Democracy." *African Governance in the 1990s: Objectives, Resources, and Constraints. Working Papers from the Second Annual Seminar of the African Governance Program.* Atlanta: the Carter Center of Emory University, March 23-25, 1990: 2-6.

Amnesty International. "Eritrea: Worsening Human Rights Crisis." *Amnesty International Index:*AFR 64/001/2002.

Amnesty International. *Amnesty International Report* London: Amnesty International, 2003.

Antunes, Marques Nuno. "The Second Stage of the Eritrea-Yemen Arbitration and the Development of International Law." *International and Comparative Law Quarterly* 50, no. 2 (2001): 299-345.

"Arab concern over alleged Israeli military presence in Eritrea." *Deutsche Prez-Agentur,* July 9, 2002.

Arendt, Hannah. *Between Past and Future: Six Exercises in Political Thought.* World Publishing Company, 1954.

Artadi, V. Elsa and Xavier Sala-i-Martin. "The Economic Tragedy of the XXth Century: Growth in Africa." *Discussion Paper # 0203-17.* New York: Columbia University, Department of Economics, May 2003.

Asmerom, Abay Ghidewon and Ogbazgy Abay Asmerom. "A Study of the Evolution of the Eritrean   Ethiopian   Border

Through Treaties and Official Maps." *Eritrean Studies Review* 3, no. 2 (1999): 43-88.

Ayele, Negussay. "EPLF/TPLF and Ethiopia-Eritrea Today: Sow the wind; reap the whirlwind." http://www.mediaethiopia.com/Views/Ethiopia_Eritrea_today.htm, (2001).

Ayittey, George B.N. *Africa in Chaos.* New York: Saint Martins Press, 1998.

"Basing U.S. Troops in Eritrea." www.jinsa.org. (July 25, 2002).

BBC News. 13 February 2001 and 17 October, 2001.

Bates, Robert. "So What Have We Learned?" *Investment and Risk in Africa.* Paul Collier and Catherine Pattillo (eds.). London: Macmillan Press, Ltd., 2000. 365-372.

Beattie, John. "Checks on the Abuse of Political Power in Some African States: A Preliminary Framework for Analysis." *Comparative Political Systems: Studies in the Politics of Pre-Industrial Societies.* Ronals Cohen and John Middleton (eds). New York: The Natural History Press, 1967. 355-373.

Bereket Habte Selassie. "Creating a Constitution for Eritrea." *Journal of Democracy* 9, no.2 (1998): 167-174.

Bohannan, Paul and Philip Curtin. *Africa and Africans.* Garden City, New York: The Natural History Press, 1971.

Boulanger, Christian: "Constitutionalism in East Central Europe: The Case of Slovakia under Meciar." *East European Quarterly* 33, no.1 (Spring 1999): 21-50.

Brazeal, Aurelia: "Capitol Hill Hearing Testimony: Federal Document Clearing House, Congressional Testimony, July 9, 2002.

Bresnahan, John: "Jack Abramoff Doubles Down." *Government Inc,* November/December, (2002).

Brownlie, Ian. *African Boundaries: A Legal and Diplomatic Encyclopedia.* London: C. Hurst & Company, 1979.

Calhoun, Craig. "Ethiopia's Ethnic Cleansing." *Dissent* (Winter 1999): 47-50.

Caporaso, James. "The State's Role in Third World Economic Growth." *The Annals of the American Academy of Political and Social Science* 459 (January 1982): 103-11.

Clapham, Christopher. *Transformation and Continuity in Revolutionary Ethiopia.* Cambridge: Cambridge University Press, 1988.

Clapham, Christopher. *Haile Selassie's Government.* London: Longman, 1968.

Clemons, Peter. "The United States and Humanitarian Demining in Eritrea: Training the Trainer, 199-1997." *Contemporary Security Policy* 21 (April 2000): 68-98.

"Clarification by the Eritrean Foreign Ministry." *Eritrea Profile* (September 21, 2002).

Cliffe, Lionel. "Regional Dimensions of Conflict in the Horn of Africa." *Third World Quarterly* 20, no.1 (February 1999): 89-111.

Cobb, Jr., Charles & Caputo, Robert. "Eritrea Wins the Peace." *National Geographic* 189, no. 6 (June 1996): 81-103.

Cohen, John and Dov Weintraub. *Land and Peasants in Imperial Ethiopia: The Social Background to a Revolution.* Assen, Netherlands: Van Gorcum, 1975.

Coleman, James S. *Foundations of Social Theory.* Cambridge, MA: Harvard University Press, 1990.

Collier, Paul, V.L. Elliott. Havard Hegre, Marta Reynal-Querol, and Nicholas Sambanis. *Breaking the Conflict Trap: Civil War and Development Policy.* Washington D.C.: Oxford University Press and The World Bank, 2003.

Connell, Dan. *Against All Odds: A Chronicle of the Eritrean Revolution.* Trenton, New Jersey: Red Press, 1993.

Connell, Dan. "Letter from Eritrea." *Nation* (March 29, 1999): 22-24.

Connell, Dan. "The Importance of Self-Reliance: NGOs and Democracy Building in Eritrea." *Middle East Report* 30, no.1 (2000): 28-32.

Connell, Dan. "Inside the EPLF: Origins of the People's Party and it's Role in the Liberation of Eritrea," Review of *African Political Economy* 89 (2001): 345-364.

Connell, Dan. *Rethinking Revolution: New Strategies for Democracy, Social Justice, the Experiences of Eritrea, South Africa, Palestine, Nicaragua.* Trenton, NJ and Asmara, Eritrea: Red Sea Press, 2002.

"Country Report: Ethiopia, Somalia, Eritrea, Djibouti." *Economist Intelligence Unit,* First Quarter, Second Quarter, Third Quarter, Fourth Quarter, 1997.

Dahl, Robert A. *Polyarchy: Participation and Opposition*. New Haven: Yale University Press,   1971.

Davis, Douglas. "Foreign Report: Mowssad Active in Africa." *The Jerusalem Post* (June 26, 1998): 4.

Davis, Douglas. "Eritrea Denies Israel Use of Strategic Islands." *Jerusalem Post* (July 18, 2000): 2.

Devlin-Brown, Arlo. "Eritrea Offers Key Lessons in Nation Building." *Christian Science Monitor* (June 18, 1996).

Dewal, Alex. "Hassan al-Turabi's Muslim Brothers: Theory in Sudan." *Covert Action Quarterly* 49 (Summer 1994): 13ff.

Diamond, Larry, et al. (eds.) *Democracy in Developing Countries: Latin America*, 2nd ed. Boulder, CO: Lynn Rienner, 1999.

Diamond, Larry. *Developing Democracy: Toward Consolidation*. Baltimore, MD: Johns Hopkins University Press, 1999.

Doornbos, Martin & Tesfai, Alemseged (eds.). *Post-Conflict Eritrea: Prospects for Reconstruction and Development*. Trenton, NJ and Asmara, Eritrea: Red Sea Press, 1999.

Easterly, William and Ross Levine. "Africa's Growth Tragedy: Policies and Ethnic Divisions." *The Quarterly Journal of Economics* 112, No. 4 (November 1997): 1203-1250.

Embassy of Eritrea. "Communique." Washington D.C. (May 1, 2003).

England, Andrew. "Eritrea: Possible U.S. Base for Action Against Iraq." Associated Press, October 13, 2002.

"Eritrea and Ethiopia, The Horn of Africa War: Mass Expulsions and the Nationality Issue (June 1998- April 2002)." *Human Rights Watch* 15, no. 3A (January 2003).

"Eritrea: Grain Production." *Africa Report* 39 (January 1994): 7.

"Eritrea: Interview with Yemane Gebreab." *Agedesti Tsuhufat* no. 8 (July 8, 2002).

"Eritrea's Next Battle Ground for Elbit Systems." *Indian Ocean Newsletter* (March 30, 2002).

"Eritrea's Non-Democracy." *The Economist* (November 23, 2002): 44-45.

"Eritrea: Persecution of Journalists and Dissidents." *Human Rights Watch* Press Release, May 16, 2002.

Eritrea Profile, monthly publication of the Eritrean government.

"Eritrea Ready to Assist U.S. Regional Presence." www.jinsa.org (March 20, 2001).

"Eritrea Rejects U.S. Claims of Religious Rights Violation." *BBC Monitoring Africa*, September 16, 2004.

"Eritrea and Sudan: We Won't Take It Anymore." *Economist* (October 14, 1995): 50-51.

"Eritrea: U.N. Agency Delivers Much Needed Food Aid." *IRIN* (October 29, 2004).

"Eritrean Lobbyists in Washington." *Indian Ocean Newsletter* (September 4, 2004).

"Eritrean President Criticizes Arab League." *BBC Monitoring Africa*, May 31, 2002.

"Eritrean President Ends Visit to Egypt." *Xinhua News Agency* (November 15, 2002).

"Eritrean President TV interview." *Africa News* (September 24, 1998).

Ethiop, Amharic daily newspaper.

Ethiopia, Office of the Government Spokesperson. "Office Issues Statement on Eritrea." *Addis Tribune* (November 19, 1999).

Evans, Malcom D. "The Maritime Delimitation Between Eritrea and Yemen." *Leiden Journal of International Law* 14, no.1 (2001): 140-170.

Everald, Yves. "Democratizing Culture or Cultural Democracy." *Journal of Arts Management, Law and Society* 27, no.3 (Fall 1997): 167-175.

Falk, Richard. "The New Bush doctrine." *Nation* (July 15, 2002): 9-10.

Fiyameta, Amharic Newspaper, Addis Ababa, Ethiopia.

"Genocides, Politicides, and Other Mass Murder Since 1945, With Stages in 2004." *Genocide Watch* (2003).

Ghebre-Ab, Habtu. *Ethiopia and Eritrea: A Documentary Study.* Trenton NJ and Asmara, Eritrea: The Red Sea Press, 1993.

Gilkes, Patrick. "Violence and Identity along the Eritrean-Ethiopian Border." *Unfinished Business: Ethiopia and Eritrea at War.* Dominique Jacquin-Berdal and Martin Plaut (eds). Lawrenceville, NJ: The Red Sea Press, Inc. 2005.

Girmai Abraham. "The Privatization of the Diesa in Independent Eritrea: towards an Agricultural Research and Policy

Agenda," *Proceedings of the International Conference on Eritrea*, EPAD, Baltimore: November 3-4, 1990. 99-116.

Gollust, David. "U.S. Voices about Human Rights Violations in Eritrea", www.voanews.com, (October 20, 2002).

Government of Eritrea. *The Constitution of Eritrea.* Asmara, 1997.

Government of Eritrea. *Proclamation 58/1994* (Land Proclamation in Tigrigna), 1994.

Government of Eritrea. Customs Office, Asmara, 1998.

Halliday, Fred. "Fighting in Eritrea." *New Left Review* no. 67 (May/June, 1971): 57-69.

Halliday, Fred and Maxine Molyneux. *The Ethiopian Revolution.* London: Verso, 1981.

Hamburg, Jill. "Eritrea's Israel Tilt." *The Jerusalem Report.* June 18, 1992.10-12.

Harbeson, W. John. "Elections and Democratization in Post-Mengistu Ethiopia." *Post conflict Elections, Democratization, and International Assistance.* Krishna Kumar (ed). Boulder: Lynne Rienner Publishers, 1998.111-131.

Hartman, Danna: "Sudan Leads Antiterrorist Push." *Christian Science Monitor* (January 14, 2002): 6.

Hayek, Friederich A. *The Road to Serfdom.* Chicago: University of Chicago Press, 1944.

"The Heart of the Matter." *The Economist* (May 11, 2000).

Heilbroner, Robert L. *21st Century Capitalism.* New York: W. W. Norton, 1993.

Henze, Paul. "A Political Success Story." *Journal of Democracy* 9, no. 4 (1998): 55-61.

Hersch, Michael. "One Year Later: Bush and the World." *Foreign Affairs* (September/October, 2002): 18-43.

Hertslet, E. Sir. *The Map of Africa By Treaty vol II and III.* London: Frank Cass & Co. Ltd. 1967.

Hill, Justin. *Ciao Asmara: A Classic Account of Contemporary Africa.* London: Abacus, 2002.

Hiwyet (monthly magazine in Tigrigna) No. 14, July 1998.

Horn of Africa Bulletin (March/April 1993): 5, 7.

Houtart, Francois. "The Social Revolution in Eritrea." *Behind the War in Eritrea.* Davidson, Basil et al (eds). Nottingham, England: Spokesman, 1980. 83-108.

Huber, Evelyn & Stephens, John D. "The Bourgeoisie and Democracy: Historical and Contemporary Perspective." *Social Research* 66, no. 3 (Fall 1999): 759-788.

Ikenberry, John G. "America's Imperial Ambition." *Foreign Affairs* (September/October, 2002): 44-60.

"International Aid Detailed." *Indian Ocean Newsletter* (February 4, 1995).

International Monetary Fund. "Eritrea: Selected Issues." *IMF Staff Country Report* no. 98/91 (September 1998).

IRIN. nwes.org.

"Isaias Meets University Students in Durban, South Africa." www.awate.com, (July 8, 2002).

"Islamic Group Says It Planted Mines." *IRIN* (March 21, 2003).

Iyob Ruth. *The Eritrean Struggle for Independence: Domination, Resistance, Nationalism, 1941-1993.* Cambridge: Cambridge University Press, 1995.

"Israeli Spies Use Africa Bases." *Times* (London), June 27, 1998.

Jordan Gebre-Medhin. *Peasants and Nationalism in Eritrea.* Trenton, NJ and Asmara, Eritrea: The Red Sea Press, 1989.

Joireman, Sandra Fullerton. "The Minefield of Land Reform: Comments on the Eritrean Land Proclamation." *African Affairs* 95, no.379 (April, 1996): 269-285.

Khadiagala, Gilbert. "Reflections on the Ethiopia-Eritrea Border Conflict." *Fletcher Forum of World Affairs* 23, no. 2 (Fall 1999): 39-56.

Kansteiner, Walter. "Sudan and Conflict Resolution in Africa." Press Statement, www.heritage.org, (November 22, 2002).

Keller, Edmond. "Ethnic Federalism, Fiscal Reform and Democratization in Ethiopia." Paper Presented at the 44th Annual Meeting of the African Studies Association, Houston: November 2001.

Kaplan, Robert D. "A Post-Saddam Scenario." *The Atlantic Monthly* (November 2002): 88-90.

Kaplan, Robert D. "A Tale of Two Colonies." *The Atlantic Monthly* (April 2003).

Kellogg, Alex P. "War Justifies All, Donald Rumsfeld Courts A Repressive Government in the Horn of Africa." *The American Prospect Online*, December 2002.

Khagram, Sanjeev. "Democracy and Democratization in Africa: A Plea for Pragmatic Possibilism." *Africa Today* 4th Quarter, 40, no.4 (1993): 55-72.

Kigotho, Wachira. "Student Program in Eritrea Turns into Forced Labor Camp." *Chronicle of Higher Education* (November 23, 2001): 13.

"Kingdom and Eritrea Sign Sr 64 million Deal." *Arab News*, July 20, 2002.

Klare, Michael T. "Endless Military Superiority." *Nation* (July 15): 12-15.

Kwiatowska, Barbara. "Current Legal Developments, Red Sea: Award of the Arbitral Tribunal in the First Stage of the Eritrea-Yemen Proceeding." *The International Journal of Marine and Coastal Law* 14, no. 1 (1999): 125-136.

Kwiatowska, Barbara. "The Eritrea-Yemen Arbitration: Landmark Progress in the Acquisition of Territorial Sovereignty and Equitable Maritime Boundary Delimitation." *Ocean Development and International Law* 32, no. 1 (January 2001): 1-25.

Lake, Anthony. "Eritrea's Shameful Deeds." *Boston Globe Online*, October 26, 2002.

Lakew, Worku. "Behind the News:Revolution in Ethiopia." *Capital and Class* 46 (Spring 19920): 7-25.

Latta, Leenco. "Ethiopia: The Path to War, and the Consequences of Peace." *Unfinished Business: Ethiopia and Eritrea at War.* Dominique Jacquin-Berdal and Martin Plaut (eds). Lawrenceville, NJ and Asmara, Eritrea: The Red Sea Press, Inc. 2005. 37- 56.

Latta, Leenco. "The Making and Unmaking of Ethiopia's Transitional Charter." *Oromo Nationalism and the Ethiopian Discourse.* Asefa Jalata (ed). Lawrenceville, NJ and Asmara, Eritrea: The Red Sea Press, 1998. 51-77.

Langsded, John. "Double Strategies in a Modem Cultural Policy." *Journal of Arts Management, Law and Society* 19, no. 4 (Winter 1990): 53-71.

Laughton, John. "Cultural Democracy: Issues of Multi-Culturalism in the Arts." *Journal of Arts Management, Law and Society* 23, no.2 (Summer 1993): 121-126.

Legesse, Asmerom. *Gada: Three Approaches to the Study of African Society.* New York: FreePress, 1973.

Lobban, Richard. "The Eritrean War: Issues and Implications." *Canadian Journal of African Studies* 10, no. 2 (1976): 335-345.

"Lobbying Contracts with Eritrea." *Indian Ocean Newsletter* (May 11, 2002).

Lesk, Gill. "Sudan: Turabi's Big Day." *Middle East International* (December 4, 1993).

Lindblom, Charles, E. "The Market as a Prison." *Journal of Politics* 44, no.2 (May, 1983):324-36.

"Links to Israel Deepen." *Indian Ocean Newsletter* (February 23, 2002).

Linz, Juan and Alfred Stephan. *Theories of Democratic Transition and Consolidation: Southern Europe, South America and Post-Communist Europe.* Baltimore, MD: Johns Hopkins University Press, 1996.

Lundstrom, Karl J. *North Eastern Ethiopia: Society in Famine. Scandinavian Institute of African Studies Research Report no. 34.* Uppsala: Scandinavian Institute of African Studies,1976.

Machida, Robert. *Eritrea: The Struggle for Independence.* Trenton, NJ and Asmara, Eritrea: Red Sea Press, 1987.

Makinda, Samuel M. "Iran, Sudan and Islam." *The World Today* (June 1994): 3-15.

Markakis, John. "Eritrea's National Charter." *Review of African Political Economy* no. 61 (1995): 126-129.

Markakis, John. *National and Class Conflict in the Horn of Africa.* New York: Cambridge University Press, 1987.

McGowan, Pat. *The Comparative Study of Foreign Policy: A Survey of Scientific Findings.* Beverly Hills: Sage Publications, 1973.

McKinley, Jr., James. "Eritrea: African Success Story Been Written." *New York Times* (April 30, 1996): A1.

"Meeting with Eritrea's President." *JINSA Report,* www.jinsa.org, (December 18, 1996).

Mengisteab, Kidane. "Eritrea's Land Reform Proclamation: A Critical Appraisal." *Eritrean Studies Review_ 2, no.2 (1998): 1-18.

Mengisteab, Kidane. "New Approaches to State building in Africa: the Case of Ethiopia's Ethnic-based Federalism." *African Studies Review* 40, no.3 (December 1997): 111-132.

Miles, William F.S. "Traditional Rulers and Development Administration: Chieftaincy in Niger, Nigeria, and Vanuatu." *Studies in Comparative International Development* 28, no.3 (Fall, 1993): 31-50.

Ministry of Land Reform, Imperial Government of Ethiopia. *Report on Land Tenure Survey: Eritrea.* Addis Ababa, 1969.

Mowbray, Joel. "Our New Ally." *National Review Online*, June 10, 2002.

"Mutual Suspicion Widens Sudan Eritrea Gulf." *Arab News* (January 13, 1993).

National Security Council. "The National Security Strategy for the United States of America." www.whitehouse.gov (September 20, 2002).

Nadel, S.F. "Land Tenure on the Eritrean Plateau." *Africa* 16, no.1 (January, 1946):1-22.

The Nation, Kenyan daily newspaper, (October 8, 1998).

Negash, Asefa. *The Pillage of Ethiopia by Eritreans and their Tigrean Surrogates.* Los Angeles: Audey Publishing Company, 1996.

"No Expenses Barred for Ethiopia's PR." *Indian Ocean Newsletter* (April 4, 2002).

Ndulo, Muna. "The Democratization Process and Structural Adjustment in Africa," *Indiana Journal of Global Legal Studies* 10, no. 1 (2003): 315-368.

The Observer. (June 15, 2003).

O'Donnell, Guillermo A. "Illusions about Consolidation." *Journal of Democracy* 7, no.2 (April 1996): 15-30.

O'Donnell, Guillermo A. *Modernization and Bureaucratic Authoritarianism: Studies in South American Politics.* Berkeley: University of California Press, 1973.

O'Donnell, Guillermo A. *Counterpoints: Selected Essays on Authoritarianism and Democracy.* Notre Dame: University of Notre Dame Press, 1999.

Ottaway, Marina. *Africa's New Leaders: Democracy or State Reconstruction?* Washington, DC: Carnegie Endowment for International Peace, 1999.

Pankhurst, Richard. *State and Land in Ethiopian History.* Addis Ababa: Haile Selassie I University and Oxford University Press, 1966.

Pankhurst, Richard. "Italian Settlement Policy in Eritrea and Its Repercussions 1889-1896." *Boston University Papers in Africa History vol. 1.* Jeffrey Butler (ed.). Boston: Boston niversity Press, 1964.

Parmelee, Jennifer. "Radicals Gain Strength in the Horn of Africa." *The Washington Post* (January 5, 1994).

Pateman, Roy. *Eritrea: Even the Stones Are Burning,* revised edition. Trenton, NJ and Asmara, Eritrea: Red Sea Press, 1998.

Peeler, John. *Building Democracy in Latin America.* Boulder, CO: Lynn Reinner, 1998.

Peninou, Jean-Louis. "The Ethiopian-Eritrean Border Conflict." *IBRU Boundary and Security Bulletin* 6, no.2 (Summer 1998): 46-50.

Peters, David; Kami Kandola; A. Edward Elmendorf; and Gnanaraj Chellaraj. *Health Expenditures, Services, and Outcomes in Africa: Basic Data and Cross-National Comparisons, 1990-1996.* Washington, D.C. World Bank Health, Nutrition, and Population Publication Series, July 1999.

"PFDJ National Charter." Adopted by the Third EPLF Congress (February 10-16, 1994).

Plaut, Martin. "The Birth of the Eritrean Reform Movement." *Review of African Political Economy* 29 No. 91 (March 2002): 119-124.

Pool, David. *From Guerrillas to Government: The Eritrean People's Liberation Front.* Athens, Ohio: Ohio University Press, 2001.

"Post-Victory Turmoil." *The Economist* (May 26, 2001): 44-45.

Reid, Richard. "'Ethiopians Believe in God, Sha'abiya Believe in Mountains': the EPLF and the 1998-2000 War in Historical Perspective." *Unfinished Business: Ethiopia and Eritrea at War.* Dominique Jacquin-Berdal and Martin Plaut (eds). Lawrenceville, NJ and Asmara, Eritrea: The Red Sea Press, Inc. 2005. 23-35.

The Reporter (Amharic weekly newspaper), November 1997.

Rice, Susan. "The Ethiopian-Eritrean War: U.S. Policy Options." Testimony before the African S Subcommittee of the House Committee on International Relations (May 25, 1999).

Rothberg, Robert I. "Failed States in a World of Terror." *Foreign Affairs* (July-August 2002: 127-141.

Sanders, A.J.G.M. "Chieftainship and Western Democracy in Botswana." *Journal of Contemporary African Studies* 2 (1983): 365-379.

Sarasohn, Judy. "Eritrea Pushed to Get U.S. Base." *The Washington Post* (November 21, 2002).

Schmitter, Philippe C. and Terry Karl. "What Democracy Is and Is Not." *Journal of Democracy* 2, no. 3 (1991): 75-88.

Sherman, Richard. *Eritrea: The Unfinished Revolution.* New York: Praeger Publishers, 1980.

Sipher, Anthony. "Eritrea Eager for Military Partnership." *Daily Yomiuri Online,* July 5, 2002.

Sklar, Richard. "Developmental Democracy." *Comparative Studies in Society and History* 23, no. 4, 1(987): 686-712.

Sklar, Richard L. "Toward a Theory of Development of Democracy." *Democracy and Development: Theory in Practice.* Leftwich, Adrian (ed.). London: Cambridge Polity Press, 1996. 25-44.

"State Department Statement Cannot be Acceptable." Eritrea Ministry of Foreign Affairs, (October 18, 2002).

Stefanos, Asgedet. "Women and Education in Eritrea: Contemporary Analysis." *Harvard Educational Review* 67, no. 4 (Winter 1997): 658-688.

Stein, David: "Israel, Ethiopia and Eritrea." *Middle East International Issue* 456 (1993): 18.

Styan, David. "Twisting Ethio-Eritrean Economic Ties: Misperceptions of War and the Misplaced Priorities of Peace." *Unfinished Business: Ethiopia and Eritrea at War.* Dominique Jacquin-Berdal and Martin Plaut (eds). Lawrenceville, NJ and Asmara, Eritrea: The Red Sea Press, Inc. 2005. 177- 200.

"Sudan: Dead On Its Feet." *Indian Ocean Newsletter* (March 15, 1997).

Sutton, Jackie. "Eritrea's Economic Problems and Progress." *Focus on Africa* 5 (April-June 1994): 46-49.

Tadesse, Kiflu. "Border or Economy." *Tobia* (monthly in Amharic) 5, no. 12 (July 1998).

Tareke, Gebru. *Ethiopia: Power and Protest.* Cambridge: Cambridge University Press, 1991.

Tash, Abdul Qader. "Why Does Afeworki Reject the Arabism of Eritrea?" *Arab News* (October 27, 1993).

Taylor, Kate and Peter De Young (eds). Business and HIV/AIDS: Who Me? A Global Review of the Business Response to HIV/AIDS, 2003-2004. World Economic Forum and UNAIDS, 2003-2004.

Teka, Tegene. "Amhara Ethnicity in the Making." *Ethnicity and the State in Eastern Africa.* M.A. Mohamed Salih and John Markakis (eds). Uppsala: Nordiska Afrikainstitutet, 1998. 116-126.

"Tension Rises with Saudi Arabia." *Indian Ocean Newsletter* (February 20, 1993).

Tigray People's Liberation Front. Kalsi *Hzbi Ertra Kabey Nabey: Gemgam.* (April 1985; Miyazya 1978 Ethiopian calendar).

Tigray People's Liberation Front. *Manifesto of the TPLF* (February 1976).

Tobia (Amharic Weekly Newspaper).

"USS Hopper Visits Massawa, Eritrea." States News Service (October 14th, 2004). "The Arabs, the U.S. and the Eritrean-Ethiopian Conflict." *Mideast Mirror* (June 9, 1998).

U.N. Africa Confronting Conflict, Secretary-General's Report to the United Nations Security Council. New York (April 16, 1988).

U.N. Development Program. "2002 Human Development Report." www.undp.org (July 24, 2002).

U.N. Office for the Coordination of Humanitarian Affairs. "Consolidated International Agency Appeal for Eritrea." Press Release (November 19, 2002).

UN Theme Group on HIV/AIDS. *Eritrea: United Nations Integrated Workplan on HIV/AIDS.* UNAIDS, 2002.

UNCTAD. *Economic Development in Africa: Performance, Prospects and Policy Issues.* New York and Geneva: UN, 2001.

UNCTAD. *The Least Developed Countries Report 2002: Escaping the Poverty Trap.* New York and Geneva: UN, 2002.

UNMEE-MACC. "Eritrea: Landmine Monitoring Report 2000." www.icbl.org/lm.

USAID. *The Health Sector Human Resource Crisis in Africa: An Issue Paper.* Washington D.C.: United States Agency for International Development, Bureau for Africa, Office of Sustainable Development, February, 2003.

U.S. Department of State. "Eritrea: Background Notes." Bureau of African Affairs (March 1998).

U.S. Department of State. "Eritrea: Country Report on Human Rights Practices." Bureau of Democracy, Human Rights and Labor (March 4, 2002).

U.S. Department of State. "Background Note: Eritrea." Bureau of African Affairs (March 2004).

"U.S. Deems Afeworki Lesser Evil." *Indian Ocean Newsletter* (May 25, 2002).

"U.S. Eritrea Military Ties." *IRIN* (July 4, 2002).

"U.S. Foreign Assistance: Africa." Congressional Research Service (Washington, D.C. January 2002).

"U.S.-Israel Offering Cash to Expand Eritrea Spy Base." *Chicago Sun Times* (March 16, 2001).

"U.S. Looks at Military Ties with Eritrea." *IRIN* (May 17, 2002).

University of Asmara. "Rehabilitation of Degraded Land." Final Report of an IDRC funded research project (1996).

Uppsala Conflict Data Program (http://www.ucdp.uu.se).

Werlin, Herbert H. "The Theory of Political Elasticity: Clarifying Concepts in Micro-Macro Administration." *Administration and Society* 20, no. 1 (May 1988): 46-70.

"What Happened to Self-Reliance?" *New African* 500 (October 2001): 12.

White, Phillip and Lionel Chile. "War and Famine in Ethiopia and Eritrea." *Review of African Political Economy* 27, no. 84 (June 2000): 329-333.

Wilson, Joseph. "A Republic or Empire." *Nation* (February 13, 2003).

World Bank. *World Development Indicators.* Washington D.C.: The World Bank, 2000-2004.

World Bank. *World Bank Atlas 1999.* Washington, D.C.: The World Bank, 1999.

World Bank. *Eritrea: Options and strategies for Growth,* vol 1. Washington, D.C.: The World Bank, November 10, 1994.

World Commission on Social Dimensions of Globalization. *A Fair Globalization: Creating Opportunities for All.* Geneva: ILO 24 February, 2004.

World Health Organization. *The World Health Report.* Geneva: 2003.

Ya'ari, Ehud. "The Land of the Sea." *The Jerusalem Report* (April 8, 2002): 28.

Young, John. "Development and Change in Post-Revolutionary Tigray." *The Journal of Modern African Studies* 35, no. 1 (1997): 81-99.

Young, John. "Ethnicity and Power in Ethiopia." *Review of African Political Economy* 23, no. 70 (December 1996): 531-542.

Young, John. "The Tigray and Eritrean Liberation Fronts: A History of Tensions and Pragmatism." *Journal of Modern African Studies* 34, no. 1, (1996):

Zekarias Ambaye. *Land Tenure in Eritrea.* Addis Ababa: Addis Ababa University Press, 1966.

INDEX

A

Abacha, 133
Abyssinia, 119
Accra, 255
Addis Ababa, 185, 231-232,
    242, 244, 285, 289, 294,
    299
Adi Murug, 244, 260
Afar, 62, 242, 281
Africa Growth and
    Opportunity Act, 184
Africa, 1-2, 4, 7-8, 11, 21, 23,
    28-29, 54, 71, 91, 107-108,
    119-121, 127, 131, 133-
    136, 138, 144, 156, 164,
    168, 170-171, 174-175,
    184, 187-188, 190, 196,
    203, 207-209, 211, 215,
    228-231, 238, 244, 257,
    265-268, 270, 272, 275,
    277-279, 285-298
African, iv-v, 1-6, 8-10, 12, 14,
    16, 18, 20-32, 36, 38, 40,
    42, 44, 46, 48, 50, 52, 54,
    56, 58, 60, 62, 64, 66, 68,
    70, 72, 74, 76, 78-80, 82,
    84-86, 88, 90, 92, 94, 96-
    98, 100-102, 104, 106-108,
    110, 112, 114, 116, 118-
    120, 122, 124-128, 131-
    140, 142, 144, 146, 148-
    150, 152, 154, 156, 158-
    159, 161-168, 170-174,
    176, 178, 180, 182, 184-
    186, 188, 190, 192-194,
    196-200, 202, 204-212,
    214, 216, 218-220, 222,
    224, 226, 228, 230, 232,
    234-236, 238-240, 242,
    244, 246, 248, 250, 252,
    254-258, 260, 262, 264-
    282, 285-288, 290-296,
    298-299
African comunitarianism, 271
African Economic
    Summit, 1
African Horn, 161, 165, 172,
    180, 185, 188, 206-209,
    211, 228
African National Congress, 136
African renaissance, 8, 163, 268
Afro-communism, 271
Akele Guzai, 63
Ala group, 44, 46
Algiers peace plan, 237
Algiers peace treaty, 231, 237
Ali Abdu Ahmed, 154
All Amhara People's
    Organization, 247
al-Qaida, 208-209, 212, 214
Amhara National Democratic
    Movement, (ANDM) 242,
    247
Amin, Idi, 133
Amnesty International, 5, 95,
    131, 285
Angola, 2, 23, 134
Arab, 66, 71, 79, 162, 165, 187-
    188, 192-195, 197, 199-
    205, 208, 210, 216, 218-